Clive Oxenden
Christina Latham-Koenig
Paul Seligson

New ENGLISH FILE

Elementary
Student's Book

Contents

		Grammar	Vocabulary	Pronunciation
6				
64	**A** **A house with a history**	*there is / there are*	houses and furniture	/ð/ and /eə/, sentence stress
66	**B** **A night in a haunted hotel**	*there was / there were*	prepositions of place	silent letters
68	**C** **Neighbours from hell**	present continuous	verb phrases	verb + *-ing*
70	**D** **When a man is tired of London…**	present simple or present continuous?	places in a city	city names
72	**Practical English**	In the street		
73	**Writing**	A postcard		
74	**Revise & Check**	What do you remember? What can you do?		
7				
76	**A** **What does your food say about you?**	*a / an, some / any*	food, countable / uncountable nouns	the letters *ea*
78	**B** **How much water do we really need?**	*how much / how many?*, quantifiers: *a lot, not much*, etc.	drinks	/w/, /v/, and /b/
80	**C** **Changing holidays**	*be going to* (plans)	holidays	sentence stress
82	**D** **It's written in the cards**	*be going to* (predictions)	verb phrases	/ʊ/, /uː/, and /ʌ/
84	**Practical English**	At a restaurant		
85	**Writing**	Instructions		
86	**Revise & Check**	What do you remember? What can you do?		
8				
88	**A** **The True False Show**	comparative adjectives	personality adjectives	/ə/, sentence stress
90	**B** **The highest city in the world**	superlative adjectives	the weather	consonant groups
92	**C** **Would you like to drive a Ferrari?**	*would like to / like*	adventures	sentence stress
94	**D** **They dress well but drive badly**	adverbs	common adverbs	adjectives and adverbs
96	**Practical English**	Going home		
97	**Writing**	Making a reservation		
98	**Revise & Check**	What do you remember? What can you do?		
9				
100	**A** **Before we met**	present perfect	*been to*	sentence stress
102	**B** **I've read the book, I've seen the film**	present perfect or past simple?	past participles	irregular past participles
104	**Grammar** Quick grammar check for each File			
106	**Vocabulary, Pronunciation** Quick check of vocabulary, sounds, and word stress			

108 **Communication**
114 **Listening**
122 **Grammar Bank**
140 **Vocabulary Bank**
154 **Irregular verbs**
156 **Sound Bank**

Look out for Study Link
This shows you where to find extra material for more practice and revision.

1 A Nice to meet you

G verb *be* [+], pronouns: *I*, *you*, etc.
V numbers 1–20, days of the week
P vowel sounds, word stress

Hi, I'm Tom. What's your name?

1 SAYING HELLO

a 1.1 Listen and read. Number the pictures 1–4.

1 **A** Hi, I'm Tom. What's your name?
B Anna.
A Sorry?
B Anna!

2 **A** Hi, Dad. This is Dave.
B Hello. Nice to meet you.
C Nice to meet you.

3 **A** Good evening. What's your name?
B My name's Janet Leigh.
A You're in room 5.

4 **A** Hello, John. How are you?
B I'm fine, thanks. And you?
A Very well, thank you.

Good morning	→ 12.00
Good afternoon	12.00–6.00 p.m.
Good evening	6.00 p.m. →

b Write the words in the chart.

Fine ~~Hi~~ I'm... thanks

Hello	My name's...	Very well	thank you
Hi	______	______	______

c Listen again and repeat. Copy the rhythm.

d 1.2 Roleplay the dialogues with the sound effects.

e Introduce yourself to five other students.

Hello. I'm Antonio. What's your name?

Carla. Nice to meet you.

2 GRAMMAR verb *be* [+], pronouns

a Complete the sentences with *are*, *is*, or *am*.

I'**m** Tom. = I ______ Tom.
My name'**s** Janet Leigh. = My name ______ Janet Leigh.
You'**re** in room 5. = You ______ in room 5.

b **p.122 Grammar Bank 1A.** Read the rules and do the exercises.

c Try to remember the names in your class.
Say *He's / She's* ______.

3 PRONUNCIATION vowel sounds, word stress

English File sound pictures help your pronunciation.

a 1.3 Listen and repeat the words and sounds.

fish	tree	cat	boot	train	bike
it this ____	he she ____	am ____	you	they ____	I Hi ____

b 1.4 Write these words in the columns above. Listen and check. Repeat the words.

name is thanks my we

A coffee, please.

Word stress is important.

c Underline the stressed syllable in these words.

d 1.5 Listen and check. Which two words are *not* stressed on the first syllable?

e Write the words from c in the chart.

food	travel	communication
coffee		

f In pairs, write two more words in each column.

4 VOCABULARY numbers 1–20

a 1.6 Listen and repeat the numbers.

1 2 3 4 5 6 7 8 9 10

11 12 13 14 15 16 17 18 19 20

b **p.140 Vocabulary Bank** *Numbers*. Do part 1.

c 1.7 Listen. Where are they? Write 1–4 in the boxes.

☐ **airport**	Gate number ____
1 **sandwich bar**	____ euros ____ cents
☐ **hotel**	Room ____
☐ **taxi**	____ Manchester Road

d Listen again. Write a number in each space.

5 SAYING GOODBYE

a 1.8 Listen and number the words.

Goodbye. ☐
Bye. *1*
Goodnight. ☐
See you. ☐
See you on Saturday. ☐
See you tomorrow. ☐

b 1.9 Complete the days of the week with a CAPITAL letter. Listen and repeat.

W F S T M

M **onday**

__**uesday**

__**ednesday**

__**hursday**

__**riday**

__**aturday**

__**unday**

G verb *be* [−] and [?]
V countries and nationalities, numbers 20–1,000
P vowel sounds

Where are you from?
I'm Irish. I'm from Dublin.

I'm not English, I'm Scottish!

1 VOCABULARY countries and nationalities

a How do you say | your country / your language / two countries near you | in English?

b ➲ **p.141 Vocabulary Bank** *Countries and nationalities.*

c 1.10 Where's the stress? Listen and underline the stressed syllable. Listen and repeat.

Japan	Japanese
Germany	German
China	Chinese
Italy	Italian
the United States	American
Russia	Russian

d In pairs, do the quiz.

The World Quiz

Hello Cześć!

1 Where are these cities?

a Kraków ______
b Glasgow ______
c Boston ______
d Shanghai ______
e Bangkok ______

¡Hola! Bom dia!

2 1.11 What languages are these?

a ______
b ______
c ______
d ______

Szia!

3 1.12 Where's this music from?

a ______
b ______
c ______
d ______

Hello Bom dia! Szia! Cześć! ¡Hola!

2 LISTENING & SPEAKING

a 1.13 Listen and number the pictures 1–4.

b Listen again and complete the dialogues.

1 **A** Are you ____________?
B No, I'm ____________. I'm from Edinburgh.

2 **A** Where are you from?
B We're from ____________.
A Are you on holiday?
B No, we aren't. We're on business.

3 **A** Where's she from? Is she ____________?
B No, she isn't. She's ____________. She's from Buenos Aires.

4 **A** Mmm, delicious. Is it ____________?
B No, it isn't. It's ____________.

c Repeat the dialogues. Copy the rhythm.

d In pairs, look at the pictures. Roleplay the dialogues.

3 GRAMMAR verb *be* [-] and [?]

a Complete the chart.

Question	Short answer	Negative
______ you English?	No, I ______.	I ______ English.
______ they from Spain?	Yes, they ______.	
______ she Portuguese?	No, she ______.	She ______ Portuguese.
______ he on business ?	Yes, he ______.	

b ➲ **p.122 Grammar Bank 1B.** Read the rules and do the exercises.

4 PRONUNCIATION vowel sounds

a 1.14 Listen and repeat the words and sounds.

b Match the sentences and pictures. Write the sound words.

1 Where's he from? *chair*
2 Ben's French. ______
3 I'm not Scottish. ______
4 I'm American. ______
5 Are you from France? ______
6 No, I'm Polish. ______

c 1.15 Listen and check.

d Repeat the sentences.

5 SPEAKING

a Ask other students.

Where are you from?
I'm Italian. I'm from Siena.

b In pairs, ask about the people and things in the pictures.

Where's it from?
Where are they from?
It's from Ireland.
They're from...
I don't know.

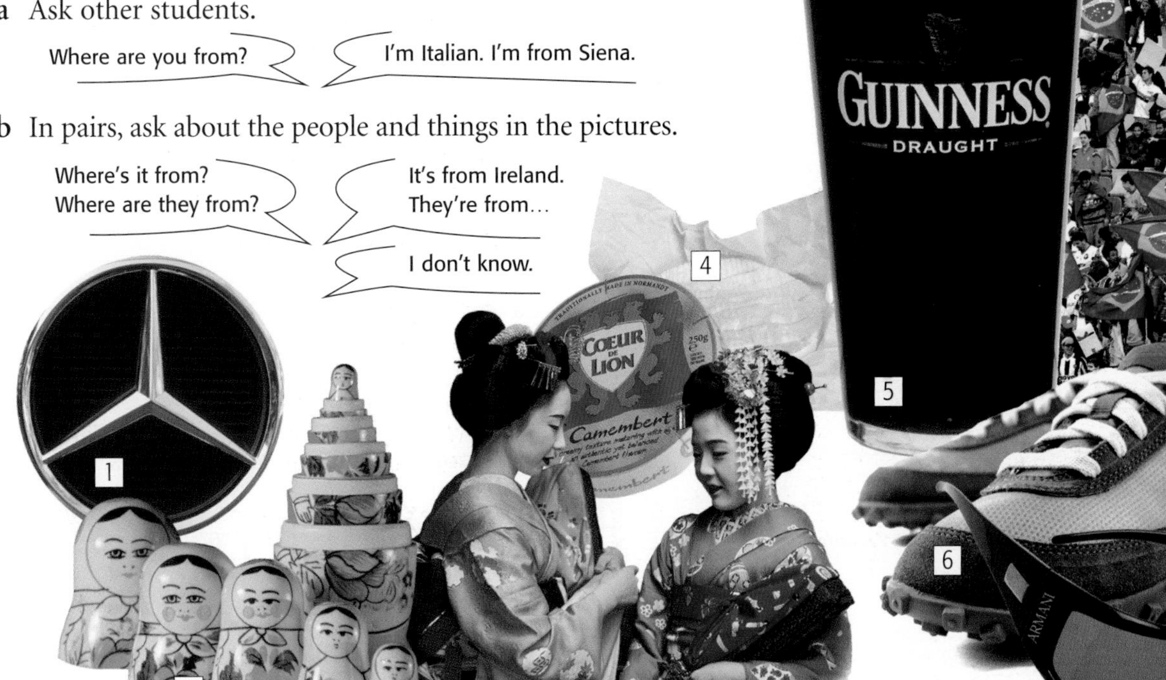

6 VOCABULARY numbers 20–1,000

a 1.16 Listen. How do you say *77* and *0* in phone numbers?

b Ask three students for their phone numbers.

c ➲ **p.140 Vocabulary Bank** ***Numbers.*** Do part 2.

d 1.17 Listen and repeat the pairs of numbers. What's the difference?

1 a 13 b 30
2 a 14 b 40
3 a 15 b 50
4 a 16 b 60
5 a 17 b 70
6 a 18 b 80
7 a 19 b 90

e 1.18 Which number do you hear? Listen and circle a or b above.

f Play *Bingo*.

1 C

G possessive adjectives: *my*, *your*, etc.
V personal information: *address*, *phone number*, etc.
P the alphabet, /ɜː/ and /aʊ/

What are their names?
His name's Jacek and her name's Ana.

His name, her name

1 LISTENING

a What do you think? Complete the sentences with one of the countries.

Australia Britain Canada Ireland the USA

Every year thousands of students travel to different countries to study English. Where do they go? Here are the Top Five countries...

600,000 study English in ________.
500,000 study English in ________.
120,000 study English in ________.
80,000 study English in ________.
40,000 study English in ________.

b 1.19 Mario goes to Ireland to study English. Listen to the interview and complete the form.

First name	*Mario*
Surname	*Benedetti*
Country / City	________ / ________
Student	Yes ☐ No ☐
Age	________
Address	*Via Foro* ________
Postcode	________
E-mail address	*mario.benedetti@hotmail.com*
Phone number	________
Mobile phone	________

@ = *at* . = *dot*

c 1.20 Listen. Complete the receptionist's questions.

1 *What's your first name?*
2 ________ your surname?
3 ________ do you spell it?
4 Where are you ________?
5 ________ you a student?
6 How old ________ you?
7 ________ your address?
8 What's ________ postcode?
9 ________ your e-mail address?
10 What's your ________ ________?

2 PRONUNCIATION the alphabet

a 1.21 Can you say the alphabet? Listen and repeat the letters.

A B C D E F G H I
J K L M N O P Q
R S T U V W X Y Z

b 1.22 Listen and repeat the words and sounds.

train	tree	egg	bike	phone	boot	car
A	B	F	___	O	Q	R
___	C	L	Y		___	
J	___	M			W	
___	E	___				
	G	S				
	___	___				
	___	Z				
	___					

c 1.23 Write the other letters of the alphabet in the correct column. Listen and check.

d In pairs, practise saying these abbreviations.

3 SPEAKING

a 1.24 Listen and repeat the questions from **1c**. Copy the rhythm.

What's your first name?

b **Communication** *Interview p.111.*

Copy the rhythm of English.

4 GRAMMAR possessive adjectives

a Look at the highlighted words. Which is an adjective? Which is a pronoun?

1 Where are you from? 2 What's your name?

b 1.25 Complete the chart with *your, my, his, her, their, our*. Listen and check.

I'm Italian.	______ family are from Rome.
You're in level 1.	This is ______ classroom.
He's the Director of Studies.	______ name is Michael.
She's your teacher.	______ name is Lucy.
We're an international school.	______ students are from different countries.
They're new students.	______ names are Tina and Daniel.

c **p.122 Grammar Bank 1C.** Read the rules and do the exercises.

5 PRONUNCIATION /ɜː/ and /aʊ/

a 1.26 Listen and repeat the words and sounds.

bird	______	______	______
owl	______	______	______

b 1.27 Write these words in the chart. Listen and repeat the words.

her how first our now surname

6 SPEAKING

Look at the photos. In pairs, ask and answer the questions.

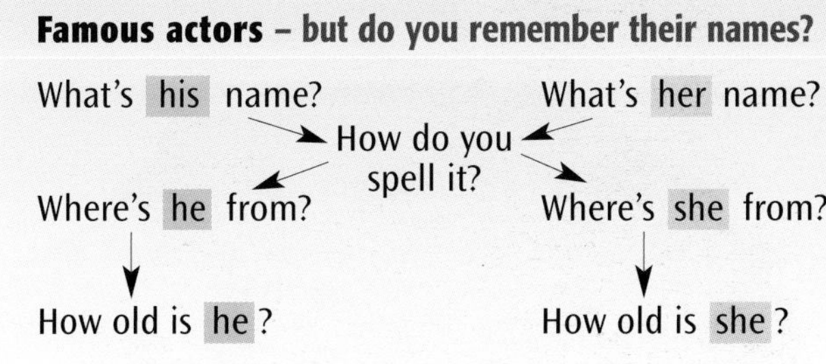

Famous actors – but do you remember their names?

What's his name? What's her name?
How do you spell it?
Where's he from? Where's she from?
How old is he? How old is she?

(I think) She's American. She's about 35.

I don't remember. I don't know.

G *a / an*, plurals, *this / that / these / those*
V the classroom, common objects, classroom language
P vowel sounds

What's this?
It's an identity card.

Turn off your mobiles!

1 VOCABULARY the classroom, common objects

a Can you see these things in your classroom? Tick (✓) or cross (✗).

a table	☐	a light	☐
a board	☐	a picture	☐
a TV	☐	a video	☐
a CD player	☐	walls	☐
a window	☐	chairs	☐
a door	☐		

b 1.28 Listen and repeat the words.

c 1.29 What's in the bag? Match the words and pictures. Listen and check.

☐ an address book	☐ keys
☐ cigarettes	☐ a lighter
☐ coins	☐ a lipstick
☐ a mobile (phone)	☐ a purse

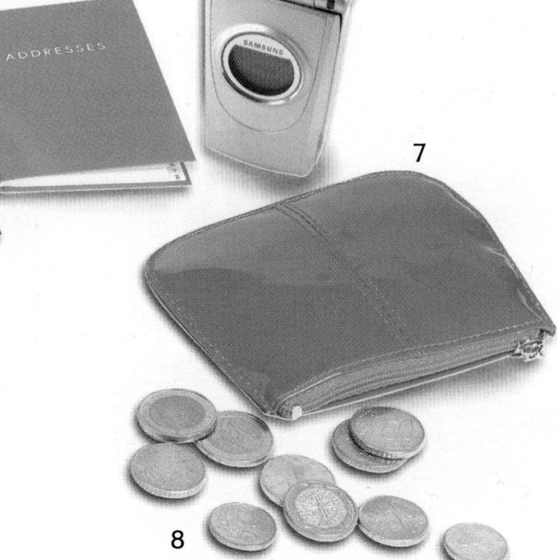

d ➲ **p.142 Vocabulary Bank** *Common objects.*

e In pairs.
A Close your eyes.
B Give **A** a thing from your bag or pocket. Ask *What's this?* or *What are these?*
A Say *It's a...* or *They're...*

2 PRONUNCIATION vowel sounds

a 1.30 Listen and repeat the six picture words and sounds.

horse	wall	door	(glasses)	
bull	book	photo	look	
up	purse	sunglasses	umbrella	
boy	coins	board	toilet	
ear	here	we're	there	
tourist	euro	Europe	e-mail	

b 1.31 Listen to the groups of words. Circle the word with a different vowel sound.

c Practise saying the words.

3 GRAMMAR *a / an*, plurals, *this / that / these / those*

a Write *a* or *an*.

1 ___ watch
2 ___ umbrella
3 ___ diary
4 ___ identity card
5 ___ file

b Write the plural.

1 stamp ________
2 match ________
3 key ________

c Complete the questions with *this*, *that*, *these*, or *those*.

What's ______? What's ______?

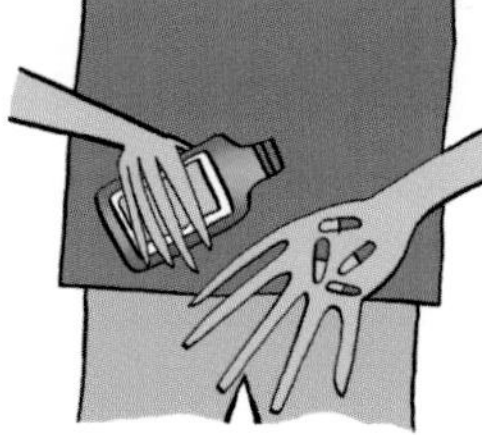

What are ______? What are ______?

d p.122 Grammar Bank 1D. Read the rules and do the exercises.

e In pairs, ask and answer. Use pictures 1–8 in **1c** for *this / these* and point to things in the class for *that / those*.

4 CLASSROOM LANGUAGE

a Match the phrases and the pictures.

- ☐ Look at the board.
- ☐ Open your books.
- *1* Close the door. ✓
- ☐ Read the text.
- ☐ Go to page (*84*).
- ☐ Turn off your mobile (phone).
- ☐ Sit down.
- ☐ Work in pairs.
- ☐ Stand up.
- ☐ Don't write.
- ☐ Listen and repeat.
- ☐ Don't speak (*Spanish*).

GIVING INSTRUCTIONS

+ Open your books (please).
− (Please) Don't write.
? Can you open the door (please)?

b **1.32** Listen. Tick (✓) the ten phrases in **a** you hear.

c **1.33** Complete the sentences. Listen and check.

What's (*bonjour*) ________ English?
________ do you spell it?
________'s the stress?
Can ________ repeat it?

I ________ know.
I ________ remember.
I ________ understand.

d Play *What's the word?*

5 1.34 SONG ♫ *Eternal Flame*

1 On a plane

VOCABULARY drinks

a Match the words and pictures.

coffee	☐	milk	☐
tea	☐	ice	☐
(*orange*) juice /ˈɒrɪndʒ dʒuːs/	☐	lemon	☐
(Diet) Coke	1	sugar /ˈʃʊɡə/	☐
mineral water	☐		

b In pairs, cover the words and test your partner.

ASKING FOR A DRINK

a 1.35 Cover the dialogue and listen. What drinks does Mark have?

YOU HEAR	YOU SAY
1 Would you like a ______, sir?	Yes, a Diet Coke, please.
2 ______ and lemon ?	Just lemon.
3 Here you ______.	Thank you.
4 Coffee? ______?	Coffee, please.
5 ______?	Yes, please.
6 ______?	No, thanks.
Here you are.	Thanks.

Mark is American. He works for MTC, a music company. He's on a plane to the UK.

b Listen again. Complete the YOU HEAR phrases.

c 1.36 Listen and repeat the YOU SAY phrases. Copy the rhythm.

d In pairs, roleplay the dialogue.

SOCIAL ENGLISH

a 1.37 Listen. Circle the correct answer.

1 What's Mark's surname? **Ryder / Wilder**
2 Where's the hotel? **at the airport / in the city centre**
3 Would Mark like a drink? **yes / no**
4 How do they go to the hotel? **by taxi / by car**

b What do you think?

1 Is Allie American?
2 Are they friends?

c Who says the USEFUL PHRASES, Mark or Allie? Listen again and check. How do you say them in your language?

USEFUL PHRASES
Welcome to the UK.
How far is it?
Great!
All right. Let's go.
Can I help you with your bags?
No, it's OK, thanks.

Allie works for MTC in the UK.

Completing a form

a Complete the form with your information.

Sydney
School of English

Student registration form

First name	
Surname	Mr / Mrs / Ms
Nationality	
Marital status	☐ Married ☐ Single ☐ Divorced ☐ Separated
Home address	
E-mail address	
Phone number	
home	
work	
mobile	
Passport / Identity card number	
Signature	Date

b In English these words start with a CAPITAL letter.

names and surnames	***M**ark **R**yder*
countries, nationalities, and languages	***F**rance, **F**rench*
towns and cities	***R**ome*
days of the week	***M**onday*
the first word in a sentence	***H**er father is from **M**ilan.*
the pronoun *I*	*She's French and **I**'m Italian.*

c Write this text again with capital letters where necessary.

my name's marta. i'm from rio in brazil, and i speak portuguese. my teacher is american. his name's gerry. my english classes are on tuesdays and thursdays.

WRITE a similar text about you.

1 What do you remember?

GRAMMAR

Circle the correct sentence, a or b.

(a) Hi. I'm Susanna.
b Hi. I Susanna.

1 a Hello. What's your name?
b Hello. What your name?
2 a She is Polish?
b Is she Polish?
3 a Where he's from?
b Where's he from?
4 a They isn't English.
b They aren't English.
5 a 'Are you from Paris?' 'Yes, I'm.'
b 'Are you from Paris?' 'Yes, I am.'
6 a She's Spanish. Her name's Ana.
b She's Spanish. His name's Ana.
7 a We're Italian. Your surname is Tozzi.
b We're Italian. Our surname is Tozzi.
8 a What are these?
b What are this?
9 a It's an umbrella.
b It's a umbrella.
10 a They're watchs.
b They're watches.

10

VOCABULARY

a prepositions

Complete with *at, from, in, off, to.*

Go *to* page 74.

1 I'm ______ Japan.
2 Nice ______ meet you.
3 What's *bonjour* ______ English?
4 Look ______ the board.
5 Please turn ______ your mobile phone.

b verb phrases

Match the verbs and phrases.

Close your books.

Answer	Listen to	Open	Read	Work

1 ______ the text.
2 ______ in pairs.
3 ______ the CD.
4 ______ the door.
5 ______ the questions.

c word groups

Circle the word that is different.

	one	three	(book)	five
1	eight	two	seven	file
2	Ireland	Chinese	Thailand	Spain
3	Polish	Italian	Japanese	France
4	sixteen	forty	ninety	eighty
5	we	you	her	he
6	they	his	our	my
7	where	how	what	watch
8	lighter	pencil	purse	address
9	newspaper	book	magazine	lipstick
10	listen	read	pen	look

20

PRONUNCIATION

a ➲ **p.156 Sound Bank.** In pairs, test each other on the vowel sounds, 1–20.

b Underline the word with a different sound.

	she	<u>her</u>	see
1	stamps	what	bag
2	key	meet	they
3	glasses	France	table
4	mobile	go	one
5	his	China	sit

c Underline the stressed syllable.

infor<u>ma</u>tion

address surname Argentina
Portuguese umbrella

10

What can you do?

CAN YOU UNDERSTAND THIS TEXT?

Where are English words from?

From Old English

Many basic English words come from Old English, e.g. England, house, woman man, child, bird, water. They sometimes have irregular pronunciation.

From Latin

Other English words come from Latin, e.g. family, wine, number, school, educate.

From French

Some English words come from French, e.g. royal, hotel, menu, beef.

From other languages

Today English is an international language. Thousands of English words come from other languages, e.g. siesta (Spanish), judo (Japanese).

New words

Every year hundreds of words come into English from new technology, e.g. Internet, text message, e-mail, modem.

a Read the text once. Do you know the highlighted words?

b Read the text again. Now cover the text. Can you remember where these words come from? Write them in the chart.

~~Internet~~ wine menu house hotel family
siesta woman judo e-mail

Old English	Latin	French	Other languages	New words
				Internet

c Where are words in *your* language from?

CAN YOU HEAR THE DIFFERENCE?

1.38 Listen. Circle a or b.

What's your name? (a) Carlos. b 21.

1 a Where's he from? b Where's she from?
2 a He's from Italy. b She's from Italy.
3 a She's French. b She isn't French.
4 a What's his name? b What's her name?
5 a the credit card b the credit cards
6 a page 13 b page 30
7 a Gate number 14 b Gate number 40
8 a Mike@info.de b Mike@info.da
9 a Mr. G. Smith b Mr. J. Smith
10 a Tuesday b Thursday

CAN YOU SAY THIS IN ENGLISH?

a Can you...? Yes (✓)

- ☐ count from 1–20
- ☐ count from 20–100 (20, 30, etc.)
- ☐ count from 100–1,000 (100, 200, etc.)
- ☐ say the days of the week (Monday, Tuesday, etc.)
- ☐ spell your address
- ☐ say five things in your bag or pocket (some keys, etc.)

b Complete with *How*, *What*, or *Where*. In pairs, ask and answer.

_____ 's your surname?
_____ do you spell it?
_____ are you from?
_____ 's your phone number?
_____ 's your address?

G present simple + and –
V verb phrases, irregular plurals
P consonant sounds, third person *-s*

They live in a flat.
He doesn't smoke.

Cappuccino and chips

1 VOCABULARY verb phrases

a 2.1 What do you think? Complete with a number, e.g. 60% (*sixty per cent*). Listen and check.

10% 25% 45% 60% 70% 90%

WHAT % OF BRITISH PEOPLE...?

read a newspaper every day	______	go to the cinema every weekend	______
smoke	______	have a pet	______
watch TV every night	______	live in a house with a garden	______

b In pairs, make true + or – sentences about you.

+ I read a newspaper every day.
– I don't smoke.

c p.143 Vocabulary Bank *Verb phrases*.

2 READING

a Look at the photos. Which things are 'typically British'?

b Read the text. Check your answer to **a**.

NO CHILDREN
UNDER 12
PERMITTED
This Is A
"Non-Smoking"
Restaurant.

Typically British?

Four foreigners in Britain talk about the people and the country...

1 **Nicolae from Romania works in a pub in Manchester**

'British people like children but not in restaurants or pubs. In my pub we have a rule: 'No children under 12'. People in Britain drink a lot of coffee – cappuccino and espresso are really popular. They drink a lot of beer too – men and women.'

2 **Alexandra from Russia is a student at Bristol University**

'This is not a good country for smokers! Many coffee bars and restaurants are 'no smoking'. I live with three British students and they don't smoke. When I want a cigarette I go into the garden.'

3 **Carlos is a tourist from Spain**

'People read the newspaper everywhere – on the train, on the bus, at the bus stop. And the newspapers are really big! Cars stop in Britain when you stand on the zebra crossing – it's incredible! Cars don't stop for you in Madrid.'

4 **Marília from Brazil works as an 'au pair' in Cambridge**

'I think my British family is typical. The woman doesn't cook – she just puts a pizza in the microwave. But she watches cooking programmes on TV every day! The man cooks at the weekend – he makes fantastic Indian curries. Their child has a terrible diet. She eats 'fish fingers' and chips and she goes to Burger King every week.'

c Find the four irregular plurals in the first text and complete the chart. How do you pronounce them?

Singular	Plural	
man	______	/men/
woman /ˈwʊmən/	______	/ˈwɪmɪn/
child /tʃaɪld/	______	/ˈtʃɪldrən/
person	______	/ˈpiːpl/

d Read the texts again. Underline three things which are the same in your country, and three things which are different.

3 GRAMMAR present simple + and −

a Answer the questions.

1 Look at the highlighted verbs. Why do the verbs in paragraph 4 end in *-s*?

2 Write the *he / she* form of these verbs.

cook ______ go ______ have ______
make ______ watch ______

3 Find three negative − verbs. Which one is different? Why?

b **p.124 Grammar Bank 2A.** Read the rules and do the exercises.

4 PRONUNCIATION consonant sounds, -s

a 2.2 Listen and repeat the words and sounds.

vase dog snake zebra leg witch

b Practise saying the sentences.

/v/ Vicky lives in Vienna.
/d/ David doesn't drive.
/s/ Sally speaks Spanish.
/z/ Liz is in Brazil.
/l/ Linda likes children.
/w/ William works as a waiter.

c 2.3 Listen and repeat the third person forms.

/s/	/z/
She smokes a lot.	She lives in a flat.
She drinks coffee.	He has a cat.
He eats chips.	She does exercise.

/ɪz/
He watches TV.
It finishes in a minute.

5 WRITING & SPEAKING

a Write *your* nationality in the title. Then ~~cross out~~ the wrong word(s), e.g. They live in a ~~**house**~~ / **flat**. Complete the sentences with your ideas.

A typical ______ family

They live in a **house** / **flat**.
They **have** / **don't have** a pet.
They have ______ **child** / **children**.
They go to ______ for their holiday.

The mother **works** / **doesn't work**.
She **cooks** / **doesn't cook**.
She **does** / **doesn't do** housework.
She reads ______.
She watches ______ on TV.
She drives a ______.
She ______.

The father **works** / **doesn't work**.
He **cooks** / **doesn't cook**.
He **does** / **doesn't do** housework.
He reads ______.
He watches ______ on TV.
He drives a ______.
He ______.

b Read your sentences to a partner. Are they the same or different?

2B When Natasha meets Darren...

G present simple ?
V common verb phrases
P consonant sounds

Do you watch TV? What programmes do you like?

1 READING

a Natasha and Darren want to meet a partner on the Internet. Look at their pictures. How old do you think they are?

b Natasha e-mails Darren and he answers. Read their e-mails. Then cover them and complete the sentences with *Natasha* or *Darren*.

1. *Darren* is 30.
2. __________ lives in north London.
3. __________ works for a magazine.
4. __________ works with computers.
5. __________ likes burgers.
6. __________ likes the cinema.
7. __________ doesn't like fast food.
8. __________ likes Japanese food.

> Dear Darren,
> My name's Natasha and I have a flat in north London. I'm 28 and I work for a magazine. I like music, good food and the cinema. Please write.
> Natasha

> Dear Natasha,
> Thanks for your e-mail. I live in London too. I'm 30 and I work with computers. Let's meet for lunch. Do you like burgers? I know a good burger restaurant in north London...
> Darren

> Hi Darren,
> Sorry, I don't like burgers, but I love Japanese food. Friday at 1.00 in Kiku? It's a Japanese restaurant in Pond Street.

> Hi Natasha
> OK. See you on Friday.

2 GRAMMAR present simple ?

Natasha and Darren meet for lunch

a 2.4 Cover the conversation and listen. What does Darren say about...?

- alcohol
- sushi
- his mother

b Listen again. Complete the conversation.

D Hi. Are you Natasha?
N Yes, and you're Darren. Nice to __________ you.
D Sorry I'm late.
N No problem. Would you like a glass of wine?
D No, thanks. I don't __________ alcohol. Mineral water for me.

D What's this?
N Sushi. It's fantastic. Don't you __________ it?
D No, I __________. Sorry.
N __________ food do you like?
D I usually __________ at home. My mother's a very good cook.
N Do you __________ with your mother?
D Yes, I do.
N Oh. Does your mother work?
D Yes, she __________.
N Where does she __________?
D She __________ in a supermarket.

c Complete the questions and short answers with *do*, *does*, and *don't*.

______ you like sushi?
No, I ______.
What food ______ you like?

______ your mother work?
Yes, she ______.
What ______ she do?

d **p.124 Grammar Bank 2B.** Read the rules and do the exercises.

3 LISTENING

a 2.5 Listen to the rest of the conversation. Is the lunch a success ☺ or a disaster ☹?

b Listen again. Complete the chart with ✓ (yes) or ✗ (no).

	Natasha	Darren
likes computers	✗	
watches TV		
goes to the cinema		
smokes		

c In pairs, ask and answer questions about Darren and Natasha.

Does Darren like computers?

Yes, he does.

4 SPEAKING

a Imagine you want to meet a new partner, and you go to an agency.
Look at the *Meeting People* form. What questions does the interviewer ask?

Meeting People
Meet a partner who's right for you

What / name?	NAME ______
How old / ?	AGE ______
work / study?	OCCUPATION ______
Where / live?	TOWN ______
/ have a car?	YES ☐ NO ☐
What languages / speak?	LANGUAGES ______
/ smoke?	YES ☐ NO ☐
What music / like?	MUSIC ______
What TV programmes / like?	TV ______
What food / like?	FOOD ______
What newspaper / read?	NEWSPAPER ______
What sports / play?	SPORTS ______

b 2.6 Listen and check. Listen again. Copy the rhythm.

c In pairs, roleplay an interview at *Meeting People*.

A You want to meet a partner.

B You are the interviewer. Ask **A** the questions and write the answers in the form.

d Change roles.

5 PRONUNCIATION consonant sounds

keys girl tie shower television right

a 2.7 Listen and repeat the words and consonant sounds.

b Practise saying the sentences.

/k/ Karen likes coffee.
/g/ Greta goes to golf classes.
/t/ Tim eats out on Tuesdays.
/ʃ/ Natasha likes sushi.
/ʒ/ Mick usually watches television.
/r/ Ricky reads Russian writers.

6 2.8 SONG ♫ *Something Stupid*

2 C

G *a* / *an* + jobs
V jobs
P consonant sounds

What do you do?
I'm a student.

An artist and a musician

1 READING

a Look at the photos of Annabel. Do you think she's a professional artist or a professional musician?

b Read the interview and match the questions with her answers.

Do you like your job? Why?
How many hours do you work?
Do you earn a lot of money?
Where do you work?
What *don't* you like about your job?
How do you relax after work?
~~**What do you do?**~~

c In pairs, guess the meaning of the highlighted words. Check with your teacher or a dictionary.

d Read the article again. <u>Underline</u> two good and two bad things about Annabel's job.

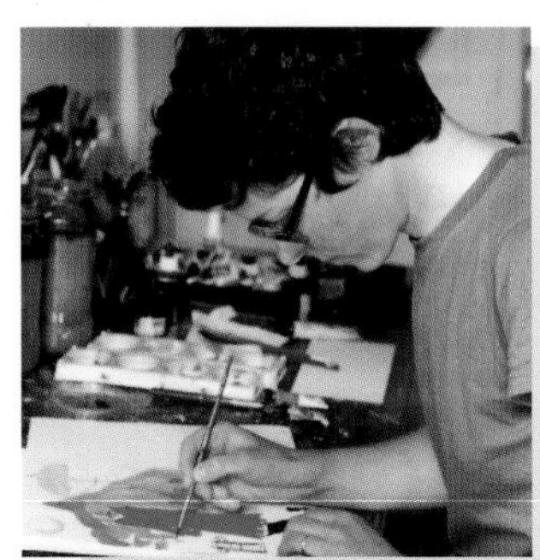

A Double Life

1 What do you do?
I'm an artist. I draw and paint pictures for magazines, books, CD covers – all kinds of things.

2 ______________________
I work at home. I have a room just for working in.

3 ______________________
I usually work about eight hours a day, from 9.30 to 5.30. Sometimes I work again in the evenings or at weekends, when I'm in a hurry to finish a picture.

4 ______________________
It depends. I earn from about £250 to £3,000 for a picture. Sometimes I have a lot of work but sometimes I don't. That's a problem. And I don't have paid holidays.

5 ______________________
Yes. I love it, because every day is different, and I like using my imagination.

6 ______________________
It's stressful when I need to work fast and the ideas don't come. And sometimes it's lonely when you don't work with other people.

7 ______________________
I play the bass in a band called International Airport. We play at weekends in pubs and clubs.

2 VOCABULARY jobs

a Look at Annabel's pictures. How many of these jobs can you say in English?

1 2

3
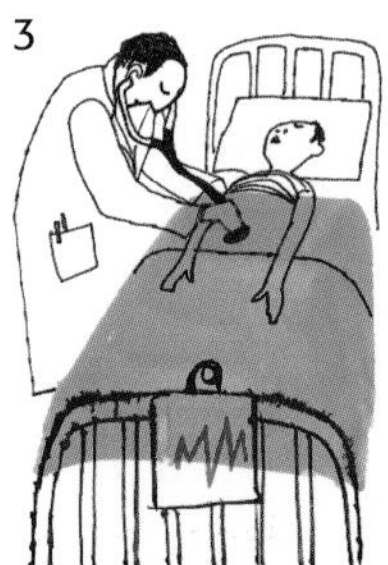

4

5

6

b Ask and answer with the pictures.

c ➲ **p.144 Vocabulary Bank *Jobs*.**

d Look at the question and answers. How do you say them in your language?

	What do you do?	
I'm **a** musician.		
I'm **an** engineer.	I work **for** a French company.	I'm **at** school.
I'm unemployed.	I work **in** a shop.	I'm **at** university.

e What do *you* do? Ask five other students in the class.

3 GRAMMAR *a / an* + jobs

Complete with *a*, *an*, or –.

1 He's ____ actor.
2 She's ____ politician.
3 They're ____ nurses.
4 We're ____ lawyers.
5 He's ____ teacher.
6 She's ____ actress.
7 Are you ____ journalist?
8 I'm ____ pilot.
9 He's ____ builder.

> ⚠ Remember! Use *a / an* + job, e.g. He's a musician. NOT ~~He's musician.~~ Don't use *a / an* with plurals, e.g. They're doctors. NOT ~~They're a doctors.~~

4 PRONUNCIATION consonant sounds

a 2.9 Listen and repeat sentences 1–9. Copy the rhythm. How do you pronounce the *-er / -or* ending?

b 2.10 Listen and repeat the words and consonant sounds.

c Practise saying the sentences.

/p/ Paul's a politician.
/f/ Phil's a fantastic footballer.
/tʃ/ Charles teaches Chinese.
/dʒ/ Jim and George are journalists.
/j/ Are you a student?
/ŋ/ A singer sings songs.

5 LISTENING & SPEAKING

When people speak fast they don't separate words.

a 2.11 Listen to a radio programme called *Guess my job*. Three people guess a person's job. Underline the ten questions they ask.

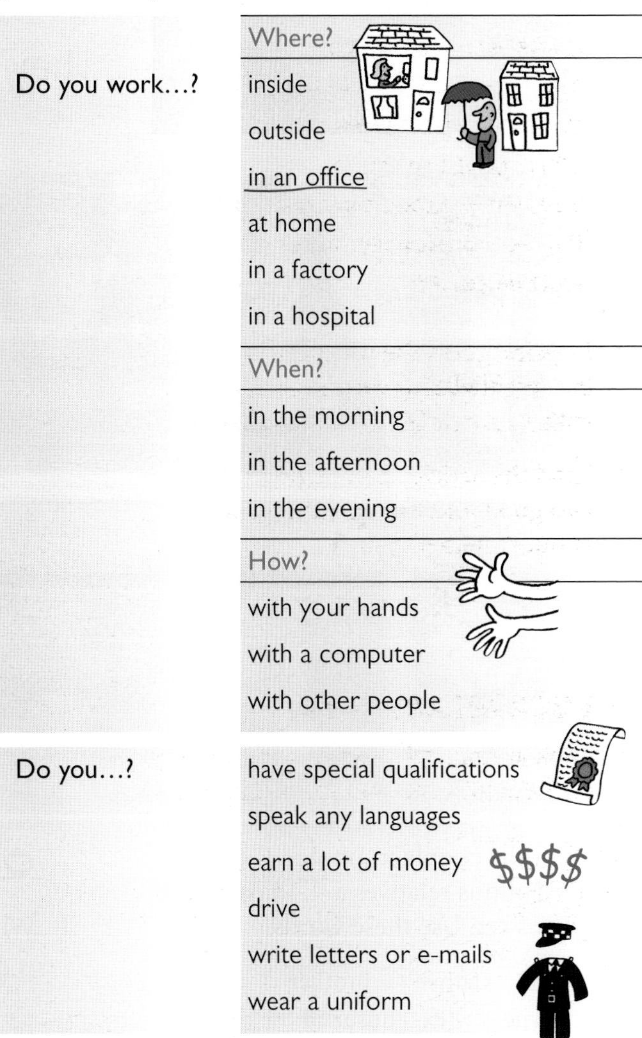

	Where?
Do you work...?	inside
	outside
	in an office
	at home
	in a factory
	in a hospital
	When?
	in the morning
	in the afternoon
	in the evening
	How?
	with your hands
	with a computer
	with other people
Do you...?	have special qualifications
	speak any languages
	earn a lot of money
	drive
	write letters or e-mails
	wear a uniform

b Listen again. What does the person answer? Write Y (yes), N (no), or D (It depends) after each question.

c Look at Phil's answers. What do you think his job is?

d 2.12 Listen to the end of the programme. What does Phil do?

e In groups of four, play the game. Choose jobs from **Vocabulary Bank** *Jobs p.144*.

2D Relatively famous

G possessive *s*
V family
P consonant sounds

Who's Joanna?
She's my boyfriend's sister.

1 GRAMMAR possessive *s*

a Look at the photo. What does *'s* mean?

Sylvester Stallone's mother at the Oscars

Who are they?

They're not famous – but their relatives are!

1 

2 

3 

4 

5 

6 

a JK Rowling

b Hugh Grant

c Will Smith

d Kate Winslet

e Naomi Campbell

f Antonio Banderas

b Match the people in photos 1–6 with their famous relatives a–f. In pairs, ask and answer. Use these words.

mother father brother sister
(ex-) wife (ex-) husband

Who's he? (picture 1)

(I think) he's Hugh Grant's brother.

c 2.13 Listen and check.

d Listen and repeat the sentences.

e ➲ **p.124 Grammar Bank 2D.** Read the rules and do the exercises.

f Whose is it? Match the people a–f with their possessions.

(I think) it's J.K. Rowling's pen.

2 VOCABULARY family

a ➲ **p.145 Vocabulary Bank** ***The family.***

b Talk to a partner.

How many	brothers and sisters cousins aunts and uncles grandparents children nieces and nephews	do you have?

3 PRONUNCIATION consonant sounds

a 2.14 Listen and repeat the words and consonant sounds.

b Practise saying the sentences.

/b/ What's your brother's job?
/θ/ I think my cousin is thirty-three.
/ð/ They live with their father.
/m/ My mother's name is Mary.
/n/ Do you know my nephew Nick?
/h/ Her husband's a hairdresser.

4 LISTENING

a 2.15 Listen to Sarah talking to her boyfriend about her family. Label the photos.

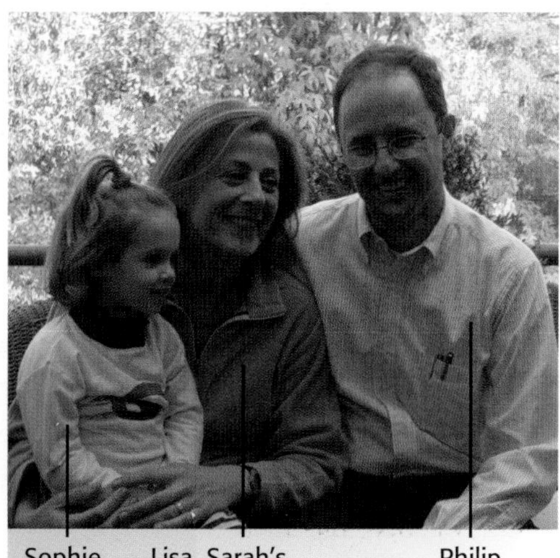

b Listen again. Answer these questions.

1 Who's Martin? Where does he work?
2 Who's Philip? How old is Sophie?
3 Where are they? What does Adam do?

5 SPEAKING

a Write on a piece of paper the first names of five people in your family. Give the piece of paper to your partner.

b Ask and answer these questions about the people.

2 At a hotel

VOCABULARY hotel words

a Match the words and symbols.

reception	☐	the lift	☐
a single room	☐	the (ground) floor /flɔː/	☐
a double room	☐	the bar	☐

b In pairs, cover the words and test your partner.

CHECKING IN

a 2.16 Cover the dialogue and listen. Answer the questions.

1 How many nights is Mark's reservation for?
2 What's his room number?

b Listen again. Complete the YOU HEAR phrases.

c 2.17 Listen and repeat the YOU SAY phrases. Copy the rhythm.

d In pairs, roleplay the dialogue. Use your name.

YOU HEAR	YOU SAY
Good evening, sir.	Hello. I have a reservation. My name's Mark Ryder.
1 Can you ______ that, please?	R-Y-D-E-R.
For five nights.	Yes, that's right.
2 Can I ______ your passport, please?	Just a moment. Here you are.
3 Can you sign here, ______?	
Do you want a smoking or non-smoking room?	Non-smoking, please.
4 Here's your ______. It's room 425, on the fourth floor.	Thank you. Where's the lift*?
5 It's over there. Do you need help with your ______?	No, it's OK, thanks.
Enjoy your stay, Mr Ryder.	Thank you.

* *lift* = British English
elevator = American English

SOCIAL ENGLISH

a 2.18 Listen and complete the chart.

	Mark	Allie
Where are they from?		
Are they married?		
Do they have children?		
How old are they?		

b Why does Allie think the phone call is from Mark's wife?

c Who says the USEFUL PHRASES, Mark or Allie? Listen again and check. How do you say them in your language?

USEFUL PHRASES

Sorry. → That's OK.
What do you think?
Would you like another drink?
I have to go now.

Study Link MultiROM

An informal e-mail / letter

To practise your English you can write to a 'penfriend' in another country. You can find penfriend websites on the Internet.

From: Rosa [rosamarquez@hotmail.com]
To: Stefan [stefan7541200@moebius.ch]
Subject: Hi from Mexico

Hi Stefan

1 My name's Rosa. 2 I'm from Mexico, and I live in Monterrey. 3 I'm a receptionist at a hotel. I study English in my free time.

4 I speak Spanish and a little English. 5 I want to learn English for my job and to travel.

6 I have a big family. I have three brothers and a sister. 7 My father is a builder and my mother doesn't work. My brothers and sisters are at school. 8 My brothers are 14, 13, and 10, and my sister is six. 9 I'm 19.

10 I like music, cinema and sport. I watch football on TV with my family every Saturday.

Please write soon.

Best wishes

Rosa

a Read the e-mail. Match Rosa's information with these questions.

Do you have a big family?	☐	What are your interests?	☐
How old are you?	☐	Why do you want to learn English?	☐
What languages do you speak?	☐	What do the people in your family do?	☐
What's your name?	1	Where are you from?	☐
What do you do?	☐	How old are your brothers and sisters?	☐

b Look at the letter. How is a letter different from an e-mail?

Los Nogales 1430
Santa Maria
Monterrey
12 October

Dear Stefan,

My name's Rosa. I'm from Mexico, and I live in Monterrey ...

WRITE a similar e-mail or letter to your teacher. Answer questions 1–10 in **a**.

2 What do you remember?

GRAMMAR

Circle the correct sentence, a or b.

(a) Hi. I'm Susanna.
b Hi. I Susanna.

1 a I not smoke.
b I don't smoke.
2 a He drinks a lot of coffee.
b He drink a lot of coffee.
3 a My cousin has a flat in Paris.
b My cousin haves a flat in Paris.
4 a Are you live with your parents?
b Do you live with your parents?
5 a Does your sister have children?
b Do your sister have children?
6 a Where does your wife work?
b Where your wife works?
7 a 'Do you play the guitar?' 'Yes, I do.'
b 'Do you play the guitar?' 'Yes, I play.'
8 a I'm an engineer.
b I'm engineer.
9 a Bill is Carla's husband.
b Bill is husband's Carla.
10 a This is my parents's house.
b This is my parents' house.

10

VOCABULARY

a prepositions

Complete with *at*, *for*, *in*, or *to*.

Look *at* the board.

1 I'm a student. I'm ______ university.
2 I work ______ IBM.
3 On Saturday nights I go ______ the cinema.
4 My brother lives ______ a flat.
5 Do you listen ______ the radio?

b verb phrases

Match the verbs and phrases.

read a newspaper.

do	have	speak	play	watch

1 ______ housework
2 ______ Russian
3 ______ TV
4 ______ the piano
5 ______ a sandwich for lunch

c word groups

Circle the word that is different.

Ireland	(Chinese)	Thailand	Spain
1 live	job	work	read
2 men	children	people	woman
3 engineer	doctor	football	pilot
4 student	factory	office	school
5 brother	uncle	niece	grandfather

d question words

Complete with *How many*, *Who*, *Why*, *What*, or *Where*.

What's your name?

1 ______ do you live?
2 ______ does your father do?
3 ______ is your favourite relative?
4 ______ hours do you work?
5 ______ do you want to learn English?

20

PRONUNCIATION

a ➲ p.158 Sound Bank. In pairs, test each other on the consonant sounds, 21–44.

b Underline the word with a different sound.

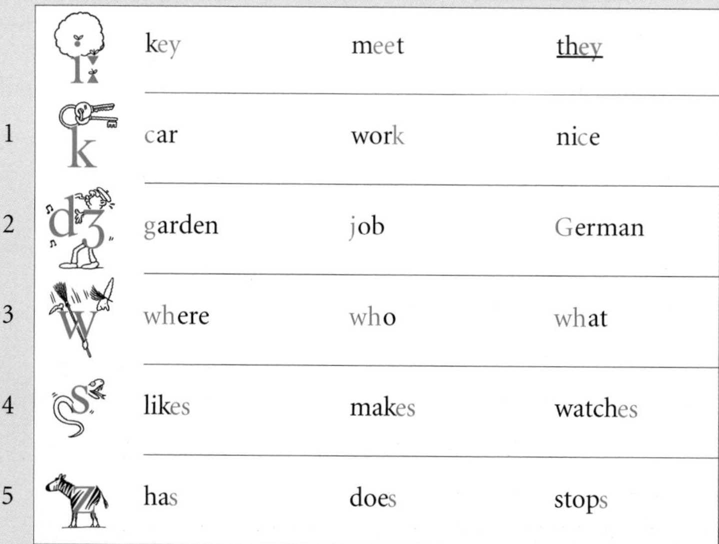

	key	meet	<u>they</u>
1	car	work	nice
2	garden	job	German
3	where	who	what
4	likes	makes	watches
5	has	does	stops

c Underline the stressed syllable.

infor<u>ma</u>tion

policeman	grandmother	receptionist	nephew	artist

10

What can you do?

CAN YOU UNDERSTAND THIS TEXT?

a Look at the picture and the title of the article. What do you think it's about?

Is a man still a child when he's 30?

Children usually live with their parents – but until what age? 20? 25?

Stephen Richardson, a social psychologist, studies the lifestyles of young people in Britain and the USA. He says that today many young people live at home when they are 25 or more. They are happy to live with their parents, go out at night, and spend their money on mobile phones and designer clothes. It's not only university students, but also young people who have jobs and earn money.

In many other European countries children leave home later. In Italy, for example, 30% of men and 18% of women between 30 and 34 live with their parents. This week in Naples a judge decided that Giuseppe Andreoli, aged 70, must pay €750 a month to his ex-wife for their son Marco. Marco lives with his mother – but he's not a child, he's a 30-year-old lawyer!

Adapted from a British newspaper

b Read the article. Mark the sentences T (true) or F (false).

1 Stephen Richardson is a student.
2 Many young people aged 25 live with their parents.
3 They don't like living with their parents.
4 In Italy 18% of 30-year-old men live with their parents.
5 Giuseppe Andreoli is divorced.

c In pairs, guess the meaning of the highlighted words. Check with your teacher or a dictionary.

CAN YOU HEAR THE DIFFERENCE?

2.19 Listen. Circle a or b.

What's your name? (a) Carlos. b 21.

	a	b
1	He's an engineer.	He's Spanish.
2	Yes, please.	Yes, I do.
3	He lives in Liverpool.	She lives in Liverpool.
4	She's fine.	She's 52.
5	I watch TV.	I'm retired.
6	He's fine.	He's my uncle.
7	No, I'm German.	Yes, a little.
8	No, they aren't.	No, she isn't.
9	Yes, I do.	Yes, they do.
10	In a school in the city centre.	On Tuesdays and Thursdays.

CAN YOU SAY THIS IN ENGLISH?

a Can you...? Yes (✓)

- ☐ say where you live and what you do
- ☐ name three relatives
- ☐ say who they are and what they do

b Ask your partner five questions. Are you similar?

What
Where
What magazines
What sports
What food
What music
What languages
What TV programmes

like
read
do
live
speak
watch
play
work

What magazines do you read?

3A Pretty woman

G adjectives
V adjectives, *quite / very*
P vowel sounds

She's very tall, with red hair.

USA quiz

1 The President of the United States lives here.
The *White* *House*

2 This city is the home of Broadway.
_______ _______

3 An important airline in the USA.
_______ _______

4 Americans eat a lot of this.
_______ _______

5 A famous Hollywood film from the 1990s.
_______ _______

6 Very popular American clothes, e.g. Levi's.
_______ _______

7 Another name for the city in number 2.
The _______ _______

8 People in this city travel in these.
_______ _______

1 VOCABULARY adjectives

a Complete the quiz using these adjectives and nouns.

adjectives	nouns
American	Woman
New	Airlines
Big	food
yellow	~~House~~
blue	Apple
Pretty	York
fast	taxis
~~White~~	jeans

b **p.146 Vocabulary Bank** *Common adjectives*. Do part 1.

2 PRONUNCIATION vowel sounds

a Put the adjectives in the correct column.

~~blue~~ cheap expensive easy slow
new white beautiful dry wet
old low empty clean high

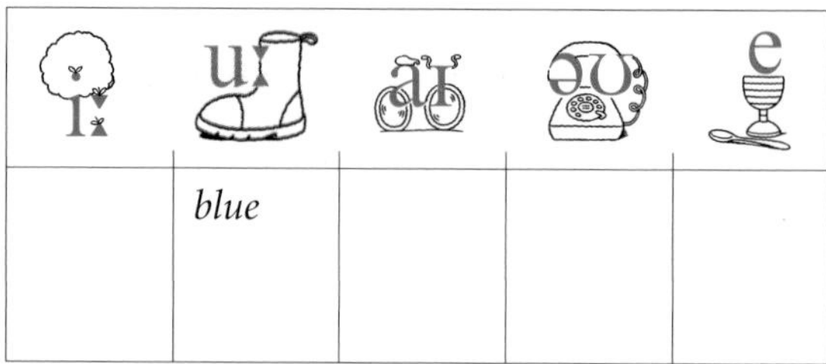

iː	uː	aɪ	əʊ	e
	blue			

b 3.1 Listen and check.

c **p.157 Sound Bank.** Look at the typical spellings for these sounds.

3 GRAMMAR adjectives

a Look at the answers to the USA quiz. Circle the correct rule.

- Adjectives go **before** / **after** a noun.
- Adjectives **change** / **don't change** before a plural noun.

b **p.126 Grammar Bank 3A.** Read the rules and do the exercises.

c **Adjective race.** In pairs, in *three* minutes make *eight* phrases (adjective + noun) for things in the picture, e.g. *a full moon*.

4 LISTENING

⚠ Remember! When people speak fast they don't separate words.

3.2 Listen and write six sentences.

1 *It's an easy exercise.*
2 ______
3 ______
4 ______
5 ______
6 ______

5 VOCABULARY & SPEAKING

a Read the descriptions and look at the pictures. Can you guess the two people?

Who are they?
He's a famous singer. He's very tall and good-looking. He has short, dark hair. He's Spanish but he lives in America. He sings in Spanish and in English.
She's a beautiful actress. She's very tall and thin. She has red hair. She lives in Australia. She has two adopted children.

b **p.146 Vocabulary Bank** *Common adjectives.* Do part 2.

c Think of a famous person. Write five clues. Tell your partner. Can he / she guess?

d Match the words and pictures.

1
2
3
4
5
6
7
8

angry	☐	hungry	☐
cold	☐	sad	☐
happy	☐	thirsty /ˈθɜːsti/	☐
hot	☐	tired /ˈtaɪəd/	☐

e 3.3 Listen and check. Repeat the phrases.

f Cover the words and look at the pictures. Tell your partner how you feel.

I'm very tired.
I'm not thirsty.
I'm quite hungry.

6 3.4 SONG ♫ *Oh Pretty Woman*

G telling the time, present simple
V daily routine
P the letter *o*

What time do you get up?
At seven o'clock.

Wake up, get out of bed...

1 GRAMMAR telling the time

a What time does your class start? What time does it finish?

b p.126 Grammar Bank 3B. Read the rules and do the exercises.

c Communication *What's the time?* *A p.108 B p.111.*

d 3.5 Listen to Vicky's morning. Write the seven times you hear. What's her job?

1 *7.00*

2 VOCABULARY daily routine

a Look at Vicky's typical morning. Match the pictures and phrases.

get dressed	☐	have a shower	☐
get up	☐	have breakfast	☐
go to (*work*)	☐	wake up	1

b In pairs, describe her morning.

She wakes up at 7.00.

c In pairs, take turns to describe *your* typical morning using pictures 1–6. Do you do things in the same order?

I wake up at (about) 7.30.

d p.147 Vocabulary Bank *Daily routine.*

3 READING & LISTENING

a Read the article. How stressed is Louisa? Why?

b In pairs, guess the meaning of the highlighted words. Check with your teacher or a dictionary.

How stressed

Professor Parker, a stress expert from the University of London, looks at two people's typical day and tries to help...

Louisa, a single mother

Louisa works as a guide at the National Gallery in London and lives with her son George, aged 9.

6.30 I get up and I make George's sandwiches. Then I do some housework. Then I wake up George and make his breakfast. I'm always in a hurry and I don't have time for breakfast at home.

8.00 We cycle to school because the bus is expensive. Then I cycle six miles* to work.

9.00 I have a sandwich for breakfast in the canteen, and then I start work. My first tour is usually at 9.30. I like my job but I don't earn much money and I stand all day.

5.00 I finish work and I go to pick up George at 5.30. We go shopping.

6.30 I cook dinner and help George with his homework. After dinner I do more housework or answer e-mails until 9.00. I don't go out in the evening because a babysitter is very expensive.

9.00 George goes to bed and I read him a story. Then I go to bed – I'm really tired!

Professor Parker's advice

Have breakfast with your son. Do all the housework in the evening. Don't cycle, get the bus. It's important to see other people. Invite a friend for a drink once a week.

* six miles = 9.6 kilometres

Adapted from a British newspaper

c Read the article again. Try to remember the information.

d **Communication** *Louisa's day A p.108 B p.111.* Test your partner's memory.

What time does Louisa get up?

She gets up at…

Simon works for a computer company. He lives in Brighton but he works in London.

are these people?

e 3.6 You are going to listen to Simon talking to Professor Parker. Listen to five things Simon says. Number the pictures 1–5.

f Listen again. What are the five sentences?

g 3.7 Now listen to Simon. Answer the questions.

1 How many children does Simon have?
2 What time does he get up?
3 Why doesn't he have breakfast?
4 What time does he start work?
5 How many cups of coffee does he drink?
6 What does he have for lunch?
7 What time does he finish work?
8 Why doesn't he have dinner with his family?
9 What time does he get home?
10 What does he do after dinner?

h 3.8 Listen. What is Professor Parker's advice?

i Who do you think is more stressed, Louisa or Simon?

4 PRONUNCIATION the letter *o*

⚠ The letter *o* has different pronunciations.

a Put these words in the correct column.

~~coffee~~ do don't go home job one school shopping son two worried

coffee			

b 3.9 Listen and check. Practise saying the words.

5 SPEAKING

In pairs, interview your partner about a typical day. Who is more stressed?

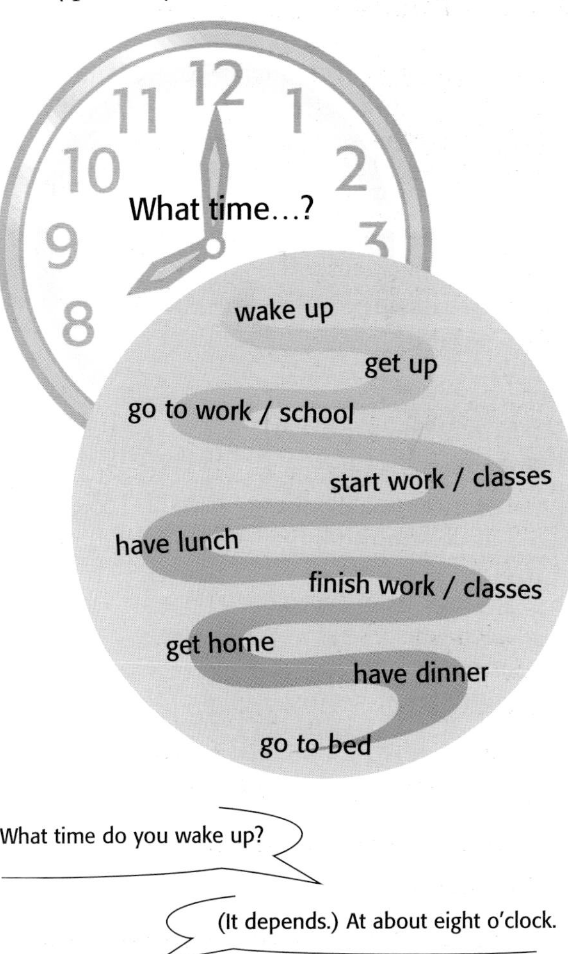

G adverbs of frequency
V time words and expressions
P the letter *h*

How often do you see your friends?
Every day.

The island with a secret

1 GRAMMAR adverbs of frequency

a Look at the photo of Takanashi. What nationality is he? How old do you think he is?

b Read the first paragraph of the article and write the highlighted words in the chart.

100	*always*
	______
	______
	sometimes
	______
0	______

c **p.126 Grammar Bank 3C.** Read the rules and do the exercises.

d Add an adverb of frequency to the sentences to make them true for you. Compare with a partner. Are you similar or different?

1 I *never* walk to work / school.
2 I do sport or exercise.
3 I use public transport.
4 I am stressed.
5 I am late.

2 READING

a Read the second paragraph of the article. What is unusual about Okinawan people? What do you think their secret is?

b Read the rest of the article. Put a heading in each gap.

Always active **Low stress** **Exercise** **A healthy diet**

c Read the article again. In pairs, guess the meaning of the highlighted words and phrases. Check with your teacher or a dictionary.

d Do people in your country live like the Okinawans? What's different? What's the same?

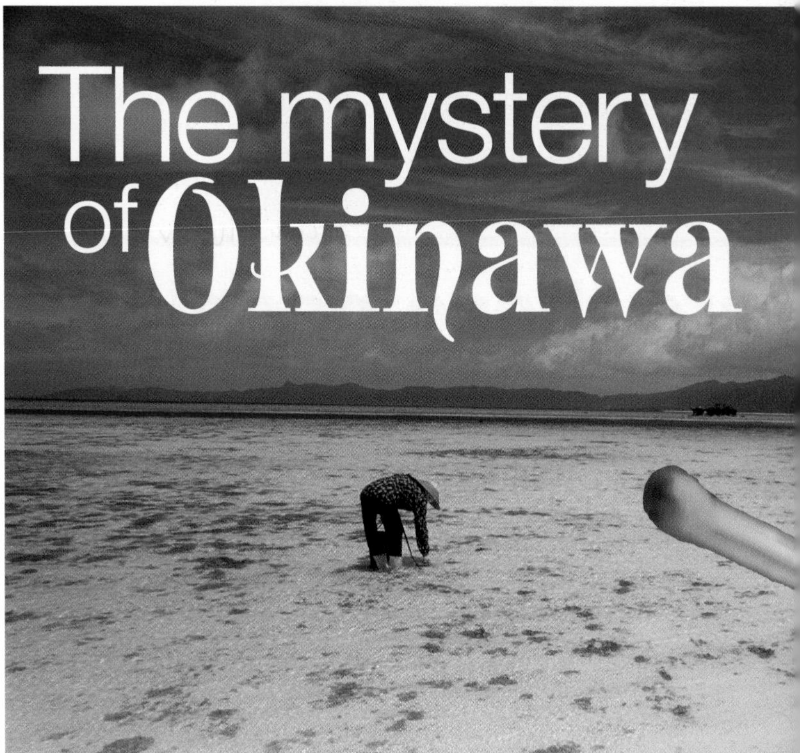

The mystery of Okinawa

Takanashi always walks three kilometres a day, and he sometimes rides a motorbike. He often works in his garden, and he usually does martial arts in the morning. He is never stressed, and he is hardly ever ill.

Not unusual you think? But Takanashi is ____ years old.

Takanashi lives on the island of Okinawa in Japan. In Okinawa people live a very long time. They are hardly ever ill. Many people live to be 100 – more people than in other parts of the world. Why? What is their secret?

1 ______________________

The Okinawans eat vegetables, fruit, fish, soya, and rice. They usually have seven portions of fruit and vegetables a day. People don't usually drink much alcohol or smoke. They don't eat much meat or fast food.

2 ______________________

Physical activity is very important for the people of Okinawa. Martial arts, walking, traditional dancing, and gardening are very popular with people of all ages.

3 ______________________

In many countries people have healthy diets and do exercise. But the unusual thing about the people in Okinawa is that they are not stressed. They are relaxed and take their time. Buses

Adapted from a British newspaper

4 GRAMMAR prepositions of time

a Can you remember? In pairs, complete the sentences with *in*, *on*, or *at*. Check with the festival texts.

1 The 'tomato battle' starts ______ 11 o'clock ______ the morning.
2 ______ January you can go to the Carnevale d'Ivrea.
3 The Thai Water Festival starts ______ April the 13th.
4 People throw water at each other all day and also ______ night.

b ➲ **p.126 Grammar Bank 3D.** Read the rules and do the exercises.

c ➲ **Communication** *When…? A p.108 B p.111.* In pairs, ask and answer the questions. Answer with a preposition + a time word.

> When do you usually read?

> I read at night, in bed.

5 READING & LISTENING

a Read the article. Complete Carla's answers with sentences A–E.

A Because it's the middle of the year – not the beginning or the end.
B Especially Christmas!
C Because I love my first coffee.
D Because I love the colours and the leaves flying in the wind.
E Because I have the week in front of me.

Times you Love

Carla Guelfenbein is a novelist. She lives in Chile.

- **What's your favourite time of day? Why?** My favourite time of the day is breakfast. ______
- **What's your favourite day of the week? Why?** Monday. ______
- **What's your favourite month? Why?** June. ______
- **What's your favourite season? Why?** Autumn. ______
- **What's your favourite public holiday? Why?** I hate all public holidays. ______

b **3.15** You're going to listen to two other people talk about their favourite times. First listen to these sentences. What do the highlighted words mean?

1 I can start to relax and enjoy the evening.
2 My family live very far away.
3 I get up early and feel full of energy.
4 In winter it's a nice temperature and it's when I feel comfortable.

c **3.16** Listen to the interviews. Complete the chart.

What's your favourite…?	Cristina, a sports coach from Spain	Udom, a manager from Thailand
1 time of day	*10 p.m.*	
2 day of the week		
3 month		
4 season		
5 public holiday		

d Listen again. Why are these their favourite times?

6 SPEAKING

In pairs, ask and answer the questions in *Times you love.*

> What's your favourite time of day? Why?

3 In a coffee shop

VOCABULARY coffee and snacks

a Look at the coffee shop menu. Match the words and pictures.

b In pairs, cover the words and test your partner.

	regular	large
☐ Filter coffee	1.50	1.70
☐ Espresso	1.65	2.85
☐ Cappuccino	1.95	2.95
☐ Chocolate chip cookies	1.50	
☐ Brownies	1.85	

BUYING A COFFEE

a 3.17 Cover the dialogue. Listen and answer the questions.

1 What do Mark and Allie get?
2 How much is it?

YOU HEAR	YOU SAY
Can I help you?	M What would you like?
	A A cappuccino, please.
1 ________ or large?	A Large, please.
	M And can I have an espresso, please?
2 To have here or ________?	M To have here.
3 ________ else?	A No, thanks.
	M A brownie for me, please.
OK.	M How much is that?
4 Together or ________?	M Together.
5 That's ________, please.	M Sorry, how much?
________. Thank you.	

b Listen again. Complete the YOU HEAR phrases.

c 3.18 Listen and repeat the YOU SAY phrases. Copy the rhythm.

d In threes, use the menu to roleplay the dialogue.

SOCIAL ENGLISH

a 3.19 Listen to Mark and Allie. Circle the correct answer.

1 There **is** / **isn't** a free table.
2 **Mark** / **Allie** spills the coffee.
3 Their next meeting is at **11.15** / **12.30**.
4 Allie **agrees** / **doesn't agree** to go shopping for a new shirt.

b Is Allie angry with Mark?

c Who says the USEFUL PHRASES, Mark or Allie? Listen again and check. How do you say them in your language?

USEFUL PHRASES

Thanks. →You're welcome.
There's a free table over there.
Here you are.
I'm really sorry.
Don't worry.

Study Link MultiROM

My favourite day

☐ My mother normally makes a big lunch. After lunch we play cards or read. My parents sometimes go for a walk, but I don't go with them. I don't like walking or doing exercise!

1 My favourite day of the week is Saturday, because it's the weekend!

☐ In the evening we often invite friends for dinner. In the summer we eat outside and people usually start singing and dancing. We never go to bed before 1.00. Nobody works on Sunday morning!

☐ I usually stay in bed until 10.30. Then I have breakfast and read the newspapers. After breakfast I often go to my parents' *dacha* near St Petersburg, especially in the summer. *Dacha* is the Russian word for a house in the country. It's a place where you relax and forget about everything.

a Read Anna's article. Number the paragraphs in the correct order 1–4.

b Read the article again. Look at the highlighted words. Complete the sentences with the connectors and sequencers.

Connectors

and or but because

1 I have coffee ______ toast for breakfast.
2 I like coffee ______ I don't like tea.
3 I like Saturdays ______ I don't work.
4 In the evening I go out with my friends ______ I watch TV at home.
5 I don't like football ______ basketball.

Sequencers

then before / after (breakfast, etc.)

6 I get up at 7.30. ______ I have a shower.
7 ______ lunch I sleep for half an hour.
8 I always have a bath ______ I go to bed.

c Complete with *and, but, or, then, after, because.*

1 I don't speak French ______ German.
2 I wake up at 8.30 ______ I don't get up – I read in bed.
3 I have dinner with my family. ______ dinner I usually watch TV.
4 On Saturday evening I sometimes go to the cinema ______ to a pub.
5 I usually get home at about 11.30, and ______ I go to bed.
6 I have two sisters ______ a brother.
7 In the winter we don't go out ______ it's very cold.

WRITE an article for a magazine: **My favourite day.**
Write four paragraphs. Answer the questions.

1 What's your favourite day of the week? Why?
2 What do you usually do in the morning?
3 Where do you have lunch? What do you usually do after lunch?
4 What do you usually do in the evening?

Check your article for mistakes.

3 What do you remember?

GRAMMAR

a Circle the correct sentence, a or b.

(a) Hi. I'm Susanna.
b Hi. I Susanna.

1 a It's a car blue.
b It's a blue car.
2 a He works in different countries.
b He works in differents countries.
3 a I'm very hungry.
b I have very hungry.
4 a What time it is?
b What time is it?
5 a It's half past seven.
b It's seven and half.
6 a It's quarter to the three.
b It's quarter to three.
7 a We often go to the cinema.
b We go often to the cinema.
8 a I'm never late.
b I never am late.
9 a My birthday is on July.
b My birthday is in July.
10 a I go to class on Tuesdays.
b I go to class at Tuesdays.

b Complete the questions.

A *Where* *are* *you* from?
B I'm from Perugia, in Italy.

1 A ______ ______ ______ your new car?
B It's green.
2 A ______ ______ ______ it?
B It's three o'clock.
3 A ______ ______ ______ you get up?
B At eight o'clock.
4 A ______ ______ ______ ______ ______ meat?
B Hardly ever. I prefer fish.
5 A ______ ______ you usually ______ TV?
B In the evening, after dinner.

15

VOCABULARY

a opposites

Write the opposite adjective.

young *old*
1 good ______
2 expensive ______
3 beautiful ______
4 tall ______
5 empty ______

b verb phrases

Match the verbs and phrases.

read a newspaper.

do get go have take

1 ______ dressed
2 ______ the dog for a walk
3 ______ a shower
4 ______ your homework
5 ______ shopping

c word groups

Circle the word that is different.

Ireland	(Chinese)	Thailand	Spain
1 hungry	tired	angry	tall
2 first	third	fifth	seven
3 one	twice	four times	six times
4 spring	nephew	autumn	summer
5 January	March	December	Easter

d prepositions

Complete the sentences with *at*, *by*, *for*, *until*, and *up*.

Look *at* the board.
1 I usually wake ______ very early.
2 He doesn't see his family ______ the evening.
3 I go home ______ bus.
4 What do you usually do ______ the weekend?
5 I often have a sandwich ______ lunch.

20

PRONUNCIATION

a Underline the word with a different sound.

b Underline the stressed syllable.

information

expensive difficult always July December

10

CAN YOU UNDERSTAND THIS TEXT?

a Read the article. Tick (✓) the things that Carl Harris says it's *good* to do in the winter.

1 Eat a lot of chocolate. ☐
2 Have a yoghurt and fruit juice for breakfast. ☐
3 Go to the gym. ☐
4 Make small changes to your diet. ☐
5 Go for a walk. ☐
6 Go running. ☐

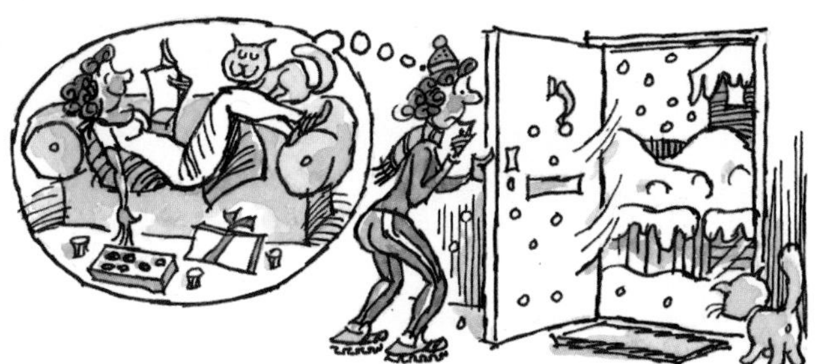

Don't go to the gym in the winter!

We all know that exercise is good for health. So on January 1st we often start the New Year with a good resolution – to go to the gym three times a week. But what happens? The first week we go three times, the second week we go twice, and the third week we stop going. The same thing happens with diets. After Christmas we start a new healthy eating plan. We are very enthusiastic at first – but after two or three weeks, we stop.

Carl Harris, a personal trainer, says this is because winter is the wrong time of the year to start new exercise routines and diets. 'In the winter the days are short and dark, and it's cold outside. Our bodies want food and sleep, not diets and exercise.' His advice for people who want to start a healthy lifestyle in January is to make small changes. 'Try to cut out chocolate and cakes for three days a week – but don't eliminate them completely. Go for short walks during the day, when it's light. But when March comes and spring begins, that's the time to get up at 7.00, have a yoghurt and fruit juice for breakfast, and go jogging!'

b In pairs, guess the meaning of the highlighted words and phrases. Check with your teacher or a dictionary.

c Read the article again. Why is it *not* a good idea to start going to the gym in the winter?

CAN YOU HEAR THE DIFFERENCE?

a 3.20 Listen. Circle a or b.

1 a I'm very angry. b I'm very hungry.
2 a It's quarter to ten. b It's quarter past ten.
3 a She gets home at five. b She goes home at five.
4 a It's on the first of May. b It's on the third of May.
5 a Today's September 12th. b Today's September 20th.

b 3.21 Listen. Circle a or b.

1 a It's red. b It's a BMW.
2 a Coffee and toast. b At half past eight.
3 a In a restaurant. b At one o'clock.
4 a Twice a week. b By car.
5 a Wednesday. b March the 13th.

CAN YOU SAY THIS IN ENGLISH?

a In English, can you...? Yes (✓)

☐ say what the date is
☐ say what time it is
☐ say what you do on a typical Monday morning
☐ describe a person in your family (age and appearance)

b Ask your partner five questions.

How often
What time
When

get up
go to the cinema
have lunch
listen to the radio
go to bed
drink champagne
use the Internet
eat meat
go on holiday

How often do you use the Internet?

4
A

G *can / can't*
V verb phrases: *buy a newspaper*, etc.
P sentence stress

Can you play the piano?
No, but I can play the guitar.

I can't dance

1 GRAMMAR *can / can't* (ability)

a Read the advertisement and look at the photos. Who do you think has 'star quality'?

POP STARS
Do you want to be a pop star?
A new Channel 6 TV programme needs young people with artistic and musical ability aged 18–25.
Call 0209 556 2453 or e-mail us at popstars@ttv.com
channel6 television

KELLY
GARETH
JUDE

b 4.1 Listen to the three people sing, play the guitar, and dance. Complete the sentences with Jude, Gareth, and Kelly.

1 *Jude* can play the guitar quite well.
2 ________ can play the guitar very well.
3 ________ can't play the guitar.
4 ________ and ________ can dance well.
5 ________ can't dance.
6 ________ can sing quite well.
7 ________ can sing very well.
8 ________ can't sing.

c 4.2 Who do you think is the winner? Why? Listen and check.

d Complete the sentences with *can* or *can't*.

[+] I ________ dance.
[−] She ________ dance.
[?] ________ he dance? ✓ Yes, he ________.
✗ No, he ________.

e In pairs, ask and answer with *sing*, *dance*, and *play the guitar*.

Can you sing?
Yes, I can. Can you?
No, I can't. Can you dance?

2 PRONUNCIATION sentence stress

a 4.3 Listen and repeat. Copy the rhythm.

A Can you sing?
B Yes. I can sing quite well.
A Can you play a musical instrument?
B Yes, I can.
A What can you play?
B I can play the guitar.
A Can you dance?
B No, I can't. I can't dance.

b When do you stress *can / can't*? Tick (✓) or (✗).

in positive [+] sentences ☐
in negative [−] sentences ☐
in *Wh*- questions [?] ☐
in short answers ☐

c 4.4 Listen. Are the sentences positive [+] or negative [−] ? Write [+] or [−].

1 ______ 3 ______ 5 ______
2 ______ 4 ______ 6 ______

3 VOCABULARY verb phrases

a ➲ **p.149 Vocabulary Bank** *More verb phrases*.

b Are you physical, creative, or practical? Interview your partner and complete the survey.

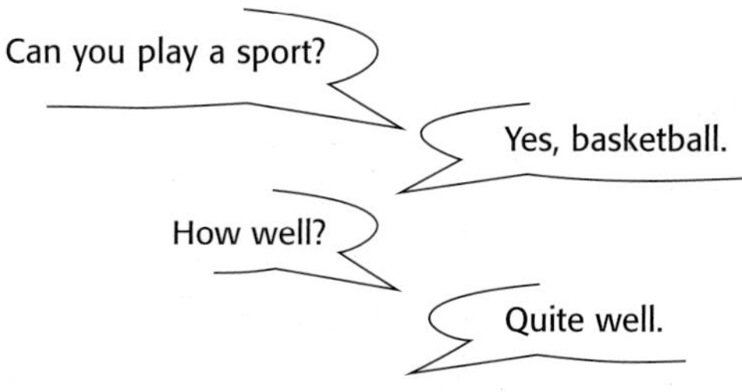

c Look at your partner's answers. Is he / she physical, creative, or practical?

Are you physical, creative, or practical?

	yes = ✓ no = ✗	*3* = very well *2* = quite well *1* = not well
Physical		
play a sport	☐	☐
swim	☐	☐
drive	☐	☐
dance	☐	☐
Creative		
take photos	☐	☐
draw or paint	☐	☐
cook	☐	☐
play a musical instrument	☐	☐
Practical		
follow instructions	☐	☐
read a map	☐	☐
programme a video	☐	☐
use a computer	☐	☐

4 GRAMMAR *can / can't* (other uses)

a 4.5 Look at the pictures. What's the problem in each one? Listen and check.

b Listen again. Write three *can / can't* sentences from each conversation.

1 *I can't...*
2 ______
3 ______

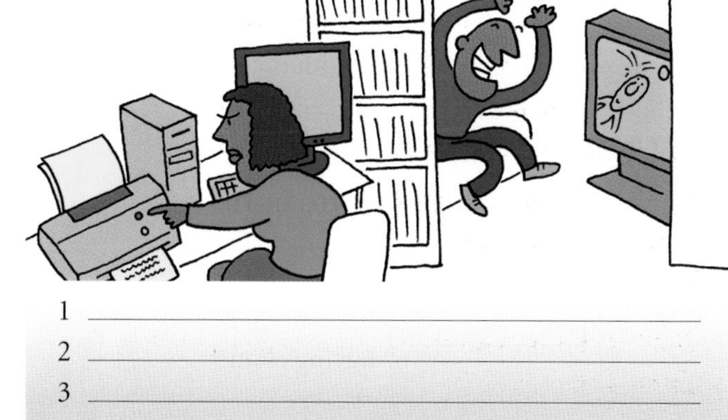

1 ______
2 ______
3 ______

c ➲ **p.128 Grammar Bank 4A.** Read the rules and do the exercises.

d Write sentences with *can / can't* for each picture.

G *like* + (verb + *-ing*)
V free time activities
P /ŋ/, sentence stress

Do you like shopping?
Yes, I love it.

4B Shopping – men love it!

1 LISTENING

a Do you like shopping? Tick (✓) the things you like buying. Tell a partner.

clothes ☐
food ☐
CDs and DVDs ☐
books ☐
presents ☐

I like buying clothes. What about you?

b Make a class survey for men and women.

Ten women like buying clothes, six men like buying clothes.

c **4.6** Listen. Match dialogues 1–4 with the pictures.

d Listen again. Complete the sentences with a verb.

trying on buying shopping going

1 I hate ________ to clothes shops with my girlfriend.
2 I don't like ________ for clothes.
3 I love ________ clothes, music, books, food – everything.
4 I like ________ clothes with my friends.

2 GRAMMAR *like* + (verb + *-ing*)

a Look at the highlighted verbs in **1d**. Complete the chart.

☺☺	I ________	buying clothes.
☺	I ________	
☹	I ________	
☹☹	I ________	

b **p.128 Grammar Bank 4B.** Read the rules and do the exercises.

c Make true sentences with *like, don't like, love,* or *hate.* Compare with a partner.

buy clothes try on clothes go shopping with my family
shop on Saturdays go to big supermarkets

I love buying clothes.

3 READING

a Read the article. Complete each paragraph with **Men** or **Women**.

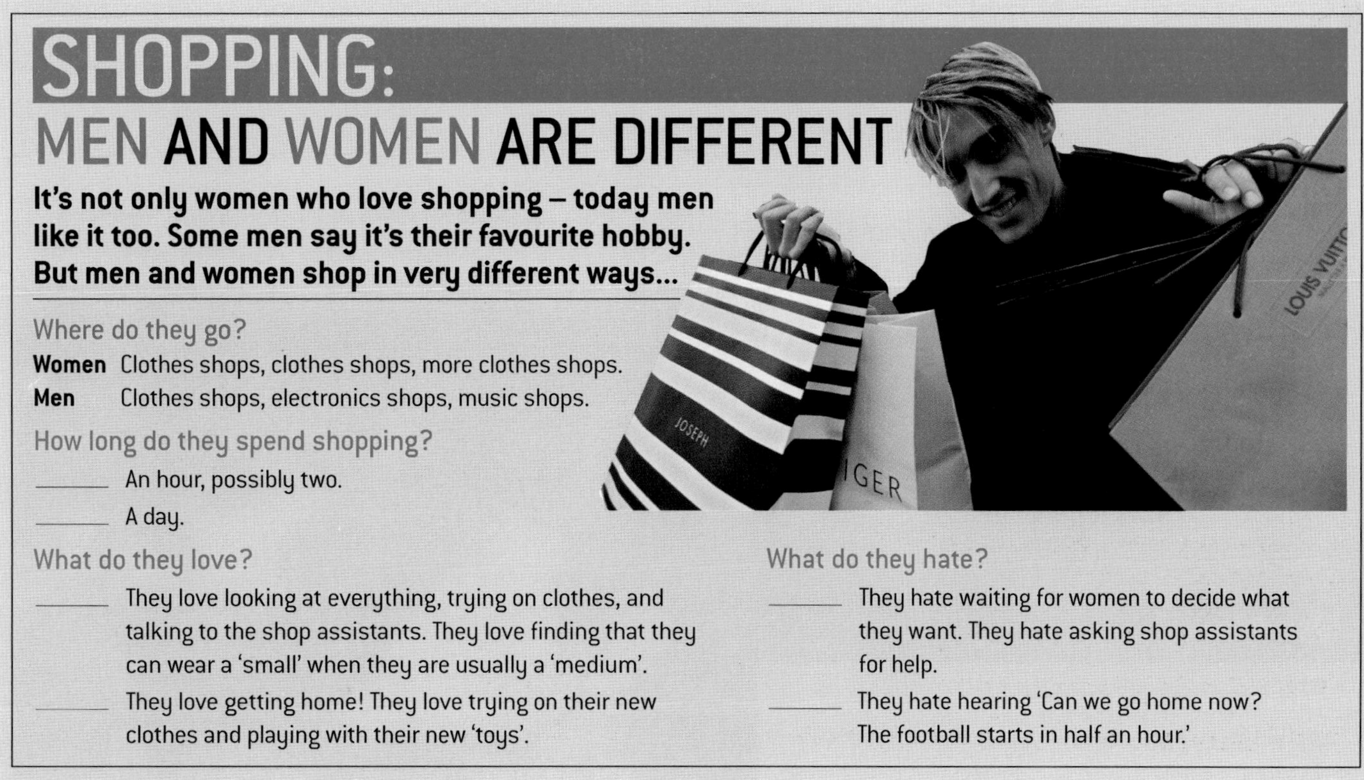

SHOPPING:
MEN AND WOMEN ARE DIFFERENT

It's not only women who love shopping – today men like it too. Some men say it's their favourite hobby. But men and women shop in very different ways...

Where do they go?

Women Clothes shops, clothes shops, more clothes shops.
Men Clothes shops, electronics shops, music shops.

How long do they spend shopping?

______ An hour, possibly two.
______ A day.

What do they love?

______ They love looking at everything, trying on clothes, and talking to the shop assistants. They love finding that they can wear a 'small' when they are usually a 'medium'.

______ They love getting home! They love trying on their new clothes and playing with their new 'toys'.

What do they hate?

______ They hate waiting for women to decide what they want. They hate asking shop assistants for help.

______ They hate hearing 'Can we go home now? The football starts in half an hour.'

Adapted from a British newspaper

b Read the article again. <u>Underline</u> one thing you think is true and one thing you think isn't true. Compare with your partner.

4 PRONUNCIATION /ŋ/, sentence stress

a 4.7 Listen and repeat the words.

b 4.8 Listen and write four sentences.

c Listen again and repeat. <u>Cop</u>y the <u>rhy</u>thm.

d **p.159 Sound Bank.** Look at the typical spellings for /ŋ/.

ŋ	shopping	waiting	think
	things	thanks	young

5 VOCABULARY & SPEAKING

a Write the *-ing* form of the activities in each picture.

b In pairs, ask and answer questions about the activities.

Do you like reading?
Yes, I do. / Yes, I love it.
It's OK.
No, I don't. / No, I hate it.
What kind of *books do you like*?
When *do you read*?
1
2
3
4
5
6
7
8
9
10
11
12

G object pronouns: *me, you, him*, etc.
V love story phrases: *she falls in love*, etc.
P /ɪ/ and /iː/

She loves him but he leaves her.

Fatal attraction?

1 GRAMMAR object pronouns

a Look at the photos and read the story of a classic film. What film is it?

Molly loves Sam. Sam loves her [1] but he never says 'I love you [2]'. Sam dies, and now he is a ghost. He watches Molly every day, but she can't see him [3]. Sam finds a psychic, Ota Mae. He uses her [4] to speak to Molly. In the end Sam says 'I love you [5]'.

b Look at the highlighted words 1–5. Who do they refer to? Write *Sam*, *Molly*, or *Ota*.

1 her = *Molly*
2 you = ______
3 him = ______
4 her = ______
5 you = ______

c Complete the chart with these words.

it me them us

subject pronouns	object pronouns
I	
you	you
he	him
she	her
it	
we	
they	

d **p.128 Grammar Bank 4C.** Read the rules and do the exercises.

2 SPEAKING

a Write four names in each circle.

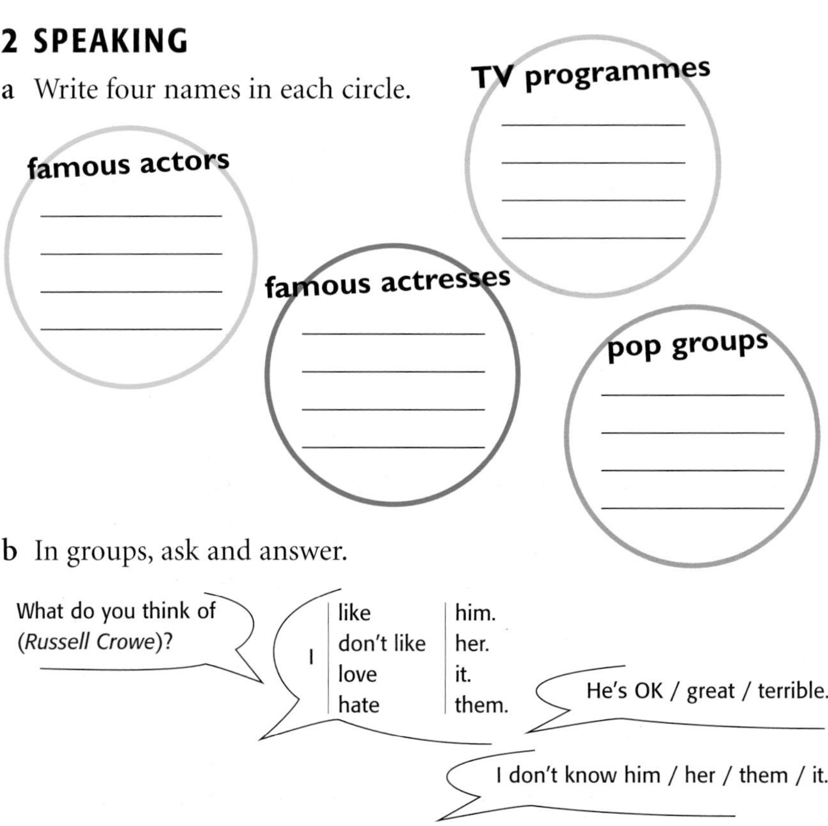

b In groups, ask and answer.

What do you think of (*Russell Crowe*)?

I like / don't like / love / hate him. / her. / it. / them.

He's OK / great / terrible.

I don't know him / her / them / it.

3 READING

a Look at the five famous films. Do they have happy endings or sad endings?

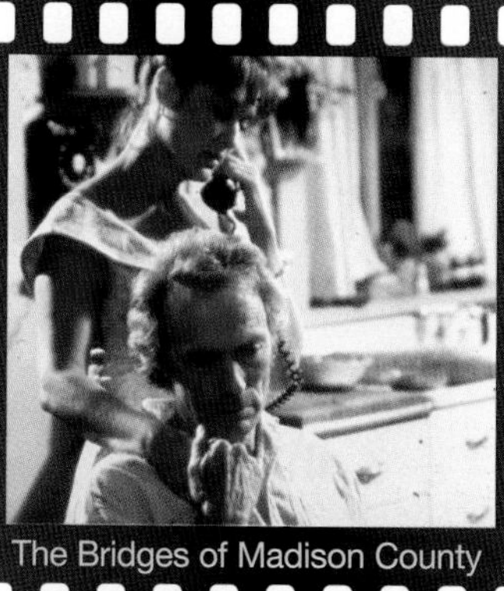
The Bridges of Madison County

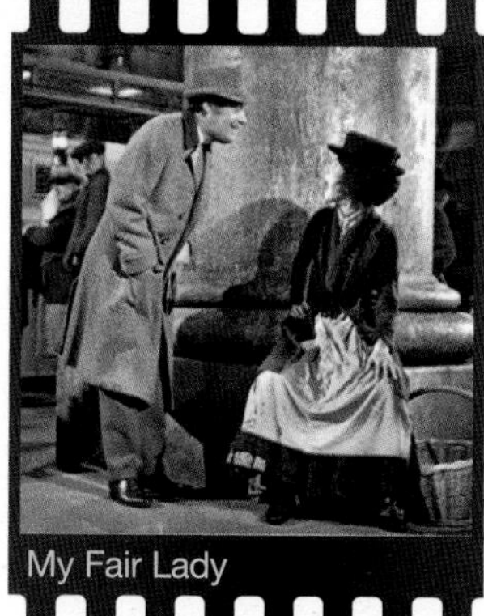
My Fair Lady

An Officer and a Gentleman

Romeo and Juliet

Fatal Attraction

b Read the newspaper article once. Write the names of the films.

Five classic love stories – which one is yours?

There are many romantic films, but there are only five basic types of love story: First love, Obsession, Teacher and pupil, Rich and poor, and Sacrifice. Here are some examples from Hollywood...

1 *My Fair Lady* **film type:** ______

She is a poor girl who sells flowers and he is a university professor. He teaches her to speak English 'like a princess'. She falls in love with him but he thinks she is only an interesting pupil. She gets angry and she leaves him. In the end he says he loves her.

2 ______ **film type:** ______

He's an American Marine. He wants to be an officer. She works in a factory. Her family are very poor. They go out together, and they fall in love. She wants to get married, but he's very ambitious, and he leaves her. But in the end he can't live without her, and he comes back to the factory for her.

3 ______ **film type:** ______

He's a happy family man. He meets a woman at work. They have a passionate love affair. He wants to finish it, but she doesn't want to stop. She follows him everywhere, and makes his life impossible. In the end his wife kills her.

4 ______ **film type:** ______

They are very young. He meets her at a party and they fall in love, but his family hate her family. They spend one night together. She says 'I love you but our love is impossible'. They want to go away and get married, but in the end they die.

5 ______ **film type:** ______

She is a housewife, married with two children. Her family go away for the weekend. A man stops at her house. They fall in love. He says 'Let's get married', but she loves her children and she can't leave them. In the end he goes away and she stays with her husband. But she never forgets him, and he never forgets her.

Adapted from a British newspaper

c Read the stories again. Guess the meaning of the highlighted phrases. Check with your teacher or a dictionary.

d What type of love story is each film? Complete the article with these film types.

First love Obsession
Teacher and pupil Rich and Poor
Sacrifice

4 PRONUNCIATION /ɪ/ and /iː/

a 4.9 Listen and repeat the words.

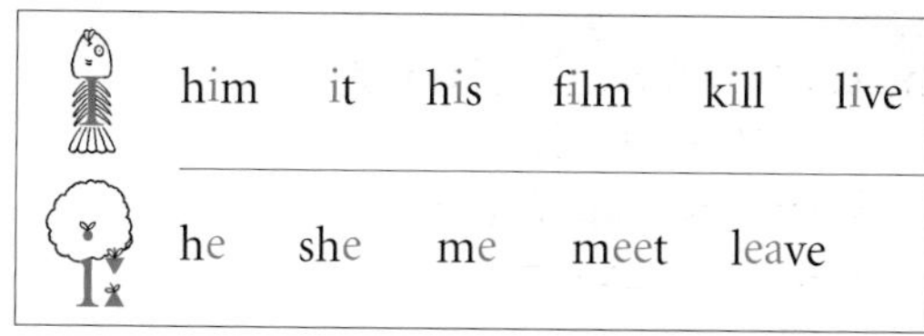

him	it	his	film	kill	live
he	she	me	meet	leave	

b 4.10 Listen to this love story. Practise telling it.

They live in a big city.
She meets him in the gym.
He works in films, she's a teacher.
She kisses him and he thinks she loves him.
But in the end she leaves him.

c **p.157 Sound Bank.** Look at the typical spellings for /ɪ/ and /iː/.

G possessive pronouns: *mine*, *yours*, etc.
V music
P rhyming words

Is this yours?
No, it's his.

Are you still mine?

1 SPEAKING

a Look at the pictures. What can you see?

b 4.11 Listen and tick (✓) the music you hear.

jazz	☐	pop	☐	dance	☐	rock	☐
classical	☐	opera	☐	blues	☐	reggae	☐

c Interview a partner with the music questionnaire. Are you similar or different?

What kind of music do you like?

What kind of music *don't* you like?

Do you...?

- sing or play in a group or orchestra ☐
- go to karaoke bars ☐
- download music from the Internet ☐

Can you...?

- play a musical instrument ☐
- read or write music ☐
- sing well ☐

How often do you...?

- buy CDs
- look for song lyrics on the Internet
- go to concerts
- watch MTV

Where do you like listening to music...?

- in the car ☐
- in the street ☐
- at home ☐

A F#m
Pretty woman, walking down the street,
A F#m
Pretty woman, the kind I like to meet,
D E
Pretty woman, I don't believe you, you're not the truth

2 GRAMMAR possessive pronouns

a Look at these song lyrics. Match them with the songs / singers. What's the difference between *my* / *your* and *mine* / *yours*?

1 I just can't get you out of my head.

2 Come with me, baby, be mine tonight.

3 You can leave your hat on.

4 I'll be yours through all the years.

a Elvis Presley, *Love me tender*

b Joe Cocker

c Kylie Minogue

d Roy Orbison, *Oh Pretty Woman*

b **p.128 Grammar Bank 4D.** Read the rules and do the exercises.

3 PRONUNCIATION rhyming words

a Pop songs often use rhyming words at the end of lines, e.g. *me – sea*. Match a pronoun from circle A with a rhyming word in circle B.

b 4.12 Listen and check. Practise saying the words.

c Cover circle A and look at the words in B. What are the rhyming pronouns?

d Play *Whose is it?*

A

mine
yours
his
hers
its
ours
theirs

B

showers
quiz
Thursday
wears
doors
fine
sits

4 LISTENING

a 4.13 Listen and complete the song with *I*, *me*, *my*, *mine*, or *your*.

b Listen again and read the song with the glossary. What does it mean? Circle 1 or 2.

1 I'm happy because you love me.
2 I'm sad because you're not with me.

c What are *your* favourite songs from films?

GLOSSARY

hunger (v) be hungry
goes by (v) passes
God speed God, please send me quickly
flow (v) move
arms (n)
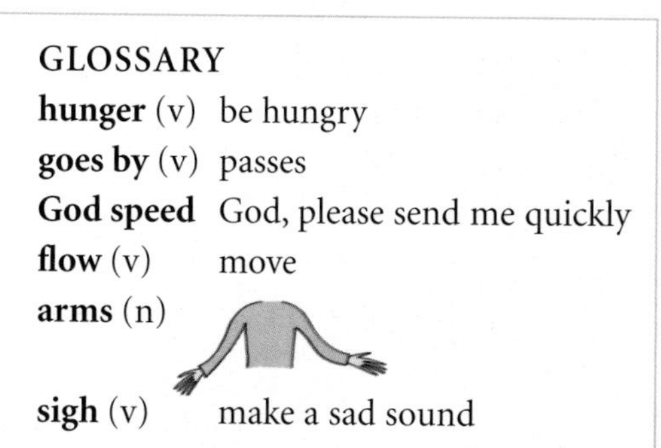
sigh (v) make a sad sound

Unchained Melody

Oh _____ love, _____ darling,
_____ hunger for _____ touch,
A long, lonely time.
And time goes by so slowly,
And time can do so much,
Are you still _____?
_____ need _____ love.
_____ need _____ love.
God speed your love to _____.
Lonely rivers flow to the sea, to the sea,
To the open arms of the sea.
Lonely rivers sigh, wait for _____, wait for _____,
_____'ll be coming home, wait for _____.

In a clothes shop

VOCABULARY clothes

a Match the words and pictures.

- a jacket ☐
- jeans ☐
- a shirt /ʃɜːt/ ☐
- shoes /ʃuːz/ ☐
- a sweater /ˈswetə/ ☐
- trousers /ˈtraʊzəz/ ☐

b In pairs, cover the words and test your partner.

BUYING CLOTHES

a 4.14 Mark and Allie are in a clothes shop. Cover the dialogue. Listen and answer the questions.

1 What size does Allie want?
2 How much is the shirt?
3 How does Mark pay?

YOU HEAR	YOU SAY
1 ______ I help you?	Yes, what size is this shirt?
2 Let's see. A small. What ______ do you want?	A medium.
3 ______ is a medium.	Thanks. Where can I try it on?
4 The changing rooms are ______ there.	Thank you.
5 ______ is it?	It's fine. How much is it?
34.99.	Do you take American Express?
Yes, sir.	

b Listen again. Complete the YOU HEAR phrases.

c 4.15 Listen and repeat the YOU SAY phrases. Copy the rhythm.

d In pairs, roleplay the dialogue.

SOCIAL ENGLISH

a 4.16 Listen and complete the sentences.

1 **Mark** I'm really sorry about the ________.
2 **Mark** We can take a ________.
3 **Allie** The ________? It's completely different!
4 **Allie** I'm sorry, but I can't have ________ tonight.
5 **Mark** Do you know a good ________?

b Does Allie really want to have dinner with Mark?

c Who says the USEFUL PHRASES, Mark or Allie? Listen again and check. How do you say them in your language?

USEFUL PHRASES

Would you like to have dinner with me tonight?
Happy birthday!
I'm busy.
How about Friday night?
Let me think.
Good idea.

Study Link MultiROM

Describing a friend

a Look at the six highlighted words in the text. They all have spelling mistakes. Write them correctly.

1 ________ 3 ________ 5 ________

2 ________ 4 ________ 6 ________

1 *This is a photo of my freind, Stephanie.*

2 *She's 18 and she's French. She lives in a village near Toulouse. She studys engineering at university.*

3 *She has short black hair and very dark eyes. She is inteligent and funny, but sometimes she's a bit sad too.*

4 *She loves music and she likes writting songs. She can play the guitar very well and she has a beautifull voice. We love listening to her. She's also crazy about computers, and she likes looking for song lyrics on the Internet. She only hates one thing – doing sport.*

5 *I like her because she's allways there when I need her.*

b Read the description of Stephanie. Match these questions with paragraphs 1–5.

- ☐ What does he / she like doing? What doesn't he / she like doing?
- ☐ How old is he / she? Where's he / she from? Where does he / she live? What does he / she do?
- ☐ Who is the person in the photo?
- ☐ Why is your friend special?
- ☐ Describe him / her.

c Read the description again. Then cover it and look at the questions. Can you remember the answers?

WRITE a similar description of a good friend. Write five paragraphs. Answer the questions in order, 1–5.

Check your description for mistakes.

4 What do you remember?

GRAMMAR

Circle the correct sentence, a or b.

(a) Hi. I'm Susanna.
b Hi. I Susanna.

1 a I can play the piano.
b I can to play the piano.
2 a Do you can come tonight?
b Can you come tonight?
3 a I hate do housework.
b I hate doing housework.
4 a Do you like swiming?
b Do you like swimming?
5 What do you think of this programme?
a I like.
b I like it.
6 a In the end she kills him.
b In the end she him kills.
7 a He doesn't love she.
b He doesn't love her.
8 a Where do your parents live?
b Where do yours parents live?
9 a This book is mine.
b This book is my.
10 a Whose is that bag?
b Who's is that bag?

☐ 10

VOCABULARY

a prepositions

Complete the sentences with *for*, *in*, *to*, or *with*.

Look *at* the board.

1 Wait ______ me.
2 Romeo falls ______ love______ Juliet.
3 I can't find my keys. Can you look ______ them?
4 I don't like talking ______ shop assistants.

b verb phrases

Match the verbs and phrases.

read a newspaper

draw	get	go	play	ride
run	take	tell	turn on	use

1 ______ the TV
2 ______ a horse
3 ______ me the secret
4 ______ chess
5 ______ photos
6 ______ a computer
7 ______ married
8 ______ a marathon
9 ______ out together
10 ______ a picture

☐ 15

PRONUNCIATION

a Underline the word with a different sound.

	 iː	key	meet	they
1	 ɪ	give	him	find
2	 iː	me	die	leave
3	 aɪ	mine	wait	try
4	 ɔː	walk	draw	turn
5	 uː	cook	use	you

b Underline the stressed syllable.

information

together	follow	instruction	classical	because

☐ 10

CAN YOU UNDERSTAND THIS TEXT?

a Read the article and answer the questions.

1 What does the writer think?

a Many young people today can't cook, and this a bad thing.

b Many young people today can't cook, but this isn't a problem.

2 Underline three reasons why young people can't cook.

TV chef Jamie Oliver

This week, journalist **Alina Wood** gives her opinion about cooking.

Cooking in Britain is now a spectator sport. We love watching famous chefs cook on TV, and we buy their books. But do we use them?

A recent study shows that 60% of British young people can't boil an egg. Four out of ten never or hardly ever cook. One teenager said 'I can't cook – but it doesn't matter. You just go to the supermarket and buy a pizza and put it in the microwave. Cooking is a waste of time.' A lot of adults think the same, and don't cook. They buy pre-cooked meals from the supermarket or take-away food. And if a mother hates cooking, then she doesn't teach her children to cook. Many schools don't teach cooking – they prefer to teach computer skills and foreign languages.

I think all this is very sad. For me, cooking is a very important skill. Everybody loves having a delicious meal but restaurants are expensive, so people who can cook well always have a lot of friends. Men love women who can cook – and women love men who can cook. Who would you prefer as a partner? Somebody who can use a computer, or a good cook?

Adapted from a British newspaper

b Read the article again. Match the highlighted words / expressions with their meaning.

1 ______________ cook in hot water
2 ______________ a young person between 13 and 19
3 ______________ a sport people like watching
4 ______________ it's not important
5 ______________ a bad use of time
6 ______________ good to eat
7 ______________ food you take home to eat, e.g. pizzas

CAN YOU HEAR THE DIFFERENCE?

a 4.17 Listen. Circle a or b.

1 a You can park here.
  b You can't park here.
2 a Is the house theirs?
  b Is the house there?
3 a Can you turn on the TV?
  b Can you turn off the TV?
4 a She doesn't like him.
  b She doesn't like them.
5 a Whose is it?
  b Who is it?

b 4.18 Listen. Circle a or b.

1 a I like it.
  b Yes, it's new.
2 a No, thanks. You can drive.
  b No, I don't. I prefer cycling.
3 a No, it's no-smoking.
  b No, thanks, I don't smoke.
4 a Yes, please.
  b Yes, but not very well.
5 a No, I think he's a terrible actor.
  b No, I think she's a terrible actress.

CAN YOU SAY THIS IN ENGLISH?

a Can you...? Yes (✓)

☐ say two things you can do well and two things you can't do

☐ say two things you love doing and two things you hate doing

b Complete these questions to interview your partner. Try to think of interesting questions.

Complete with a verb
What time do you ______?
Do you like ______?
How often do you ______?
Where do you ______?
Can you ______?

Complete with a noun (or the name of a person, programme, etc.)
What kind of ______ do you like?
What do you think of ______?
What's your favourite ______?
Who's your favourite ______?

c Interview your partner. Then change roles.

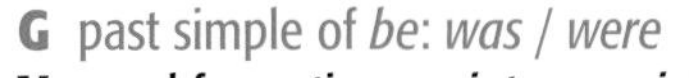

G past simple of *be*: *was* / *were*
V word formation: *paint* → *painter*
P sentence stress

Who was he?
He was a famous musician.

5 A Who were they?

1 LISTENING

a Look at the photo of Mount Rushmore. Who are the men? Match their first names and surnames.

George	Jefferson
Thomas	Lincoln
Theodore	Washington
Abraham	Roosevelt

b 5.1 Listen to an American tour guide. Check your answers.

c 5.2 Listen. Complete with numbers and dates.

Guide The second head is of Thomas Jefferson. He was President of the United States from *1801* to ______.

Tourist 1 When was he born?

Guide He was born in ______, in Virginia. His parents were very rich.

Tourist 1 Was he President after Washington?

Guide No, he was the ______ President.

Tourist 2 What's Jefferson famous for?

Guide Well, he's famous for writing the Declaration of Independence – that was when he was ______, before he was President – and for buying the state of Louisiana from Napoleon in ______.

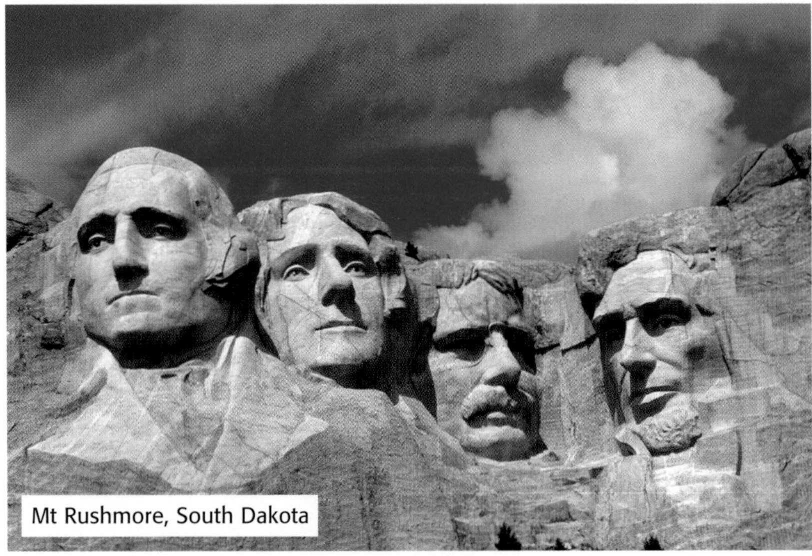

Mt Rushmore, South Dakota

2 GRAMMAR *was* / *were*

a Complete the sentences with *was* or *were*.

Present simple	Past simple
The heads **are** of four famous Americans.	They ______ all Presidents of the USA.
The first head on the left **is** Washington.	He ______ the first American President.

b **p.130 Grammar Bank 5A.** Read the rules and do the exercises.

3 PRONUNCIATION sentence stress

a 5.3 Listen and repeat. Copy the rhythm.

+ He was born in Virginia. His parents were very rich.
− He wasn't the second President. They weren't all famous.
? Where was he born? When was he born?
Was he famous? No, he wasn't.
Were they good Presidents? Yes, they were.

b **Communication** *Three Presidents A p.109 B p.112.*
Ask and answer about Washington, Lincoln, and Roosevelt.

c In pairs, ask and answer.

- When were you born?
- Where were you born?
- Where was your mother / father born?
- Where were your grandparents born?

1

The statue of ___________ in ___________.

______ was born in Mazovia in P______ in 1810. When he was seven years old he was already a brilliant pianist. He was a great composer and his piano music is world-famous and very popular.

2

The statue of ___________ in ___________.

______ was born in 1412 in the village of Domrémy in F______. She was only a young girl but she was also a soldier and a famous leader in the war against the English.

3

The statue of ___________ in ___________.

______ was born in Norfolk, E______, in 1758. He was a great sailor. He was famous for his victory against the French at the Battle of Trafalgar in 1805. His statue is in Trafalgar Square.

4

The statue of ___________ in ___________.

______ was born in 1807. His family were from Genoa, in I______. He was a famous politician and soldier, and a great leader.

4 READING

a Look at the four statues. Who are they? Where are they? Label the photos with the people and cities.

Nelson	Garibaldi	Chopin	Joan of Arc
Rome	Warsaw	Paris	London

b Complete the biographies with the names of the people and the countries they were from.

c 5.4 Listen and check. Cover the texts. What can you remember about the people?

5 VOCABULARY word formation

a You can often make the word for a person by adding an ending to a verb or noun. Look at the examples. What letters do you add?

verb →	**person**
paint	painter
act	actor
write	writer

noun →	**person**
art	artist
science	scientist
music	musician

b Read the texts again and find the words for people from these verbs and nouns.

1 piano ________
2 compose (v) ________
3 lead (v) ________
4 sail (v) ________
5 politics ________

c Underline the stressed syllable and practise saying the words.

d Think of a famous statue of a person in your town, or in the capital of your country. Write a short text about it. Say where it is, who it is, and what the person was famous for.

***The statue of* ______ *in* ______.**
He / She was…

6 SPEAKING

Who was the top British person of all time?

In a BBC survey the winner was Winston Churchill. Other people in the top ten were William Shakespeare, Lord Nelson, John Lennon, and Queen Elizabeth I.

a In groups of three, decide who you think are the top three people of all time from *your* country.

b Tell the class about them.

We think number 1 is ________.
He / She was a famous…

5B Sydney, here we come!

G past simple regular verbs
V past time expressions
P *-ed* endings

We wanted to go to Sydney.

1 READING

a 5.5 Read and listen to the true story about Raoul and Emma. Answer the question at the end.

A tale of two Sydneys

Last April two British teenagers wanted to go to Australia for their summer holiday. But it was a 24-hour journey by plane and tickets were very expensive. So, Raoul Sebastian and Emma Nunn, aged 19, looked for cheap tickets on the Internet. They were lucky, and they booked two tickets to Sydney.

On August 4th they arrived at Heathrow airport. They checked in and waited for the plane to leave. Six hours later they landed at a big airport and changed planes.

Emma: 'I was a bit worried because the second plane was very small, but I didn't want to say anything to Raoul.'

Raoul: 'After only an hour the plane landed. We looked out of the window. It was a very small airport. We walked to the information desk and I showed our tickets to the woman.'

'When is our next flight?' I asked.

She looked at our tickets. 'The next flight? This is the end of your journey. Where did you want to go?'

'Where are we?' I asked.

Do you think they were in Sydney?

Adapted from a news website

b Read the story again and number the pictures 1–9.

c 5.6 Listen to the end of the story. Where were they?

d **Communication** *Sydney p.112* and read about what happened to Emma and Raoul in the end. Is it easy to make a mistake like this?

2 GRAMMAR past simple regular verbs

a Look at the highlighted verbs in the text and complete the chart.

Present simple	Past simple
They want to go to Australia.	They ___________ to go to Australia.
I don't want to say anything.	I ___________ to say anything.
Where do you want to go?	Where ___________ to go?

b p.130 Grammar Bank 5B. Read the rules and do the exercises.

c Complete the questions with *Was / Were* or *Did*.

1 _____ they want to go to Australia?
2 _____ it a long journey?
3 _____ they book their tickets at a travel agent's?
4 _____ the tickets expensive?
5 _____ they check in at Heathrow airport?
6 _____ they change planes three times?
7 _____ the second plane big?
8 _____ Emma worried?
9 _____ the plane land in Australia?
10 _____ they stay in Nova Scotia for a long time?

d 5.7 Listen and check. Then listen and repeat. Copy the rhythm.

e In pairs, ask and answer the questions about Raoul and Emma.

Did they want to go to Australia?

Yes (they did).

3 PRONUNCIATION *-ed* endings

⚠ Past simple regular verbs end in *-ed* in + sentences. *-ed* can be pronounced in three ways.

a 5.8 Listen and repeat the verbs. In which group do you pronounce the *e* in the *-ed*? Why?

1 *-ed* = /d/	2 *-ed* = /t/	3 *-ed* = /ɪd/
arrived	booked	wanted
changed	checked	landed
showed	looked	waited
tried	walked	
	asked	

b 5.9 Listen and repeat Emma and Raoul's story.

1 They wanted to go to Australia.
2 They booked two tickets on the Internet.
3 They arrived at Heathrow airport.
4 They checked in.
5 They landed at a big airport.
6 They changed planes.
7 They looked out of the window.
8 They walked to the information desk.
9 They showed their tickets to a woman.

c Use the pictures in **1b** to re-tell the story from memory. Try to pronounce the past simple verbs correctly.

4 VOCABULARY & SPEAKING

a Number the past time expressions 1–7.

I booked the tickets
- yesterday morning. ☐
- five minutes ago. [1]
- last November. ☐
- a year ago. ☐
- last night. ☐
- three days ago. ☐
- last week. ☐

⚠ *last April*, NOT ~~*the last April*~~,
last week, NOT ~~*the last week*~~
yesterday morning / afternoon / evening
BUT *last night* NOT ~~*yesterday night*~~

b Stand up and move around the class. Ask *Did you...?* questions. When somebody answers *Yes, I did* write down their name and ask the next question, e.g. *Where to?*

Find a person who...

travelled by plane last year.	_____	Where to?
started learning English a long time ago.	_____	When?
played football last weekend.	_____	Who with?
studied last night.	_____	What?
cooked a meal yesterday.	_____	What?
arrived late for class today.	_____	Why?
listened to the radio this morning.	_____	What programme?
invited a friend to dinner last weekend.	_____	Who?
finished work late last night.	_____	Why?
watched TV last night.	_____	What programme?

Did you travel by plane last year?

Yes, I did.

Where to?

5C Girls' night out

G past simple irregular verbs
V *go, have, get*
P sentence stress

Where did you go?
We went to a restaurant.

1 VOCABULARY *go, have, get*

a Can you remember? Write *go*, *have*, or *get*.

_____ lunch   _____ shopping   _____ up

b ➲ **p.150 Vocabulary Bank** *Go, have, get*.

2 READING

a Do women go out together in your country? Where do they go?

b Look at the photos and read the reports. Where do you think the women are? Write **Rio de Janeiro**, **Beijing**, or **Moscow**.

The magazine ***Marie Claire*** asked its women journalists in **Rio**, **Beijing**, and **Moscow** to go out for the evening and then write a report.

	SABINA lives in ________. She went out with her friends Lali and Anna on a Friday night.	**SHARON lives in ________. She went out with her friends Nicole and Hujia on a Saturday night.**
1	I wore a black sweater and trousers and a lot of make-up. Girls here like wearing sexy clothes!	I wore a long dress. People are quite traditional here but young people want to wear new fashions and have new hair colours.
2	We went to Piramida. It's a bar and restaurant that's open 24 hours a day, and it's the 'in' place at the moment. There's a DJ and we saw a lot of interesting people.	First I drove to Bar Street, a street with about 50 bars. We met in the Pink Loft, a Thai restaurant. After dinner we went to a tea house because it's a good place to talk.
3	We had coffee and apple cake and then wine.	We had typical Thai food, like green curry. Then we had tea. Women here don't drink a lot of alcohol.
4	We talked about Lali's problems with her boyfriend. She was a bit sad. Then some men at the next table started talking to us and they bought us a drink. This is a very macho country and men always pay for women's drinks.	We talked about our love lives, especially Hujia's. She has a problem with her partner. We talked about men, fashion, and literature.
5	We got a taxi. It can be quite dangerous here at night and the metro closes at about 12.30.	We went home by car. I didn't drink any alcohol so I could drive.
6	We left Piramida at about 1.30, and I got home at 2.00.	We left at 12.00 and I got home at about 12.30.
7	Fantastic. 10 points. We had a great time and Lali was happy again.	It was a very good night. 8 points.

c Match the questions with the women's answers.

Did you have a good time?	☐
How did you go home?	☐
What did you do?	☐
What did you have to eat and drink?	☐
What did you wear?	1
What time did you get home?	☐
What did you talk about?	☐

d Read the reports again. Complete the chart with ✓ (= yes) or ✗ (= no).

	Sabina	Sharon
wear a dress?	✗	
go to a bar?		
drink alcohol?		
talk about men?		
talk about clothes?		
go home by taxi?		
get home after 1.30?		

e Compare your answers with a partner. A ask about Sabina, B ask about Sharon.

3 GRAMMAR past simple irregular verbs

a Look at the reports again and find the past tense of these irregular verbs.

wear	________	/wɔː/
go	________	/went/
see	________	/sɔː/
have	________	/hæd/
buy	________	/bɔːt/
get	________	/gɒt/
leave	________	/left/
drive	________	/drəʊv/
meet	________	/met/
can	________	/kʊd/

b 5.10 Listen and check. Practise saying the verbs.

c p.130 Grammar Bank 5C. Read the rules and do the exercises.

4 LISTENING

a Look at the third picture in *Girls' Night Out*. Where are they?

b 5.11 Listen to Sílvia talking about their 'girls' night out'. Listen once. Did they have a good time? How many points out of 10?

c Listen again. Answer questions 1–6 from 2c.

5 SPEAKING & PRONUNCIATION

a Look at the questions below. What words are missing?

b 5.12 Listen and repeat the questions. Copy the rhythm.

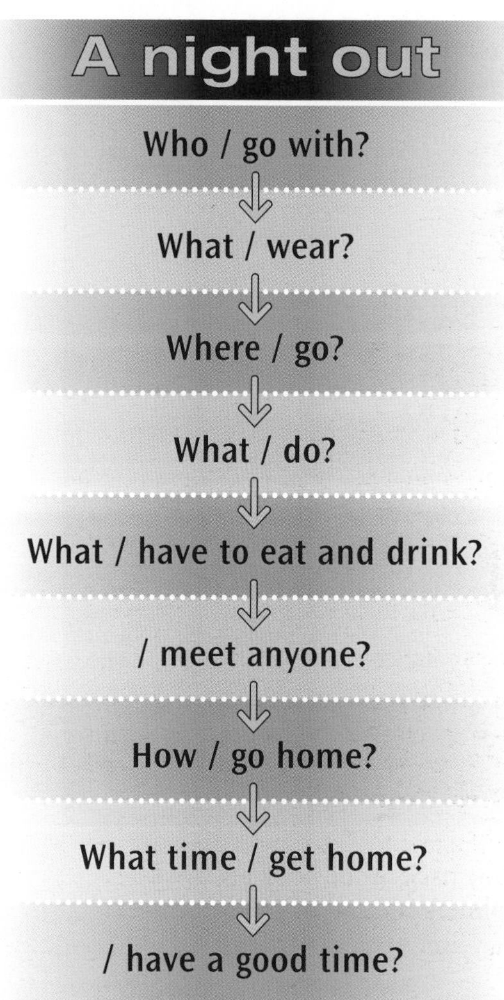

c Think about the last time you went out with friends. Look at the questions and plan your answers.

d Interview your partner about their night out. Did they have a good time? How many points out of 10?

6 5.13 SONG ♫ *Dancing Queen*

5 D

G past simple regular and irregular
V irregular verbs
P past simple verbs

Did you hear anything during the night?
No, I didn't. I was very tired.

Murder in a country house

1 READING

a Read the information on the back of the book. What's it about?

MURDER IN A COUNTRY HOUSE

The true story of the murder of a rich businessman. June 22nd 1938 was Jeremy Travers' sixtieth birthday. He had dinner at his country house with his wife, Amanda, his daughter, Barbara, his business partner, Gordon Smith, and his secretary, Claudia Simeone. Next morning when Amanda Travers went to her husband's bedroom she found him in bed ... dead.

ISBN 0-19-433846-0

Inspector Granger arrived at about 9.00. He was a tall man with a big black moustache. Amanda, Barbara, Claudia, and Gordon were in the living room. The inspector came [1] in.

'Mr Travers died between midnight last night and seven o'clock this morning,' he said [2]. 'Somebody in this room killed him.' He looked at them one by one but nobody spoke [3].

'Mrs Travers. I want to talk to you first. Come into the library with me, please.'

Amanda Travers followed the inspector into the library and they sat [4] down.

'What did your husband do after dinner last night?'

'When we finished dinner Jeremy said he was tired and he went to bed.'

'Did you go to bed then?'

'No, I didn't. I went for a walk in the garden.'

'What time did you go to bed?'

'About quarter to twelve.'

'Was your husband asleep?'

'I don't know, inspector. We... we slept [5] in separate rooms.'

'Did you hear anything when you were in your room?'

'Yes, I heard [6] Jeremy's bedroom door. It opened. I thought [7] it was Jeremy. Then it closed again. I read [8] in bed for half an hour and then I went to sleep.'

'What time did you get up this morning?'

'I got up at about 7.15. I had breakfast and at 8.00 I took [9] my husband a cup of tea. I found [10] him in bed. He was... dead.'

'Tell me, Mrs Travers, did you love your husband?'

'Jeremy is... was a difficult man.'

'But did you love him, Mrs Travers?'

'No, inspector. I hated him.'

138

b Cover the back of the book and look at the photographs. Can you remember who they are?

Who's Amanda?

She's Jeremy's wife.

Jeremy Travers

Amanda

Barbara

Gordon Smith

Claudia Simeone

c 5.14 Read and listen to the story. Mark the sentences T (true) or F (false). Correct the false sentences.

1 Somebody killed Jeremy at 8.00.
2 The inspector questioned Amanda in the living room.
3 Jeremy went to bed before Amanda.
4 Amanda and Jeremy slept in the same room.
5 Somebody opened and closed Jeremy's door.
6 Amanda got up at 7.00.
7 Amanda didn't love Jeremy.

d Look at the ten highlighted irregular verbs in the story. What are the infinitives?

1 *come*

e ➲ **p.154 Irregular verbs** and check.

2 PRONUNCIATION past simple verbs

a 5.15 Put these **irregular** verbs in the correct column. Listen and check.

~~bought~~ came could drove
found had heard read
said sat saw slept
spoke thought took wore

æ	ɔː	ʊ	ɜː	e	eɪ	əʊ	aʊ
	bought						

b 5.16 Find and underline nine past simple **regular** verbs in the story. How do you pronounce them? Listen and check.

3 LISTENING

a 5.17 Listen to the inspector question Barbara. Write the information in the chart. Listen again and check.

	Amanda	Barbara	Gordon	Claudia
What did they do after dinner?	She went for a walk.			
What time did they go to bed?	11.45.			
Did they hear anything?	Jeremy's door opened and closed.			
Possible motive?	She hated him.			

b 5.18 Listen to the inspector question Gordon. Write the information in the chart.

c 5.19 Listen to the inspector question Claudia. Write the information in the chart.

d Compare your chart with a partner.

e Who do you think was the murderer? Amanda, Barbara, Gordon, or Claudia? Why?

f 5.20 Now listen to what happened. Were you right?

4 SPEAKING

➲ **Communication** *Police interview A p.109 B p.112.*
Interview your partner about yesterday.

5 VOCABULARY irregular verbs

➲ **p.154 Irregular verbs.** Tick (✓) the irregular verbs you know. Choose three new ones and learn them.

A very good way to improve your English and learn irregular verbs is by reading Graded Readers. Buy or borrow a Stage 1 Graded Reader in the past tense (with a cassette or CD if possible).

5 In a gift shop

VOCABULARY shopping

a Match the words and pictures.

- postcards ☐
- batteries ☐
- a (camera) film ☐
- T-shirts ☐
- a mug ☐

b In pairs, cover the words and test your partner.

BUYING A PRESENT

a 5.21 Allie is in a gift shop. Cover the dialogue and listen. What does she buy?

YOU HEAR	YOU SAY
Can I help you?	How much is that T-shirt?
1 It's ______.	Sorry, how much did you say?
______.	And how much are those mugs?
2 The big mugs are ______ and the small ones are ______.	Can I have a big mug, please?
3 Sure. ______ you are. ______ else?	Do you have birthday cards?
4 Sorry, *we've only got ______.	Oh well, just the mug then.
5 That's ______.	Here you are.
6 *Have you got the ______?	Yes, here.
Thanks.	Thank you.
Bye.	Bye.

* In Britain people often use *I've got* (*I have got*) or *Have you got…?* as an alternative to *I have* or *Do you have…?*

b Listen again. Complete the YOU HEAR phrases.

c 5.22 Listen and repeat the YOU SAY phrases. Copy the rhythm.

d In pairs, roleplay the dialogue.

SOCIAL ENGLISH

a 5.23 Listen. Mark the sentences T (true) or F (false).

1 Mark likes Allie's dress.
2 Mark breaks the mug.
3 They get a taxi to the restaurant.
4 Allie reserved a table for 8.30.

b Why is Allie stressed?

c Who says the USEFUL PHRASES, Mark or Allie? Listen again and check. How do you say them in your language?

USEFUL PHRASES

Wow! You look great.
I don't believe it!
No problem.
Come on, it's time to go.
Relax.

A holiday report

a Read Alex's questionnaire and report. Which questions does Alex answer in each paragraph?

paragraph 1 questions *1,* ________
paragraph 2 questions ________
paragraph 3 questions ________
paragraph 4 questions ________

b Plan your report. Answer the questionnaire for your last holiday. Write short notes (not complete sentences).

Questionnaire

Where did you go for your last holiday?
What did you do?
Please tell us your experiences…

1 **Where did you go?**
To Rome.

2 **When did you go there?**
Last August.

3 **Who did you go with?**
My girlfriend.

4 **How did you get there?**
By plane – British Airways

5 **How long did you stay?**
A week.

6 **Where did you stay?**
In a small hotel near the Colosseum. Nice and quite cheap.

7 **What did you do?**
During the day: walked around the city, saw famous places, took photos.

At night: went to restaurants – pasta and wine.

8 **Did you buy anything?**
Yes, painting and shoes.

9 **Did you have a good time?**
Fantastic – city full of history, special atmosphere, great food.

10 **Did you have any problems?**
Very hot, difficult to cross the road.

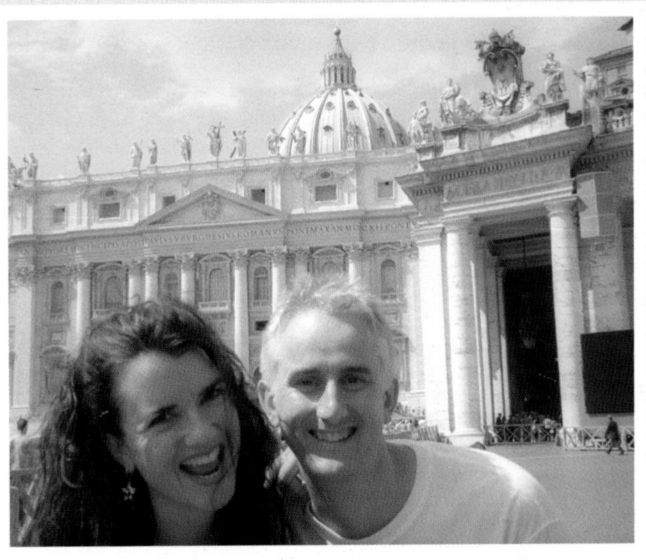

1 I went to Rome last August with my girlfriend. We flew to Rome with British Airways.

2 We stayed for a week in a small hotel near the Colosseum. The hotel was nice and quite cheap.

3 During the day we walked around the city. We saw all the famous places like the Colosseum and St Peter's, and we threw a coin in the Trevi Fountain. We took a lot of photos. At night we went to restaurants and had fantastic pasta and red wine. Our favourite restaurant was in the Piazza Navona. We bought a painting of Trastevere (the old town) and my girlfriend bought some very expensive shoes.

4 We had a great time. Rome is full of history and has a special atmosphere, and Italian food is wonderful. We only had two problems: it was very hot, and it was very difficult to cross the road.

WRITE a report of your holiday. Write four paragraphs. Answer questions 1–10 in the questionnaire.

Read your report carefully. Check spelling, punctuation (CAPITAL letters and full stops), and grammar (are the verbs in the past tense?). Attach a photo if you have one.

5 What do you remember?

GRAMMAR

a Circle the correct sentence, a or b.

(a) Hi. I'm Susanna.
b Hi. I Susanna.

1 a They was Presidents of the USA.
b They were Presidents of the USA.

2 a Where you were born?
b Where were you born?

3 a Were the tickets expensive?
b Did the tickets be expensive?

4 a They booked the tickets last April.
b They book the tickets last April.

5 a They didn't arrive in Australia.
b They didn't arrived in Australia.

6 a When does the plane landed?
b When did the plane land?

7 a Had they a good time last night?
b Did they have a good time last night?

8 a They leaved the bar very early.
b They left the bar very early.

9 a I didn't see anything.
b I didn't saw anything.

10 a What time did you go to bed?
b What time you did go to bed?

b Write the past simple.

get *got*

1 study studied
2 go went
3 drive drove
4 can could
5 wait waited
6 say said
7 think thought
8 write wrote
9 stay stayed
10 hear heard

20

VOCABULARY

a people

Complete with *-er*, *-or*, *-ist*, or *-ian*.

lead *er*

1 act er
2 art ist
3 paint er
4 music ___
5 scient ist

b verb phrases

Complete with *have*, *go*, or *get*.

have a shower

1 have a good time
2 go an e-mail
3 get away for the weekend
4 go a taxi
5 have a drink

c prepositions

Complete the sentences with *by*, *for*, *in*, *out*, or *to*.

Look *at* the board.

1 We went ______ a walk in the park.
2 I went ______ with my friends on Saturday night.
3 They went home ______ car.
4 What time did you get ______ the restaurant?
5 I was born ______ 1982.

d past time expressions

~~Cross out~~ the wrong expression.

She phoned him **yesterday** / ~~**the yesterday**~~.

1 She saw him **ago three weeks** / **three weeks ago**.
2 What time did you get up **yesterday morning** / **last morning**?
3 My birthday was **last month** / **the last month**.
4 We watched TV **last night** / **yesterday night**.
5 The concert was **in last April** / **last April**.

20

PRONUNCIATION

a Underline the word with a different sound.

	iː	key	meet	<u>they</u>
1	t	looked	asked	waited
2	d	landed	died	called
3	ɔː	saw	told	bought
4	ʊ	could	took	found
5	e	said	heard	met

b Underline the stressed syllable.

infor<u>ma</u>tion

politician musician restaurant ago somebody

10

What can you do?

CAN YOU UNDERSTAND THIS TEXT?

a Read the article once and complete the questions with a verb in the past simple.

cry ~~go~~ go smoke

First times, Last times

Ben Silverstone in *The Browning Version*.

This week our interview is with Ben Silverstone, a young actor with a great future. His films include *The Browning Version*, *Lolita*, and *Get Real*.

1 When was the first time you *went* **out with a girl?**
When I was 12. I took a girl from school to the cinema and then to McDonald's – very romantic! But I didn't have a serious girlfriend until I was 18.

2 When was the first time you ______ a cigarette?
When I was 14. I was in a film called *The Browning Version*. One night after we finished filming I sat with some of the other young actors on the roof of our hotel and I had my first cigarette under the stars. I didn't really enjoy it because I was frightened of falling off the roof.

3 When was the last time you ______ in the cinema?
A long time ago! I don't remember the film. But I remember seeing *Dead Poets' Society* with my father when I was about ten. I thought I was very adult because I didn't cry at the end. Then I looked at my father and he was crying! Very confusing when you're ten years old.

4 When was the last time you ______ to a party?
Last Saturday. It was a barbecue. When summer comes, the English love barbecues in the sun. But as usual it rained, and in the end we ate hamburgers and sausages in the kitchen.

b Read the article again and answer the questions.

1 Was his first date really romantic? Why (not)?
2 Was he inside or outside when he had his first cigarette?
3 Did he cry at the end of *Dead Poets' Society*?
4 Why wasn't the party very good?

c Underline any words or expressions you don't know. Try to guess them from the context. Check with your dictionary. Try to learn *five* new words.

CAN YOU HEAR THE DIFFERENCE?

a **5.24** Listen. Circle a or b.

1 a My mother is a writer.
  b My mother was a writer.
2 a We book tickets on the Internet.
  b We booked tickets on the Internet.
3 a Where do you study English?
  b Where did you study English?
4 a We meet every week.
  b We met every week.
5 a They have a lot of money.
  b They had a lot of money.

b **5.25** Listen. Circle a or b.

1 a He was born in France.
  b He was born in Argentina.
2 a She bought some expensive shoes.
  b She bought some cheap shoes.
3 a He didn't think the film was very good.
  b He thought the film was very good.
4 a They went out on Saturday night.
  b They went out on Friday night.
5 a She got up at 7.00.
  b She got up at 7.30.

CAN YOU SAY THIS IN ENGLISH?

a Can you...? Yes (✓)

- [ ] say where and when you were born
- [ ] say five things you did yesterday morning
- [ ] say five things you did last weekend

b In pairs, choose three questions and ask a partner. Ask for more information.

When was the last time you...?

- saw a film in the cinema
- bought flowers for somebody
- went to a party
- sent a text message
- went away for the weekend
- spent a lot of money

When was the last time you went away for the weekend?

A month ago.

Where did you go?

6 A

G *there is / there are*
V houses and furniture
P /ð/ and /eə/, sentence stress

Is there a television?
No, there isn't.

A house with a history

1 VOCABULARY houses and furniture

a Order the letters to make three rooms in a house.

chitken ________ redboom ________ thorobam ________

b Name two things you usually find in these rooms.

c ➲ **p.151 Vocabulary Bank** *Flats and houses.* Do parts 1 and 2.

2 LISTENING

a Read the advert and look at the photo.
Would you like to live in this house? Why (not)?

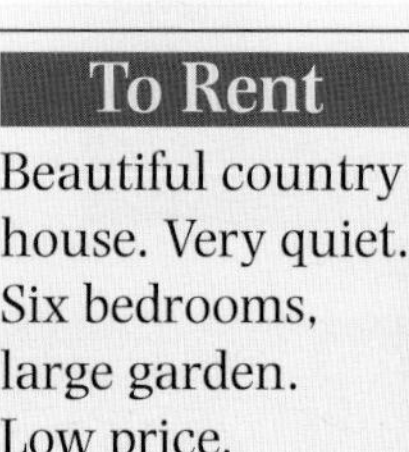
To Rent
Beautiful country house. Very quiet. Six bedrooms, large garden. Low price.

b 6.1 Larry and Louise are from the USA. They want to rent the house. Cover the dialogue and listen. Which three rooms in the house do they go into?

c Listen again and complete the dialogue.

Estate agent Well, this is the hall. There are six rooms on this floor. There's a kitchen, a [1] ______, a living room, a [2] ______, a library...
Larry Wow! There's a library, Louise!
Louise What's that room?
Estate agent That's a [3] ______, madam.
Larry How many bathrooms are there?
Estate agent There's one downstairs and three [4] ______.
Louise Are there any [5] ______?
Estate agent No, there aren't, madam. This is an old house.

Estate agent This is the living room.
Louise Are those paintings original?
Estate agent Yes, I think so, madam.
Larry Is there a [6] ______?
Estate agent No, there isn't, sir. But there's a [7] ______.

Estate agent And the kitchen.
Louise There isn't a [8] ______.
Estate agent Yes, there is. It's over there,
Louise You call that a fridge! Are there any [9] ______? I need a glass of water.
Estate agent Yes, madam. There are some glasses in that [10] ______. Now let's go upstairs.

d 6.2 Larry and Louise and the estate agent go upstairs. Listen. What problem is there with one of the bedrooms? Do they decide to rent the house?

3 GRAMMAR *there is / there are*

a Read the dialogue in 2c. Complete the chart.

	singular	plural
+	There's a piano.	There ______ some glasses in the cupboard.
−	There ______ a fridge	There aren't any showers.
?	______ ______ a TV?	______ ______ any glasses?

b What's the difference between...?

1 There are **four** glasses in the cupboard.
2 There are **some** glasses in the cupboard.

c **p.132 Grammar Bank 6A.** Read the rules and do the exercises.

4 PRONUNCIATION /ð/ and /eə/, sentence stress

a 6.3 Listen and repeat. Copy the rhythm.

A Where's the bathroom?
B It's upstairs.
A Is there a lift?
B No, there are stairs.
A Where are the stairs?
B They're over there.

b In groups of three, roleplay the dialogue in 2c between the estate agent and Louise and Larry.

5 SPEAKING

a Complete the questions with *is there* or *are there*. In pairs, ask and answer.

In your house / flat

1 How many bedrooms ________?
2 How many bathrooms ________?
3 ________ a study?
4 ________ a garden?
5 ________ a garage?
6 ________ central heating?

In your bedroom

7 ________ a TV?
8 ________ any pictures on the wall?
9 ________ any plants?
10 ________ a mirror?
11 ________ any cupboards?
12 ________ a computer?

b Quickly draw a plan of your living room. 'Show' the room to your partner.

This is the living room. There are two sofas and an armchair...

6 LISTENING

6.4 On their first night in the house, Larry and Louise go to the local pub. Listen and answer the questions.

1 What do they have to drink? Why?
2 What does the barman tell them?
3 What happens in the end?

6B A night in a haunted hotel

G *there was / there were*
V prepositions of place
P silent letters

Was there a ghost in the room?

1 VOCABULARY prepositions of place

a Match the words and pictures.

in	☐	between	☐
in front of	☐	opposite	☐
on	☐	next to	☐
under	☐	over	☐
behind	☐		

1 

2 

3, 4 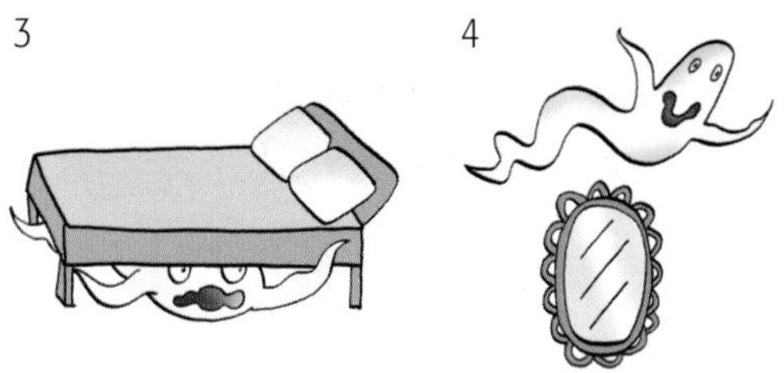

5, 6, 7 

8, 9 

b In pairs, ask and answer with the pictures.

Where's the ghost? It's under the bed.

c **p.151 Vocabulary Bank** *Flats and houses.* Play *Where's the ghost?*

2 READING

a Look at the photos and read the introduction below. Answer the questions.

1 Where is Gosforth Hall Hotel?
2 Who is Stephen Bleach?
3 What is special about Room 11?
4 What did Stephen do?
5 What *couldn't* he do?
6 How did he feel before he went to the hotel?
7 Does he believe in ghosts?

b Do *you* believe in ghosts? Would you like to spend a night in Room 11 of Gosforth Hall Hotel? Why (not)?

Would you like to spend a night in this room?

THERE ARE MANY old houses, pubs, and hotels in Britain which people say have ghosts. A British newspaper, the *Sunday Times*, sent one of its journalists, **Stephen Bleach**, to investigate Gosforth Hall Hotel, a small hotel in Cumbria in the north of England. People say that the hotel has the ghost of a seventeenth century Catholic priest. The ghost always appears in Room 11.

Stephen's job was to spend the night alone in Room 11. He couldn't phone or speak to anybody. Before he went to the hotel, Stephen said 'I feel a bit nervous, but I don't believe in ghosts.'

c 6.5 Read and listen about Stephen's experience. Label the three pictures with words from the article.

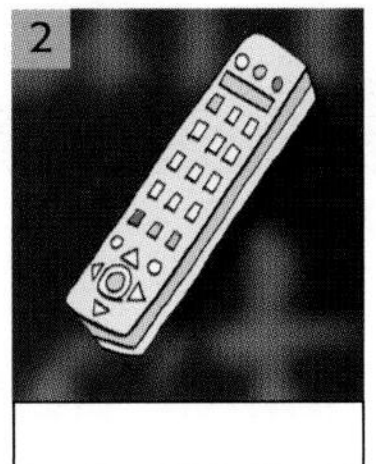

I arrived at Gosforth Hall late in the evening. It was a very dark night but I could see there was a church with a cemetery next to the hotel. I checked in, and the receptionist gave me the key and showed me to my room.

I left my things in the room and came downstairs. There weren't many guests. There were only three including me. I sat in the sitting room and I talked to the manager, Sara Daniels, about her hotel. I had a drink and then at 12.00 I went upstairs to my room.

Room 11 was on the top floor. I opened the door and turned on the light. It was a very big room, quite old, and yes, it was a bit spooky. There was an old television on a table – but there wasn't a remote control. I turned on the TV. There was a film on. I was happy to see that it wasn't a horror film. I decided to watch the film and have the light on all night. But I was tired after my long journey and after half an hour I went to sleep.

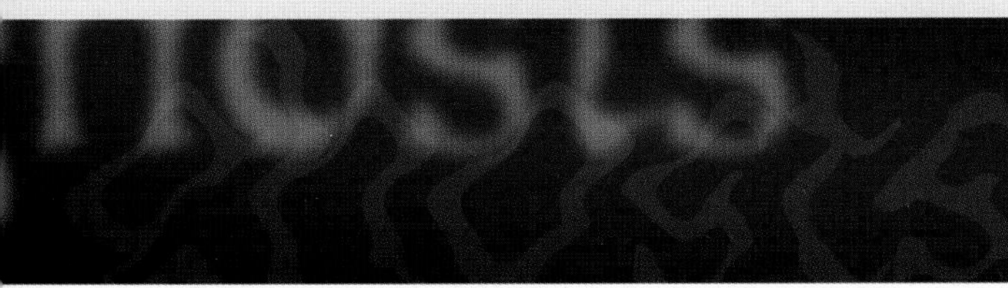

d From memory, correct the information in these sentences. Quickly read the article again to check.

1 There was a cemetery ~~behind~~ the hotel. *next to*
2 There were three other guests in the hotel.
3 He talked to one of the guests.
4 Room 11 was on the first floor.
5 The room was quite small.
6 There was a horror film on TV.
7 When he want to sleep, the TV and the lights were turned off.

e Do you think Stephen saw the ghost?

3 LISTENING

a 6.6 Listen to Stephen describing what happened. Did he see the ghost?

b Listen again. Complete his report.

Journalist:	Stephen Bleach
The hotel:	Gosforth Hall Hotel
The ghost:	17th century Catholic priest
Did you wake up during the night?	1 Yes / No
If yes, what time?	2 ______
Did anything strange happen?	3 Yes / No
If yes, what?	The 4 ______ and the 5 ______ went off.
Did you see the ghost?	6 Yes / No
Did you 'feel' the ghost?	7 Yes / No
Were you frightened?	8 ☐ very ☐ a little ☐ not at all
Would you like to go back?	9 Yes / No
Why (not)?	10 ______

4 GRAMMAR *there was / there were*

a Complete the sentences from the article with *was*, *wasn't*, *were*, or *weren't*.

1 There ______ many guests in the hotel.
2 There ______ only three including me.
3 There ______ an old TV on a table.
4 There ______ a remote control.

b **p.132 Grammar Bank 6B.** Read the rules and do the exercises.

5 SPEAKING

Communication *Room 11 p.111.*
Look at the picture for one minute. Try to remember what's in the room.

6 PRONUNCIATION silent letters

Some English words have a 'silent' letter, e.g. in *cupboard* /ˈkʌbəd/ you don't pronounce the *p*.

a Practise saying these words. ~~Cross out~~ the 'silent' letter in each one.

g~~u~~est	ghost	half	could	know
building	listen	friend	write	hour

b 6.7 Listen and check.

6 C

G present continuous
V verb phrases
P verb + *-ing*

What are they doing?
They're having a party.

Neighbours from hell

1 VOCABULARY & SPEAKING

a Read the article about neighbours. Complete the list of problems with these verbs.

argue bark cry have move play talk watch

Love your neighbour?
Sometimes it can be difficult!

You can choose your friends but you can't choose your neighbours. The people who live upstairs, downstairs, and next door can have a very big influence on our lives – and it isn't always positive! The typical problem that people have with their neighbours is that they make a lot of noise.

In a European newspaper survey these were the top eight problems.

- They ______ loudly.
- Their babies ______.
- They ______ noisy parties.
- Their dogs ______.
- They ______ TV late at night.
- They ______ furniture.
- They ______ a musical instrument.
- They ______ with their partner.

b In groups of two or three, answer the questions in the survey.

Do you have good neighbours?
Do you live in a house or a flat?
What floor do you live on?
Where do you have neighbours? upstairs ☐ downstairs ☐ next door ☐
Do you know your neighbours?
Are they friendly? Do they help you?
Do they make a lot of noise? What kind of noise?
Do you have any other problems with your neighbours?

2 GRAMMAR present continuous

a Match the sentences with flats 1–8.

He's listening to music. ☐
The baby's crying. ☐
They're having a party. ☐
She's playing the violin. ☐
The dog's barking. ☐
They're arguing. ☐
He's watching football. ☐
They're moving furniture. ☐

b 6.8 Cover the sentences and listen. What's happening? Where?

c Complete the chart.

[+] The baby's crying.
She's playing the violin.
They're having a party.

[−] The baby ______ crying.
She ______ ______ the violin.
They ______ ______ a party.

[?] ______ the baby ______?
Is ______ ______ the violin?
______ they ______ a party?

d 6.9 Listen and repeat the sentences in the chart. Copy the rhythm.

e ➲ **p.132 Grammar Bank 6C.** Read the rules and do the exercises.

f In pairs, point and ask and answer about the people in the flats.

What's he doing?

He's watching football. What are they doing?

g 6.10 Listen to the sounds. Write six sentences to say what's happening.

3 PRONUNCIATION verb + *-ing*

a Practise saying the words in the six sound pictures. Then put two words from the box in each column.

ɑː	eɪ	ɔː	aɪ	uː	əʊ
					smoking

~~smoking~~ dancing going playing
asking calling doing moving
talking crying driving raining

b 6.11 Listen and check. Practise saying the words.

c 6.12 Listen to a man on a mobile. Write the six present continuous sentences.

4 SPEAKING

Communication *They're having a party!* *A p.110 B p.113*. Describe the pictures and find ten differences.

6D When a man is tired of London...

G present simple or present continuous?
V places in a city
P city names

Look! The bridge is opening!
It only opens twice a month.

1 GRAMMAR present simple or present continuous?

a Look at the photos of four top tourist attractions in London. What are they? Imagine you have one morning in London. Which two would you like to go to?

b 6.13 Where are Ivan and Eva? Cover the dialogues and listen. Number the pictures 1–4.

1 **Ivan** Look! It ________ (open)! A ship ________ (go) through!
Eva We're lucky. The guidebook says that it only ________ (open) two or three times a month!

2 **Eva** The flag ________ (fly) – that means the Queen is at home. She ________ (not live) here all the time. She often ________ (stay) at Windsor Castle or in one of her other homes.

3 **Eva** That's Napoleon. He ________ (look) at a model of the Battle of Waterloo.
Ivan Come on – let's go and see the next room.
Eva Yes, we ________ (not have) much time. It ________ (close) in twenty minutes.

4 **Ivan** We ________ (go up)! Wow! Look – there's the Houses of Parliament! And Buckingham Palace over there!
Eva What a pity it ________ (rain). The guidebook ________ (say) you can see Windsor Castle on a clear day.

c Listen again. Put the verbs in brackets into the present continuous or the present simple. What's the difference between the two tenses?

d **p.132 Grammar Bank 6D.** Read the rules and do the exercises.

Ivan and Eva are tourists in London

2 READING

a Quickly read the guidebook extract about the London Eye and answer the questions.

1 How high is the London Eye? ______
2 How far can you see on a clear day? ______
3 How many capsules are there? ______
4 How many passengers are there in each capsule? ______
5 How long is the trip? ______
6 How fast does it move? ______
7 What time does it open / close? In the summer ______
In the winter ______
8 Can you get tickets on the day you want to go? ______
9 Where is the ticket office? ______
10 Which underground station is near the London Eye? ______

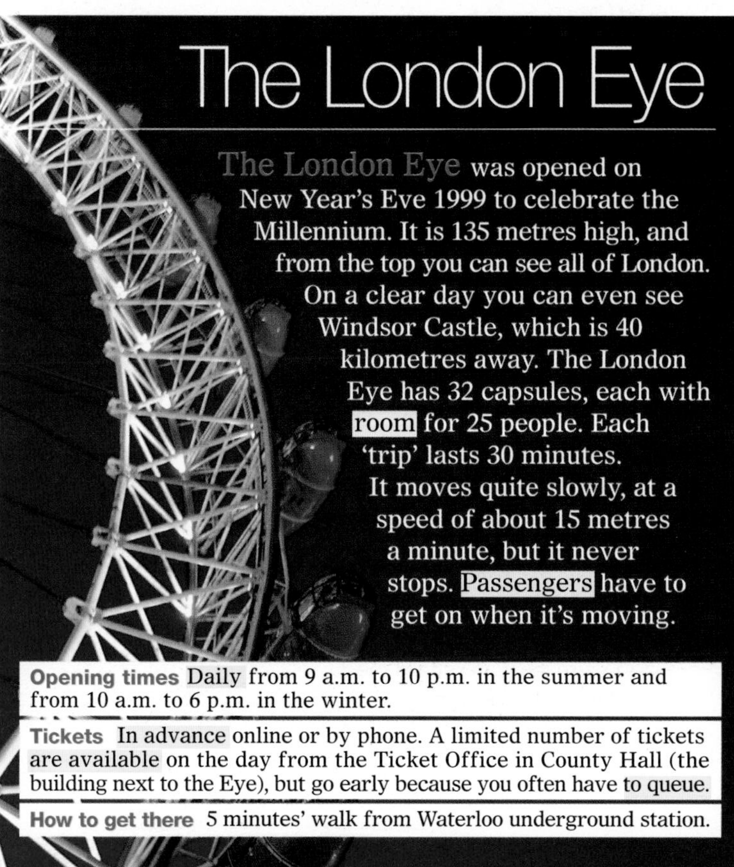

The London Eye

The London Eye was opened on New Year's Eve 1999 to celebrate the Millennium. It is 135 metres high, and from the top you can see all of London. On a clear day you can even see Windsor Castle, which is 40 kilometres away. The London Eye has 32 capsules, each with room for 25 people. Each 'trip' lasts 30 minutes. It moves quite slowly, at a speed of about 15 metres a minute, but it never stops. Passengers have to get on when it's moving.

Opening times Daily from 9 a.m. to 10 p.m. in the summer and from 10 a.m. to 6 p.m. in the winter.

Tickets In advance online or by phone. A limited number of tickets are available on the day from the Ticket Office in County Hall (the building next to the Eye), but go early because you often have to queue.

How to get there 5 minutes' walk from Waterloo underground station.

www.londoneye.com

b Match the highlighted words and expressions with their meanings.

1 ______ before you go
2 ______ you can buy them
3 ______ every day
4 ______ to wait in a line
5 ______ space (for people or things)
6 ______ people who are travelling

c Would you like to go on the London Eye? Why (not)?

3 VOCABULARY places in a city

a Is there a building in your town with a very good view? Where is it? What's its name?

b p.152 **Vocabulary Bank** *Town and city.*

4 SPEAKING

In pairs, answer these questions.

Your town
Tourist information

1 Do you live in a village, town, or city?
2 Do many tourists visit? When do they come?
3 Are there any important tourist areas near where you live?
4 Where you live, is there...? Write the name.
   - an interesting museum ______
   - a famous street ______
   - a beautiful square ______
   - a famous bridge ______
   - a good art gallery ______
   - an old castle ______
   - an important church or mosque ______
   - a good department store ______
   - a good, cheap hotel ______
   - a street market ______
5 What are the top three tourist attractions in your town?

5 PRONUNCIATION city names

Place names in the UK and Ireland are sometimes difficult for visitors to pronounce and understand, e.g. *Leicester* /ˈlestə/.

a 6.14 Listen. What are the eight cities?

b Listen again and repeat the city names. Which city names have an /ə/ sound?

c Practise saying the city names.

d p.157 **Sound Bank.** Look at the spellings for /ə/.

6 6.15 SONG ♫ *Waterloo Sunset*

VOCABULARY directions

a Match the words and pictures.

on the corner ☐
at the traffic lights ☐
a roundabout ☐
opposite ☐

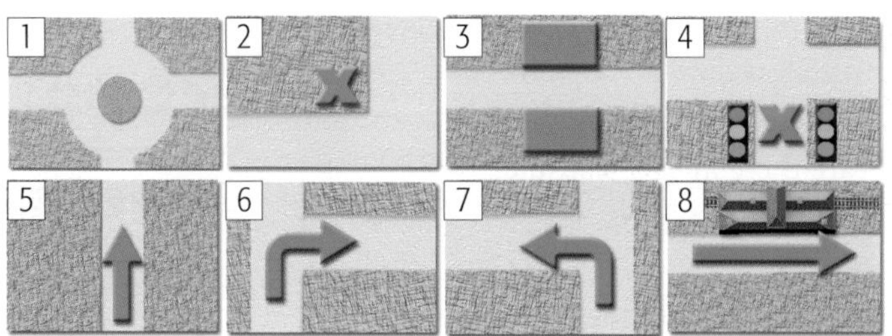

turn left ☐
turn right ☐
go straight on ☐
go past (*the station*) ☐

b In pairs, cover the words and test your partner.

ASKING FOR DIRECTIONS

a 6.16 Allie and Mark are trying to find the restaurant. Cover the dialogue and listen. Can you mark King Street on the map?

YOU SAY	YOU HEAR
Excuse me. Where's King Street, please?	1 Sorry, I _______ know.
Excuse me. Is King Street near here?	2 King Street? It's _______ here but I don't know exactly _______. Sorry.
Thank you.	
Excuse me. Can you tell me the way to King Street?	3 Yes. Go _______ on. Go past the church, and then turn _______ at the traffic lights. And then I think it's the _______ on the right.
Sorry, could you say that again, please?	Yes, go…
Thank you.	

b Listen again. Complete the YOU HEAR phrases.

c 6.17 Listen and repeat the YOU SAY phrases. Copy the rhythm.

d In pairs, roleplay asking for and giving directions. A ask for the art gallery and the car park, B ask for the museum and the station. Start where Allie's car is.

Excuse me. Can you tell me the way to the art gallery?

Yes, go…

SOCIAL ENGLISH

a 6.18 Listen and complete the sentences.

1 **Allie** I'm sure she said the _______ on the right.
2 **Mark** I don't think he knows. He's a _______.
3 **Allie** Can you see anywhere to _______?
4 **Mark** Do you think you can park in that _______?
5 **Allie** Are you saying I _______ park?

b Do they enjoy their dinner?

c Who says the USEFUL PHRASES, Mark or Allie? Listen again and check. How do you say them in your language?

USEFUL PHRASES

Let's ask that man there.
Excuse me! We're lost.
You see. I was right. (opposite = *wrong*)
Here it is.
I'm only joking.

A postcard

a Look at the two postcards. Do you know which city it is?

1

2

b Quickly read Melanie's postcard. Which postcard is it?

Dear Kim,

Hope you're OK. We ___ (have) a great holiday here! We ___ (arrive) four days ago, and we ___ (stay) in a small hotel in the old town. Yesterday morning we ___ (go) to see the castle, and in the afternoon we ___ (visit) a beer factory.

At the moment we ___ (sit) in a café in the main square. It's really beautiful. There ___ (be) a wonderful old clock – you can see it in the picture.

My favourite area is Mala Strana. It's the old part of Prague and it's fantastic. There ___ (be) a lot of nice restaurants, and we usually ___ (go) for a walk there in the evening and then ___ (have) dinner. You'd really like it.

See you next week!

Love,
Melanie

PS Matthew sends his love.

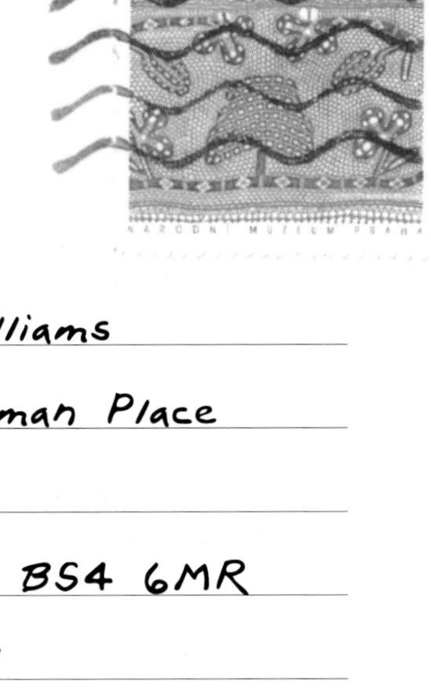

Kim Williams
8 Freeman Place
Clifton
Bristol BS4 6MR
England

c Read the postcard again. Put the verbs in the correct form (present simple, present continuous, or past simple).

WRITE a postcard to another student. Imagine you're on holiday in another town or city. Give this information.

- Are you having a good time?
- When did you arrive?
- Where are you staying?
- What did you do yesterday?
- Where are you at the moment?
- What are you doing?
- Say something about the town / city.
- Say what you usually do in the evening.

Check your postcard for mistakes.

6 What do you remember?

GRAMMAR

Circle the correct sentence, a or b.

(a) Hi. I'm Susanna.
b Hi. I Susanna.

1 a There is two tables in the living room.
b There are two tables in the living room.

2 a How many bedrooms are there?
b How many bedrooms there are?

3 a There aren't some glasses.
b There aren't any glasses.

4 a There were only three guests.
b There was only three guests.

5 a How many people there were in the hotel?
b How many people were there in the hotel?

6 a We having a great time.
b We're having a great time.

7 a They aren't arguing.
b They not arguing.

8 a What you are doing?
b What are you doing?

9 a Look! The bridge opens!
b Look! The bridge is opening!

10 a The museum closes at 2.00 on Mondays.
b The museum is closing at 2.00 on Mondays.

10

VOCABULARY

a verb phrases

Match the verbs and phrases.

have a shower

book	play	have	make	take

1 ______ a noise
2 ______ a musical instrument
3 ______ a party
4 ______ theatre tickets
5 ______ photos

b word groups

Circle the word that is different.

Ireland	(Chinese)	Thailand	Spain
1 kitchen	bathroom	shelf	hall
2 armchair	cooker	sofa	carpet
3 there	behind	opposite	between
4 village	city	town	town hall
5 supermarket	square	bank	chemist's

c prepositions

Complete the sentences with *of*, *on*, *to*, or *with*.

Look *at* the board.

1 She's arguing ______ her husband.
2 They have their TV ______ very loud.
3 I live ______ the second floor.
4 The TV is in front ______ the cupboard.
5 The table is next ______ the sofa.

15

PRONUNCIATION

a Underline the word with a different sound.

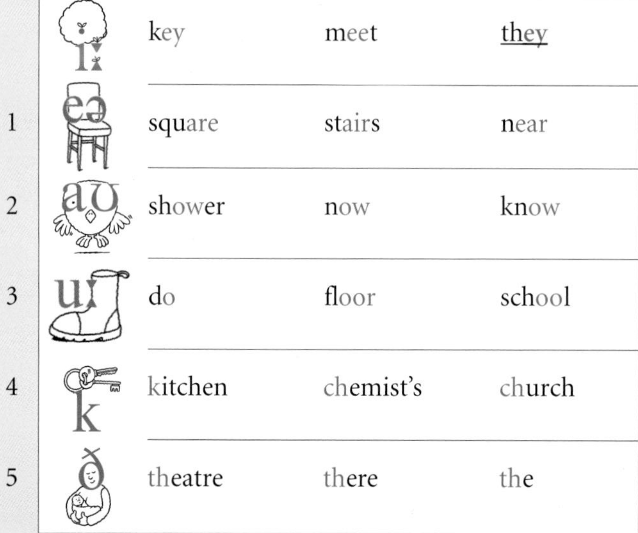

	key	meet	they
1	square	stairs	near
2	shower	now	know
3	do	floor	school
4	kitchen	chemist's	church
5	theatre	there	the

b Underline the stressed syllable.

information

opposite	between	behind	cupboard	museum

10

CAN YOU UNDERSTAND THIS TEXT?

Our little piece of pop history

Andrew Holgate and his family bought a house at number 59 Lyndhurst Grove, in London. On their first morning in their new house they were very surprised. They looked out of the window and saw some people taking photographs of their front door. Every week more people came and took photographs. Andrew and his family couldn't understand it. Then they solved the mystery...

The British pop group Pulp have a song on their album *PulpIntro* called 59 *Lyndhurst Grove* (written by the singer, Jarvis Cocker). The people who came to see their house were Pulp fans. But why did Pulp sing about 59 Lyndhurst Grove? This is the story. One night Jarvis Cocker came to a party at the house. He argued with the owner, an architect, and the owner threw him out of the house. Jarvis went home and wrote an angry song about the house, the party, and the architect owner.

There are other pop songs about streets. For example, the Beatles wrote a song about Penny Lane in Liverpool. But what is unusual is that Jarvis Cocker's song gives the number of the house. Fortunately, Andrew and his family are quite happy that their house is famous.

Adapted from a British newspaper

a Read the article. Number the sentences in order.

A Jarvis wrote a song about the house. ☐
B Jarvis Cocker went to a party. *1*
C The Holgates found out about the song. ☐
D Andrew's family bought the house. ☐
E The owner of the house threw Jarvis out. ☐
F Jarvis argued with the owner of the house. ☐
G Andrew's family saw people taking photos of the house. ☐

b Read the article again. Mark the sentences T (true) or F (false).

1 There aren't many songs about houses.
2 Jarvis wrote the song because he liked the house.
3 Andrew doesn't like people taking photos of his house.

c Underline five words you want to learn in the text.

CAN YOU HEAR THE DIFFERENCE?

a 6.19 Listen. Circle a or b.

1 How far is the house from Cambridge?
a 30 miles b 13 miles
2 How many bathrooms are there?
a two b three
3 How old is it?
a 19 years b 90 years
4 What day can she see the house?
a Tuesday b Thursday
5 What time can she see the house?
a at 5.45 b at 6.15

b 6.20 Listen. Circle a or b.

1 a There were five guests at the hotel.
b There were seven guests at the hotel.
2 a Their neighbours are arguing.
b Their neighbours are watching TV.
3 a Jim is at his friends' house.
b Jim is at a restaurant.
4 a Maria usually reads in English.
b Maria doesn't usually read in English.
5 a The gallery closes at 4.00 on Sundays.
b The gallery closes at 4.00 every afternoon.

CAN YOU SAY THIS IN ENGLISH?

a Can you...? Yes (✓)

☐ say what rooms there are in your house
☐ say what there is in your bedroom
☐ say what you think people in your family are doing now

b Re-order the words to make questions.

1 TVs house are there in many your
How ______________________?
2 on was last TV there night
What ______________________?
3 computer there your in a bedroom
Is ______________________?
4 banks time in the do your open country
What ______________________?
5 you today wearing are
What ______________________?

c In pairs, ask and answer.

7 A

G *a / an, some / any*
V food, countable / uncountable nouns
P the letters *ea*

Is there any beer?
No, but there's some orange juice.

What does your food say about you?

1 VOCABULARY food

a Look at the picture. Write the missing letters. What did Laura have to eat and drink yesterday?

She had an apple, ...

b Food words are countable or uncountable. Write the words in the correct column.

countable nouns (singular or plural)	**uncountable nouns** (singular)
an apple	*some butter*

c ➲ **p.153 Vocabulary Bank** *Food.*

1 an *a* pple
2 a __anana
3 some __utter
4 an __gg
5 some __eat
6 some __ice
7 some __ugar
8 a __omato
9 a __iscuit
10 some __offee

2 GRAMMAR *a / an, some / any*

a In pairs, ask and answer.

1 How often do you go to the supermarket?
2 Which supermarket do you go to? Why?
3 Do you look at the food other people are buying? Does it say anything about them?

b Match the people with the baskets.

Fast Food Frank ☐

Healthy Hannah ☐

Luxury Lucy ☐

c Read the sentences. Which basket is it? Circle 1, 2, or 3.

a There's **some** ice cream.	1	②	3
b There isn't **any** fruit.	1	2	3
c There aren't **any** vegetables.	1	2	3
d There are **some** biscuits.	1	2	3
e There's **a** lettuce.	1	2	3
f There isn't **a** pineapple.	1	2	3

d Look at the sentences and complete the rules with *some*, *any*, or *a* / *an*.

Use ______ with singular countable nouns, e.g. *pineapple*
Use ______ (+) and ______ (− and ?)
with plural nouns, e.g. *vegetables*
with uncountable nouns, e.g. *cheese*

e ➲ **p.134 Grammar Bank 7A.** Read the rules and do the exercises.

f In pairs, A say + and − sentences about the baskets. B say which basket it is. Change roles.

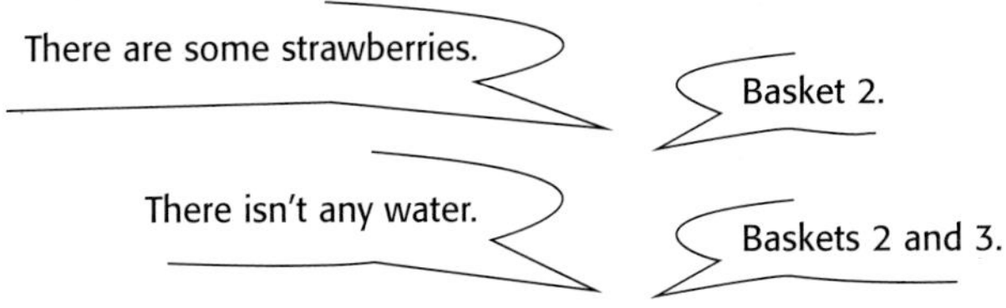
There are some strawberries.
Basket 2.
There isn't any water.
Baskets 2 and 3.

3 PRONUNCIATION the letters *ea*

a How is *ea* pronounced in these words? Put them in the correct column.

bread breakfast eat health
ice cream meat peas steak tea

iː	e	eɪ

b 7.1 Listen and check. Practise saying them. Which is the most common pronunciation of *ea*?

4 SPEAKING

a Make a food diary for yesterday. Write down exactly what food and drink you had. Use **Vocabulary Bank** *Food p.153* to help you.

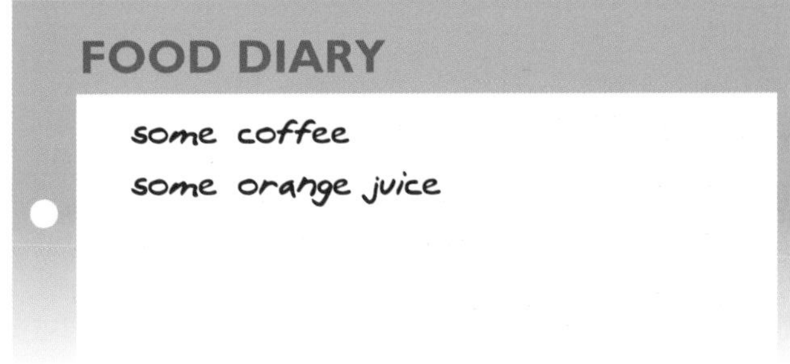
FOOD DIARY
some coffee
some orange juice

b In pairs, A tell B exactly what food you had. B say if you think A is like Fast Food Frank, Healthy Hannah, or Luxury Lucy. Then change roles.

5 LISTENING

a Can you make spaghetti bolognese? What do you need to make it?

CAN MEN COOK?

b 7.2 Listen to a TV cooking programme. What nine things does Colin use to make spaghetti bolognese?

1 *some spaghetti*
2 an ______
3 some ______
4 a ______
5 some ______
6 some ______
7 some ______
8 some ______
9 some ______

c Listen again and check. Does Belinda like Colin's spaghetti bolognese?

d In pairs, think of a famous dish from your country. Write the ingredients you need. Tell the class.

G *how much / how many?*, quantifiers: *a lot, not much*, etc.
V drinks
P /w/, /v/, and /b/

How much water do you drink?
Not much.

How much water do we really need?

1 PRONUNCIATION /w/, /v/, and /b/

a 7.3 Listen and repeat the sounds and words.

water

vodka

beer

b 7.4 Listen and practise the dialogue.

V Would you like a beer, Bill?
B No, thanks, Vicky. A whisky and water.
V Do you want some biscuits or a sandwich?
B A sandwich.
V Brown bread or white bread?
B Brown bread. It's very good for you.

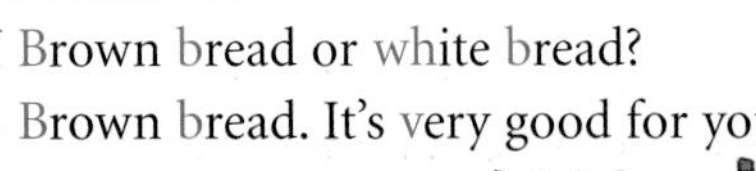

2 SPEAKING

a Read the introduction and the questionnaire.

b In pairs, interview your partner. Who drinks more water?

3 GRAMMAR *how much / how many?*, quantifiers

a Complete the questions with *How much* or *How many*.

1 ________ litres of water do you drink?
2 ________ mineral water do you drink?

b Match the sentences and pictures.

1 I **don't** drink **any** water. ☐
2 I **don't** drink **much** water. ☐
3 I drink **quite a lot of** water. ☐
4 I drink **a lot of** water. ☐

A B C D

c **p.134 Grammar Bank 7B.** Read the rules and do the exercises.

How much water do YOU drink?

What do many people take with them everywhere these days? A bag? A mobile? A credit card? Yes, but also a bottle of mineral water. In magazines today there are many articles telling us that we need to drink a lot of water to be healthy and beautiful.

1 How much water do you drink a day?
a I drink a lot of water. (2+ litres)
b I drink quite a lot of water. (1–2 litres)
c I don't drink much water. (0–1 litre)
d I don't drink any water. (0)

2 When do you drink water?
a Very often.
b Only with my meals.
c Hardly ever.

3 What kind of water do you drink?
a Only mineral water.
b Only tap water.
c Mineral water and tap water.

4 Do you think water is...?
a healthy but boring
b healthy and nice
c perfect when you're thirsty

5 Do you think you need to drink more water?
a Yes.
b No.
c I don't know.

d Complete the questions with *How much* or *How many*.

1 ____________ cups of coffee
2 ____________ milk
3 ____________ glasses of wine
4 ____________ cups of tea
5 ____________ fruit juice
6 ____________ beer
7 ____________ mineral water
8 ____________ Coke

do you drink a day?

A lot.
Quite a *lot*.
Not much/many.
None.

e In pairs, ask and answer. Answer with an expression from **d** or a number.

How many cups of coffee do you drink a day?

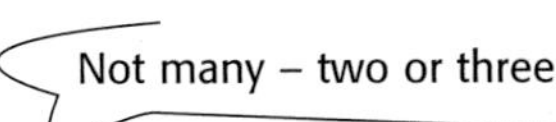

4 READING

a Cover the magazine article *Water – facts and myths*. In pairs, look at these questions. Can you answer any of them?

1 ~~**Why do we need to drink water?**~~
2 **Do people need less water when the weather's cold?**
3 **Can we drink *too much* water?**
4 **Can we get the water we need from other drinks or food?**
5 **How much water do we need to drink a day?**
6 **Do Coke and coffee make us dehydrated?**

b Read the article. Put the questions in **a** in the gaps.

c Read the article again. Match the highlighted words with these phrases.

1 ____________ how hot or cold it is
2 ____________ when water comes out of your body when you are hot
3 ____________ scientists do these
4 ____________ not a long time ago
5 ____________ things people believe which are not true
6 ____________ a minimum of
7 ____________ have in it
8 ____________ the truth is

d Look at the questions in **a** again. In pairs, answer them from memory.

e Is there anything in the article you don't agree with?

Water – facts and myths

A Why do we need to drink water?

We all know that our bodies need water. Water cleans our body, controls our temperature, and helps to keep us healthy. About 70% of our body is water.

B ____________________

We often read that we need to drink at least eight glasses of water a day (about two litres). The idea probably came from mineral water companies! In fact, how much water we need depends on the weather and on what we're doing. When we are hot, or if we do sport or exercise, we need to drink more. Some experts say that, in normal conditions, we only really need about one litre a day.

C ____________________

No. When temperatures are very low we also need to drink more than on a normal day. This is because we wear a lot of clothes so we sweat a lot and lose water.

D ____________________

Yes, of course. We get water from food, especially fruit and vegetables (an apple is 85% water, an onion is 87%). We can also get water from other drinks like fruit juice, coffee and colas, which contain a lot of water.

E ____________________

No. In experiments in America some people drank only water and other people drank water, cola, and coffee. Their levels of hydration were more or less the same.

F ____________________

Yes. It can be dangerous to drink a lot of water. Recently a British actor nearly died after drinking eight litres of water a day for several months.

7 C

G *be going to* (plans)
V holidays
P sentence stress

What are you going to do?
We're going to see the sights.

Changing holidays

1 READING

Read about this TV programme. What's it about?

Tonight's TV Don't miss...
Changing Holidays 8.30 p.m.
* * * *
In this new holiday programme we ask two couples to plan their holiday for the same week. Then these two couples change holidays – they go on the holiday the other couple planned! But they don't know where the holiday is until the last moment...
Tonight's couples are Lisa and Jon, and Jerry and Sue.
Lisa
Jon
Jerry
Sue

2 GRAMMAR *be going to* (plans)

a 7.5 The presenter from *Changing Holidays* calls Lisa Carter. Cover the dialogue. Listen. What are Lisa and Jon's holiday plans?

b Listen again and complete the dialogue.

Couple 1 **Lisa and Jon**

Lisa Hello?
Peter Hi! Lisa? This is Peter Douglas from *Changing Holidays.*
Lisa Oh! Hello!
Peter Lisa, what are your holiday plans for next week?
Lisa Er... I'm going to [1] *fly* to New York with my boyfriend, Jon.
Peter Great. And where are you going to [2] ______?
Lisa We're going to [3] ______ in the Hotel Athena in Manhattan.
Peter What are you going to [4] ______ in New York, Lisa?
Lisa We're going to [5] ______ ______ – the shops in New York are fantastic – and in the evening we're going to [6] ______ clubbing and [7] ______ a show on Broadway.
Peter Are you going to [8] ______ the sights too?
Lisa Oh yes, we want to see the Empire State Building, the Statue of Liberty, Central Park...
Peter Well, Lisa, say goodbye to New York. Because we're going to [9] ______ your holiday!

c Underline the examples of (*be*) *going to* in the dialogue.

1 What form is the verb after *going to*?
2 Do we use *going to* to talk about the past, the present, or the future?

d p.134 Grammar Bank 7C. Read the rules and do the exercises.

e 7.6 Listen to Peter Douglas calling Jerry Harte and complete the chart.

Couple 2	Jerry and Sue
1 Where / go?	
2 Who / with?	
3 How / get there?	
4 What / do?	
5 Where / stay?	

3 PRONUNCIATION sentence stress

a 7.7 Listen and repeat Peter's questions in e. Copy the rhythm.

b In pairs, use the chart in e to roleplay the dialogue between Peter and Jerry.

Where are you going to go?

We're going to go to Norway.

4 LISTENING & READING

a 7.8 Listen. The two couples are at the airport. Peter is going to tell them where their holidays are. Are they happy? Why (not)?

b Read the two couples' holiday diaries for the first three days. Are they happy?

MONDAY

It's raining and it's cold. Today we met the other people on the work camp – they're friendly but they're very different from us. Dinner was a disaster – we can't cook.

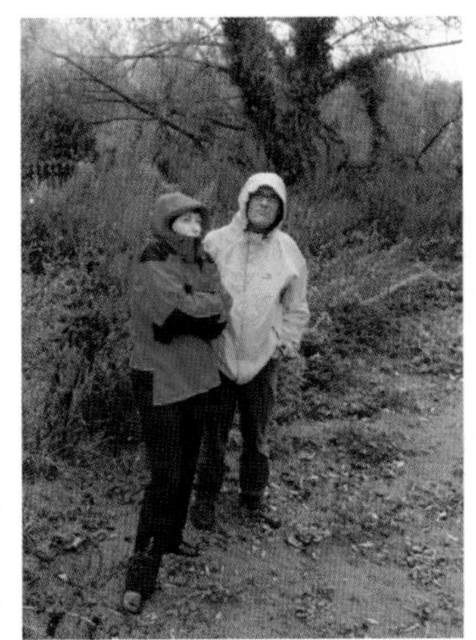

Lisa and Jon in Norway

TUESDAY

We got up at 6.00 and started cleaning the river. In the afternoon we planted 20 trees. It's still raining and all our clothes are wet and dirty.

WEDNESDAY

This morning the sun came out!! We had the morning free and we went on a boat trip – we stopped work and relaxed! In the afternoon – back to work. And it started raining again.

MONDAY

The hotel's OK but there's no view.

In the morning we went shopping – but we didn't buy anything. In the afternoon we went up the Empire State Building – a great view from the top…

Sue and Jerry in New York

TUESDAY

We like the food very much – there are so many different restaurants. We walked in Central Park – really beautiful. In the afternoon we went to the Guggenheim Museum – incredible.

WEDNESDAY

Today was a great day. We saw the sights – Brooklyn Bridge, the Statue of Liberty. In the evening we went to The Village, a famous nightclub – we went to bed at 3 a.m.!

c 7.9 Listen to the end of the programme. Did they have a good time? Where are they going to go next year?

d Listen again. Tick (✓) what they liked, cross (✗) what they didn't like.

Lisa and Jon

the work	✗	the weather	☐
camping	☐	going to bed early	☐
the people	☐		

Jerry and Sue

the hotel	☐	the food	☐
the sights	☐	the nightlife	☐
the people	☐		

5 SPEAKING

Play ***Changing Holidays.***

a In pairs, plan your ideal summer holiday. Decide…

- where / go?
- how / get there?
- where / stay?
- what / do there?

OK. Where are we going to go?

Why don't we go to…?

That's a good idea.

b Write down your plans. Give them to your teacher. He / She is going to 'change your holiday'.

c Look at your new holiday. Work with another pair. Ask about their new holiday. Use the questions in **a**. Ask *Are you happy with your new holiday? Why (not)?*

6 7.10 SONG ♫ *La Isla Bonita*

G *be going to* (predictions)
V verb phrases
P /ʊ/, /uː/, and /ʌ/

You're going to be very happy.

7D It's written in the cards

1 READING & LISTENING

a Match the cards and verb phrases.

- ☐ be <u>fa</u>mous
- ☐ get a new job
- ☐ get <u>ma</u>rried
- ☐ fall in love
- ☐ <u>tra</u>vel
- ☐ get a lot of <u>mo</u>ney
- ☐ have a sur<u>prise</u>
- [A] be <u>lu</u>cky
- ☐ move house
- ☐ meet <u>some</u>body new

b 7.11 Cover the story. Read and listen to the first paragraph only. In pairs, answer the questions. Then do the same with the other four paragraphs.

It's written in the cards

'Come in,' said a voice. Jane Ross opened the door and went into a small room. There was a man sitting behind a table.

'Good afternoon,' said Jane. 'I want to see Madame Yolanda, the fortune teller.'

'Madame Yolanda isn't here today,' said the man. 'But don't worry. I'm going to tell you about your future. What questions do you want to ask?' Jane looked at the fortune teller. She couldn't see him very well because the room was very dark.

1 Who does Jane want to see?
2 Who is going to tell her about her future? Why?
3 Why can't she see the man very well?

7.12

Well,' she said, 'I have a problem with my boyfriend. We argue all the time. I don't think he loves me. I want to know if we're going to stay together.'

'Please choose five cards, but don't look at them.'

Jane took five cards. The fortune teller put them on the table face down. He turned over the first card.

'Ah, this is a good card. This means you're going to be very lucky.'

'But am I going to stay with my boyfriend?' Jane asked.

'Maybe,' said the fortune teller. 'We need to look at the other cards first.'

4 What's Jane's problem?
5 How many cards does she take?
6 What is her first card? What does it mean?

7.13

He turned over the second card.

'Mm, a house. A new house. You're going to move, very soon, to another country.'

'But my boyfriend works here. He can't move to another country.'

'Let's look at the next card,' said the fortune teller. He turned over the third card.

'A heart. You're going to fall in love.'

'Who with?' asked Jane.

'Let me concentrate. I can see a tall man. He's very attractive.'

'Oh, that's Jim,' said Jane.

'Who's Jim? Your boyfriend?'

'No. Jim's a man I met at a party last month. He's an actor, and he says he's in love with me. It was his idea for me to come to Madame Yolanda.'

'Well, the card says that you're going to fall in love with him.'

'Are you sure?' asked Jane. 'But what about my boyfriend?'

'Let's look at the fourth card,' said the fortune teller.

7 What's the second card? What does it mean?
8 Why is this a problem for Jane?
9 What's her third card? What does it mean?
10 Who's Jim? Where did Jane meet him?
11 What do you think the fourth card is going to be?

7.14

The fortune teller turned over a card with two rings.

'Now I can see everything clearly. You are going to leave your boyfriend and go away with the other man, to another country. You are going to get married.'

'Married? But am I going to be happy with him?'

'You're going to be very happy.'

Jane looked at her watch. 'Oh no, look at the time. I'm going to be late.'

She stood up, left a £50 note on the table, and ran out of the room.

12 What is her fourth card? What does it mean?
13 Why is she in a hurry?
14 How much does she pay?

7.15

The fortune teller stood up. He turned on the light. At that moment an old woman came in. 'So, what happened?' she asked.

'She believed everything,' said Jim. 'I told you, I'm a very good actor!'

He gave the woman £100.

'That's Jane's £50 and another £50 from me. Thanks very much, Madame Yolanda.'

Madame Yolanda took the money. The fifth card was still on the table, face down. She turned it over. It was the ship. She looked at it for four or five seconds and then she said:

'Young man! Don't travel with that girl – you're going to…'

But the room was empty.

15 Who was the fortune teller?
16 Why does he pay the fortune teller £50?
17 What's the fifth card? What do you think is going to happen?

2 GRAMMAR *be going to* (predictions)

a Look at these two sentences. Which one is a plan? Which one is a prediction?

1 She's going to be very lucky.
2 She's going to go to New York next week.

b p.134 Grammar Bank 7D. Read the rules and do the exercises.

3 PRONUNCIATION /ʊ/, /uː/, and /ʌ/

a Put these words from the story in the correct column. Be careful, *oo* can be /ʊ/ or /uː/.

good look love lucky money
move put couldn't argue you
new young but soon woman

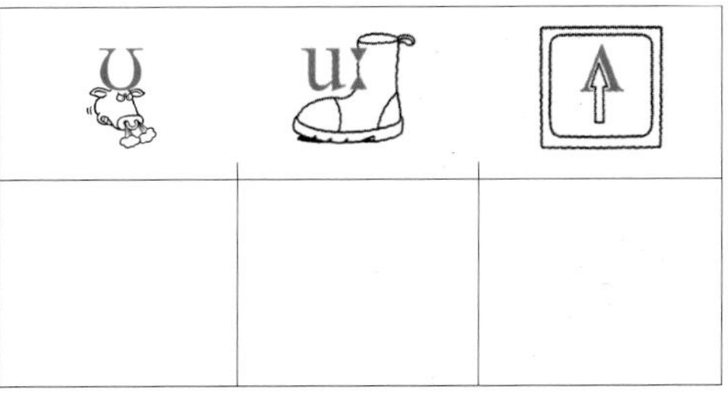

b 7.16 Listen and check.

c p.157 Sound Bank. Look at the typical spellings for these sounds.

4 SPEAKING

Roleplay fortune telling.

A Look at the ten cards in exercise 1. Secretly, number the cards in a different order.

B Choose five numbers.

A Predict **B**'s future using those cards. Then change roles.

I'm going to tell you about your future. Your first card is a star. You're going to be famous. Maybe you're going to be on TV…

At a restaurant

VOCABULARY a menu

a Complete the menu.

Main courses Desserts Starters

b What do the highlighted words mean? How do you pronounce them?

c Cover the menu. In pairs, try to remember what's on the menu.

Donatella's

Onion soup
Goat's cheese salad

Steak and chips
Roast chicken with vegetables
Fresh lasagne

Home-made vanilla ice cream with hot chocolate sauce
Fresh fruit salad
Tiramisu

2 courses £15.00
3 courses £22.50

ORDERING A MEAL

a 7.17 Allie and Mark are having dinner. Cover the dialogue and listen. What do they order?

YOU HEAR	YOU SAY
1 Good ______. Do you have a reservation?	**A** Yes, a table for two. My name's Allie Gray.
2 ______ or non-smoking?	**A** Non-smoking, please.
3 Come this ______, please.	
4 Are you ______ to order?	**M** Yes, I'd like the onion soup and then the steak, please.
	A The goat's cheese salad and the lasagne for me, please.
5 What would you like to ______?	**M** Would you like some wine?
	A No, thanks. Just mineral water for me.
	M OK. A glass of red wine and a bottle of mineral water, please.
Thank you, sir.	**M** Thank you.

b Listen again. Complete the YOU HEAR phrases.

c 7.18 Listen and repeat the YOU SAY phrases. Copy the rhythm.

d In groups of three, use the menu to roleplay ordering a meal. A is the waiter, B and C are customers.

SOCIAL ENGLISH

a 7.19 Listen and answer the questions.

1 What do they order for dessert / coffee?
2 What does Mark ask Allie?
3 What does she answer?
4 What does Mark ask the waiter at the end?

b What do you think?

1 Why does Mark want Allie to go to the conference?
2 Is Allie going to say yes?

c Who says the USEFUL PHRASES, Mark or Allie? Listen again and check. How do you say them in your language?

USEFUL PHRASES

It was delicious.
What is there?
Nothing for me, thanks.
The same for me, please.
I'm not sure.
Could we have the bill, please?

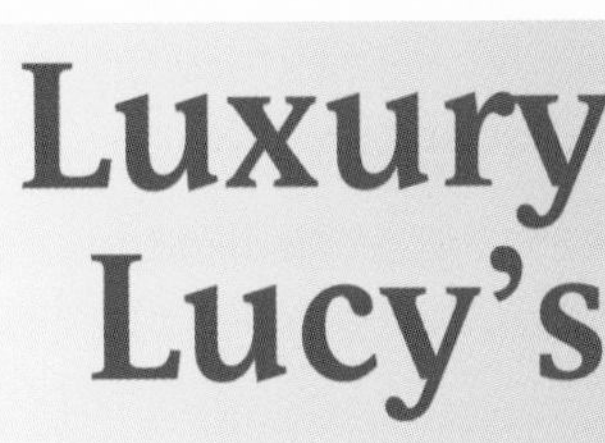

Luxury Lucy's favourite sandwich

a Match the ingredients and pictures.

You need:

- ☐ some brown bread
- ☐ some smoked salmon
- ☐ some cream cheese
- ☐ a lemon
- ☐ some black pepper

b Read the instructions. Complete them with *cut* or *put*.

1 First ____ two thin pieces of brown bread.

2 Then ____ some cream cheese on one of the pieces.

3 ____ some pieces of smoked salmon on the cream cheese.

4 ____ the lemon in half.

5 ____ a little lemon juice and black pepper on the salmon.

6 Now ____ the other piece of bread on top.

7 Finally – eat the sandwich! It's delicious!

WRITE instructions to make *your* favourite sandwich.

- Invent a name for it.
- Say what ingredients you need (some bread, etc.).
- Write the instructions.

Check your instructions for mistakes.

7 What do you remember?

GRAMMAR

Circle the correct sentence, a or b.

(a) Hi. I'm Susanna.
b Hi. I Susanna.

1 a Are there any onions?
b Are there an onions?
2 a There's a butter in the fridge.
b There's some butter in the fridge.
3 a We don't need some bread.
b We don't need any bread.
4 a How much fruit do you eat a day?
b How many fruit do you eat a day?
5 a I drink quite a lot coffee.
b I drink quite a lot of coffee.
6 a She doesn't drink much water.
b She doesn't drink many water.
7 a I go to buy my ticket today.
b I'm going to buy my ticket today.
8 a Are they going to get married?
b Do they going to get married?
9 a What you are going to do this summer?
b What are you going to do this summer?
10 a It's going to rain next week.
b It's going to rain the next week.

VOCABULARY

a verb phrases

Match the verbs and phrases.

get a taxi

get meet move stay see

1 ______ in a hotel
2 ______ the sights in a city
3 ______ a new job
4 ______ somebody new
5 ______ house

b food

Circle the word that is different.

Ireland	(Chinese)	Thailand	Spain
1 breakfast	lunch	dessert	dinner
2 mushrooms	strawberries	onions	peas
3 orange juice	sugar	milk	mineral water
4 crisps	chips	tomatoes	potatoes
5 fruit salad	ice cream	coffee	cake

c prepositions

Complete the sentences with *for*, *in*, *of*, *on*, or *with*.

Look *at* the board.

1 Is there any water ______ the fridge?
2 I drink a lot ______ coffee.
3 Water is good ______ you.
4 Who are you going to New York ______?
5 They're going to go ______ holiday together.

15

PRONUNCIATION

a Underline the word with a different sound.

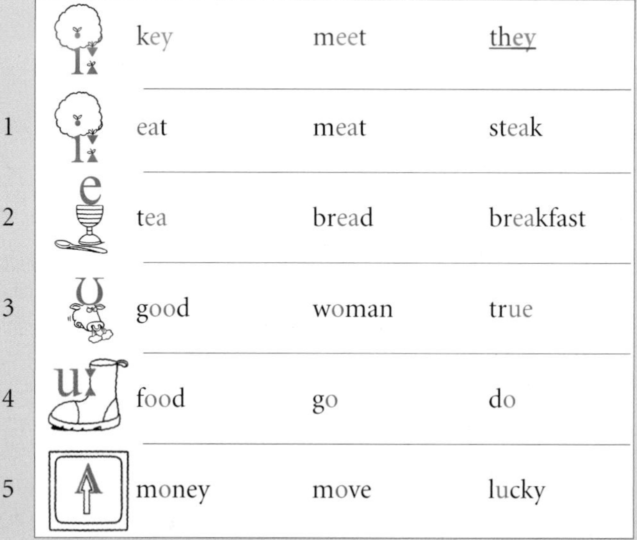

	key	meet	<u>they</u>
1	eat	meat	steak
2	tea	bread	breakfast
3	good	woman	true
4	food	go	do
5	money	move	lucky

b Underline the stressed syllable.

infor<u>ma</u>tion

dessert menu vegetables banana biscuit

10

CAN YOU UNDERSTAND THIS TEXT?

Food can be dangerous for your health!

WHEN you go to a restaurant you often think that the food you are ordering is good for you. But many restaurants serve healthy food, like fish or salad, with a sauce or dressing that uses a lot of oil, fat, or sugar.

The British Food Standards Agency wants all restaurants to say in their menus exactly what is in each dish, how many calories, how much fat, and what additives. They think that restaurants don't give their customers enough information, and that this new plan could help people to have a healthier diet.

But chefs are not happy with the Agency's plan. One top chef said, 'People are not stupid. They know that many sauces have butter and cream in them. But if we put on a menu that a dish has 1,000 calories, nobody is going to order it!'

However, many doctors agree with the plan. Bruce Ward, Professor of Medicine, said, 'People know that cigarettes are bad for them, because it tells you on the packet. But when they go to a restaurant they often have no idea if the food is healthy or not. Food products that have a lot of calories, fat, and sugar need a health warning, exactly like cigarettes.'

Adapted from a British newspaper

a Read the article. Circle a, b, or c.

1 Many restaurants…
  a serve healthy food.
  b only serve fish and salad.
  c serve healthy food but with unhealthy sauces.

2 The British Food Standards Agency wants restaurants…
  a to serve healthy food.
  b to give more information about their dishes.
  c not to use fat and additives.

3 Chefs think that…
  a people are not going to order their dishes.
  b people are stupid.
  c cream and butter are good for you.

4 Doctors think that people…
  a need more information about cigarettes.
  b need more information about food.
  c need to stop eating in restaurants.

b Read the article again. Underline and learn five new words connected with food or cooking.

CAN YOU HEAR THE DIFFERENCE?

a 7.20 Listen. Circle a or b.

1 a There's some milk in the fridge.
  b There isn't any milk in the fridge.
2 a The woman doesn't drink much coffee.
  b The woman drinks a lot of coffee.
3 a She's going to go to Australia.
  b She's going to go to Italy.
4 a They're going to go to a restaurant.
  b They're going to go to the cinema.
5 a She thinks they're going to get married.
  b She doesn't think they're going to get married.

b 7.21 Listen to a woman shopping. Answer the questions.

1 What does she buy? Tick (✓) the boxes.

carrots	☐	oranges	☐
peas	☐	onions	☐
strawberries	☐	tomatoes	☐
grapes	☐	mushrooms	☐

2 How much does she pay?

CAN YOU SAY THIS IN ENGLISH?

a Can you...? Yes (✓)

☐ say five things that there are in your fridge
☐ say three *healthy* things that you eat or drink a lot of
☐ say three *unhealthy* things that you eat or drink a lot of

b In pairs, ask and answer questions about your plans.

Tonight / study English? What / have for dinner? What / do after dinner?	**Next weekend** / go away? / stay at home on Saturday night?
Tomorrow What time / get up? Where / have lunch? What / do in the evening?	**Next summer** / go abroad? Where / go?

Are you going to study English tonight?

G comparative adjectives
V personality adjectives
P /ə/, sentence stress

The True False Show

1 SPEAKING & LISTENING

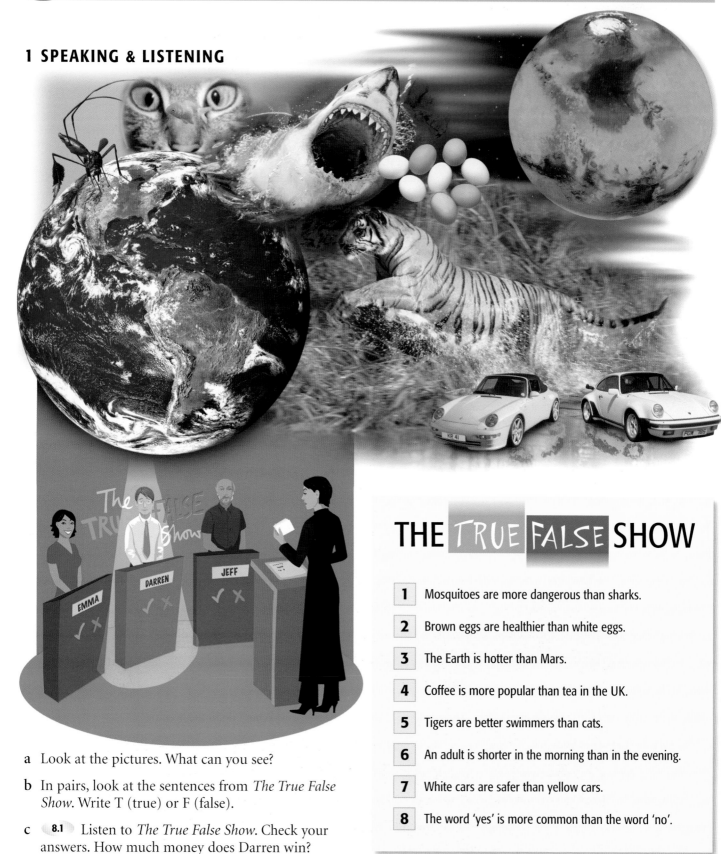

THE TRUE FALSE SHOW

1 Mosquitoes are more dangerous than sharks.

2 Brown eggs are healthier than white eggs.

3 The Earth is hotter than Mars.

4 Coffee is more popular than tea in the UK.

5 Tigers are better swimmers than cats.

6 An adult is shorter in the morning than in the evening.

7 White cars are safer than yellow cars.

8 The word 'yes' is more common than the word 'no'.

a Look at the pictures. What can you see?

b In pairs, look at the sentences from *The True False Show*. Write T (true) or F (false).

c 8.1 Listen to *The True False Show*. Check your answers. How much money does Darren win?

2 GRAMMAR comparative adjectives

a Look at the adjectives in the quiz sentences. In pairs, answer the questions.

Using adjectives to compare two things:

1 What two letters do you put at the end of one-syllable adjectives (e.g. *short*)?
2 Why is *hot* different?
3 What happens when an adjective ends in *-y*?
4 What word do you put in front of long adjectives (e.g. *popular*)?
5 What's the missing word?
China is bigger ______ *Japan.*

b **p.136 Grammar Bank 8A.** Read the rules and do the exercises.

3 PRONUNCIATION /ə/, sentence stress

a **8.2** Listen and repeat the comparative adjectives. Underline the stressed syllable. How is *-er* pronounced at the end of a word?

healthier
hotter
better
shorter
safer

b **8.3** Listen and repeat the eight quiz sentences from **1b**. Copy the rhythm.

c **Communication** *True False Show A p.110 B p.113.* Write eight quiz sentences. Then play *The True False Show.*

4 VOCABULARY personality adjectives

Match the adjectives of personality with their meaning.

aggressive careful stylish ~~friendly~~
generous quiet serious

1 a *friendly* person is open and kind
2 a ______ person doesn't make mistakes or have accidents
3 a ______ person thinks a lot and doesn't make jokes
4 a ______ person doesn't talk a lot
5 a ______ person likes giving people things
6 a ______ person dresses well
7 an ______ person likes arguing and can be violent

5 LISTENING

a What colour is your / your family's car? Do you like the colour?

b **8.4** You're going to listen to a radio programme about car colours and personality. Listen once and write the colours in the chart.

your car colour	your personality
1 *yellow*	very ______ (more popular with women than men)
2 ______	______ (very popular with doctors)
3 ______	more ______ than normal
4 ______	______
5 ______	______
6 ______	______ (popular with business people)
7 ______	______

c Listen again and complete 'your personality' with the adjectives from **4**.

d Think of three people you know who have a car. What colour are their cars? Is their personality the same as in the chart?

8 B

G superlative adjectives
V the weather
P consonant groups

What's the coldest place in the world?

The highest city in the world

1 READING

a Look at the photos. Where do you think the places are?

b Read the article and complete each heading with a phrase.

The coldest **The highest** **The hottest**

EXTREME LIVING

Welcome to the coldest, highest, and hottest places in the world!

_______________ **country in the world**

How do people live in **Mali**, West Africa, where the temperature is often 50°? John Baxter, a BBC journalist in Mali, says, 'People get up very early and they don't move very much in the afternoon. Surprisingly, they wear a lot of clothes (usually cotton) as this helps them not to get dehydrated. Houses are very hot and don't have air conditioning – the best place to sleep is on the roof!'

_______________ **capital city in the world**

La Paz in Bolivia is 4,090 metres above sea level. It can be difficult to breathe because there isn't much oxygen. Liz Tremlett, a travel agent who lives there, says, 'When people arrive at El Alto airport we sometimes need to give them oxygen.' It is also the worst place to be if you drink too much beer. The next day you feel terrible because you get more dehydrated. But La Paz is a very good place to play golf. At this altitude, when you hit a golf ball it goes further!

_______________ **place in the world**

Can you imagine living in a place which is four times colder than your freezer? This is **Yakutia** in Siberia, where in winter it is often –50° or lower. Valeria Usimenko, a housewife, says, 'After a few minutes outside your nose fills with ice. It snows a lot and there is always a lot of ice and snow on top of the houses. The most dangerous time is the spring – when the ice falls it can kill people! The winter is very boring because we can't go out much. A lot of babies are born here in the autumn!'

Adapted from a magazine

c Read the article again. Answers these questions.

1 Where do people wear a lot of cotton clothes? *Mali*
2 Where is a good place to play golf? _______
3 Where do people sleep on the roof? _______
4 Where can you have a problem with your nose? _______
5 Where do you need to be careful in spring? _______
6 Where is a bad place to drink a lot of alcohol? _______

d In pairs, guess the meaning of the highlighted words. Check with your teacher or a dictionary.

e Choose five new words to learn from the article.

2 GRAMMAR superlative adjectives

a Complete the chart with superlatives from the article.

adjective	comparative	superlative
cold	colder	*the coldest*
high	higher	________
hot	hotter	________
dangerous	more dangerous	________
good	better	________
bad	worse	________

b **p.136 Grammar Bank 8B.** Read the rules and do the exercises.

3 PRONUNCIATION consonant groups

a 8.5 Listen and repeat the adjectives in **2a**.

b 8.6 Words which have two or three consonants together can be difficult to pronounce. Listen and repeat these superlatives.

the most expensive	the most beautiful
the most crowded	the smallest
the driest	the fastest
the coldest	the strongest

c Complete the questions with superlative adjectives. Then ask and answer the questions with a partner.

World Capitals Quiz

1 What's the ________ capital city in the world? (noisy)
a Tokyo b Madrid c Rome

2 What's the ________ capital city in the world? (big)
a Buenos Aires b Mexico City c Tokyo

3 What's the ________ capital city in the world? (dry)
a Nairobi b Lagos c Cairo

4 What's the ________ capital city in the world? (expensive)
a London b Tokyo c Washington

5 What's the ________ capital city in the world? (safe)
a Copenhagen b Canberra c Oslo

6 What's the ________ capital city in the world? (crowded)
a Beijing b Bangkok c New Delhi

4 VOCABULARY the weather

a What's the weather like? Match the sentences and pictures.

1 It's raining / wet. ☐
2 It's sunny / dry / hot. ☐
3 It's snowing / cold. ☐
4 It's cloudy. ☐
5 It's windy. ☐

A B C D E

b What's the weather like where you are today?

5 SPEAKING

In pairs or small groups, ask and answer these questions about your country.

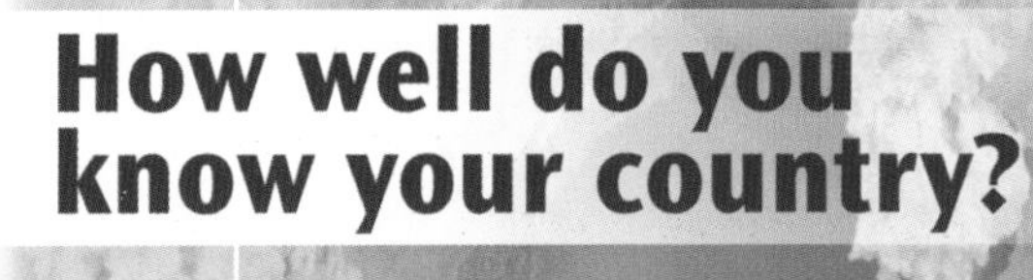
What's the wettest place?
I think it's...

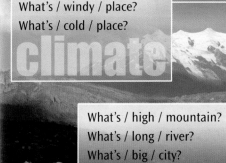

How well do you know your country?

climate

What's / wet / place?
What's / hot / place?
What's / windy / place?
What's / cold / place?

geography

What's / high / mountain?
What's / long / river?
What's / big / city?

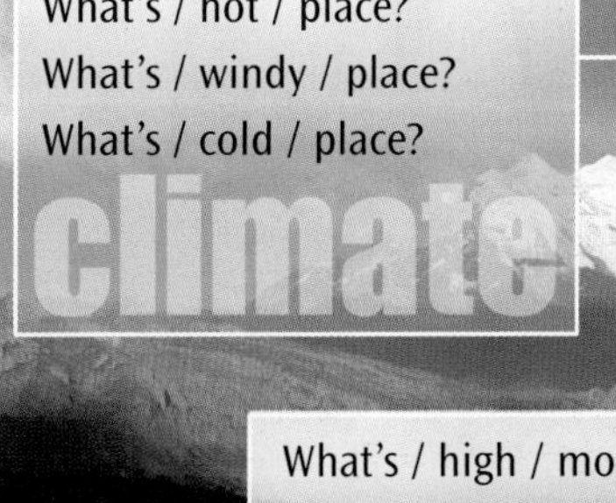

tourism

What's / beautiful / city?
What's / popular / place for tourists? Why?
What's / good / time of year to visit? Why?
What's / bad / time of year to visit? Why?
What's / good / way to travel round the country?
What's / dangerous / city?

6 8.7 SONG ♫ *The Best*

8C

G *would like to / like*
V adventures
P sentence stress

Would you like to fly a plane?
No, I don't like flying.

Would you like to drive a Ferrari?

1 READING & SPEAKING

a Do you like buying presents? Who's the easiest person in your family to buy presents for? Who is the most difficult?

b Read the advert. Match the *Experience* presents with paragraphs A–F.

Are you looking for
A REALLY SPECIAL PRESENT?

WHSmith's Amazing Adventures are the perfect original present

Do you know somebody who would like to drive a real Ferrari, salsa dance, or fly in a balloon? There are more than 40 'experience presents' to choose from. Each Amazing Adventure comes in an attractive box including a book and video.

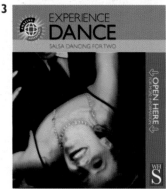

1
EXPERIENCE BALLOONING
GO ON A HOT-AIR BALLOON FLIGHT

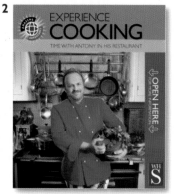

2
EXPERIENCE COOKING
TIME WITH ANTONY IN HIS RESTAURANT

3
EXPERIENCE DANCE
SALSA DANCING FOR TWO

4

5
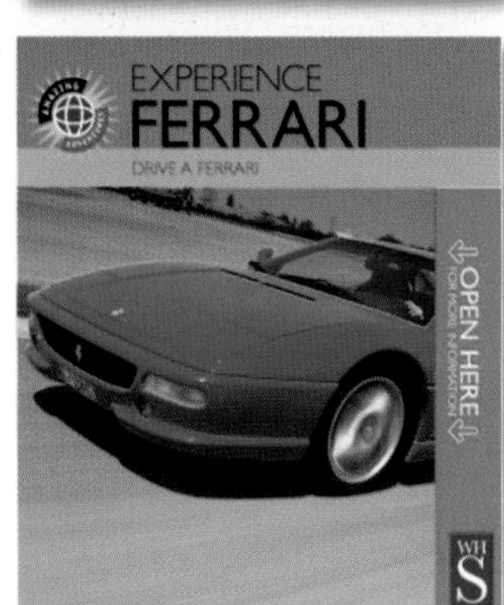

6

A Do you like singing in the shower? Would you like to be a pop star? Now you can record the song of your dreams at a real recording studio. Price £249.99 ☐

B Do you like seeing historic cars and planes? Would you like to go back in time and learn to fly an authentic World War II plane?
Price £139.99 ☐
* For people of maximum weight 102 kg, maximum height 1.92 m

C Do you like cooking? Would you like to spend a day with a famous chef and learn new recipes and techniques? Then this is the adventure for you. The day includes a delicious lunch (with wine).
Price £149.99 ☐

D You like driving fast, but your car is very slow. Now you too can drive this famous Italian sports car.
Price £229.99 ☐
* Minimum age 19, with driving licence

E It's easy! It's fun! Everybody's doing it! Wouldn't you like to learn, and be the star of the dance floor?
Price £39.99 ☐

F Would you like to have the experience of a lifetime and go up into the sky in a hot-air balloon? The flight lasts about one hour, and the adventure ends with a glass of champagne.
Price £189.99 ☐

c Read paragraphs A–F again. Answer these questions.

Which amazing adventure is…?
- the cheapest
- the most expensive

Which do you think is…?
- the most dangerous
- the most exciting
- the most boring
- the most difficult
- the most useful

d Which one…
- would you like as a present? Why?
- would you like to give to someone in your family? Why?

2 GRAMMAR *would like to / like*

a Look at the dialogue. In pairs, answer the questions.

A **Would you like to learn** salsa?
B No, I wouldn't. **I don't like dancing**. But **I'd like to drive** a Ferrari.

1 What's the form of the verb after *would like*?
2 Does *Would you like…?* mean…
a Do you like…? b Do you want…?
3 What's the difference between *I like dancing* and *I'd like to dance?*

b **p.136 Grammar Bank 8C.** Read the rules and do the exercises.

3 PRONUNCIATION sentence stress

a 8.8 Listen and repeat the dialogue. Copy the rhythm.

A Would you like to learn to fly a plane?
B No, I wouldn't.
A Why not?
B Because I don't like flying, and I think it's dangerous.

b 8.9 Listen to this dialogue. Underline the stressed words.

A Would you like to drive a Ferrari?
B Yes, I'd love to.
A Why?
B Because I like driving, but my car's very slow.

c In pairs, practise the dialogues.

d In pairs, use the pictures in **1b**. Ask *Would you like to…? Why (not)?*

4 LISTENING

a You're going to listen to Russell talking about an 'experience present'. Look at the photo. What was the present? Do you think he enjoyed it?

b 8.10 Listen to these phrases. Match them with the pictures.

1 We learned how to land.
2 I sat on the floor and waited.
3 Then the instructor said 'Jump!' and I jumped.
4 Suddenly the parachute opened, and I floated down.
5 One of the people in my group broke his leg.

c 8.11 Listen to the interview with Russell. Did he enjoy the jump? Would he like to do it again? Why (not)?

d Number the sentences 1–9 in the correct order. Listen again and check.

☐	He fell very fast.	☐	He went up in the plane.
☐	He felt fantastic.	☐	He jumped.
☐	He landed.	☐	His parachute opened.
1	He had some classes.	☐	He felt frightened.
☐	He waited to jump.		

8D

G adverbs
V common adverbs
P adjectives and adverbs

They drive slowly and work hard.

They dress well but drive badly

1 READING & SPEAKING

a Look at these cities. What countries are they in?

Rio de Janeiro   Milan   Tokyo   Los Angeles   Barcelona   Sydney

b Imagine you are going to live in one of these cities. Mark them **E** (easy for me to live in) or **D** (difficult for me to live in). Compare with a partner. Say why.

c Read the article. Where are the three people living? Complete the gaps with cities from **a**.

d Read the article again. Then cover it and try to remember three things about each city. Did anything surprise you?

The inside story

Three people who live abroad talk about their 'new' countries.

Nuria from Spain lives in ________

Driving 8/10 I was surprised – people drive quite slowly. People use their cars for everything. You never see people walking in the street.

Social life 5/10 People don't go out during the week because they work very hard. It's normal to work twelve hours a day and people usually only have one or two weeks' holiday. Work is the most important thing here, more important than family and social life.

People 9/10 People are really nice here. It's easy to talk to them. And in shops the shop assistants are very helpful. They always say 'Have a good day!'

Chic Boutique
Have a good day!

Mónica from Argentina lives in ________

Safety 10/10 There is almost no crime here. You can walk safely in the city late at night. And you can leave things in your car and nobody steals them!

Driving 7/10 People drive carefully, but the big problem is that there aren't any street names. It's impossible to find where you want to go. Even taxi drivers don't know! Also traffic lights are horizontal and they are difficult to see.

People 9/10 They are shy and polite and they speak very quietly. But when they drink some of them change completely! Last Friday night I went out with people from work and we ended up in a karaoke bar. My boss is usually quite serious but he sang 'My Way' very loudly and badly.

2 GRAMMAR adverbs

a Look at these sentences. How do you make an adverb from an adjective?

adjectives
They are slow drivers.
They are careful drivers.

adverbs
They drive slow**ly**.
They drive careful**ly**.

b Look at the article again. Find and underline nine verb + adverb phrases. Which adverbs don't end in *-ly*?

c ➲ **p.136 Grammar Bank 8D.** Read the rules and do the exercises.

d 8.12 Listen and say what is happening. Use an adverb.
They're speaking quietly.

Kevin from the UK lives in ________

Clothes 8/10 Appearance is very important. Everybody dresses well, but especially the men. They are very elegant and wear very stylish clothes. It is easy to see who the British people are here!

Food 9/10 They love food here and it is fantastic! But times are changing. Today many people under 35 can't cook. Supermarkets are full of food now which you can put in the microwave. When I first came to live here there weren't any McDonald's but now they are everywhere.

Driving 5/10 People here are in love with their cars and they drive very fast. Even the nicest people become more aggressive when they drive.

3 PRONUNCIATION adjectives and adverbs

a Underline the stressed syllable in the adjectives.

adjectives	adverbs
aggressive	aggressively
stylish	stylishly
dangerous	dangerously
polite	politely
beautiful	beautifully
quiet	quietly
careful	carefully
complete	completely

b 8.13 Listen and check. Repeat the adjectives.

c 8.14 Now listen to the adverbs. Does the stress change?

d Practise saying the adverbs.

4 SPEAKING

a In pairs, complete with a country or city (not yours).

They drive dangerously in ______.
They dress very stylishly in ______.
You can eat very well in ______.
People in ______ talk loudly.
They play football badly in ______.
They work hard in ______.
People speak English very well in ______.
People dance beautifully in ______.

b Compare your sentences with other students. Do you agree?

c What about in *your* country or city? How do people...?

VOCABULARY verb phrases

a Match the verbs and phrases.

ask	call	check out	pay	sign	need

1 ______ of a hotel
2 ______ for the bill
3 ______ by credit card
4 ______ your name
5 ______ help with your luggage
6 ______ a taxi (*for somebody*)

b In pairs, test your partner.

CHECKING OUT

a 8.15 Mark is leaving the hotel. Cover the dialogue and listen. What does he ask for? What two things doesn't he need?

YOU HEAR	YOU SAY
Good morning, sir.	Good morning. Can I have my bill, please? I'm checking out.
1 Which room ______ it?	Room 425.
2 ______ you have anything from the minibar last night?	Yes, a mineral water.
Here you are.	
3 How ______ you like to pay?	American Express.
4 Thank you. OK. ______ you sign here, please? Thank you.	
5 ______ you like me to call a taxi for you?	No, thanks.
6 ______ you need any help with your luggage?	No, I'm fine, thanks.
Have a good trip, Mr Ryder.	Thank you.
Goodbye.	Goodbye.

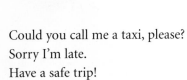

b Listen again. Complete the YOU HEAR phrases.

c 8.16 Listen and repeat the YOU SAY phrases. Copy the rhythm.

d In pairs, roleplay the dialogue.

SOCIAL ENGLISH

a 8.17 Listen. Circle the correct answer.

1 Allie says the traffic is **terrible / horrible**.
2 Mark gets a **taxi / train** to the airport.
3 Allie is going to meet Mark at the **station / airport**.
4 Mark's flight leaves in **30 / 40** minutes.
5 Allie's boss said she **can / can't** go to the conference.

b What do you think is going to happen to Mark and Allie in the future?

c Who says the USEFUL PHRASES, Mark or Allie? Listen again and check. How do you say them in your language?

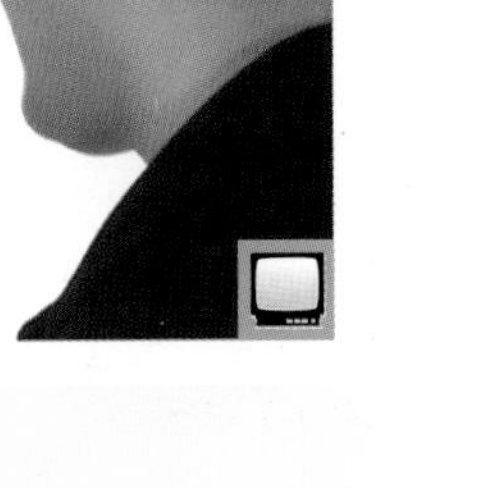

USEFUL PHRASES

*I'll call a taxi.
Well, thanks for everything.
*I'll meet you (*at the airport*).
Where can we meet?
Could you call me a taxi, please?
Sorry I'm late.
Have a safe trip!

*I'll = I will (future)

Making a reservation

a Read about the three hotels. Which one would you most like to go to?

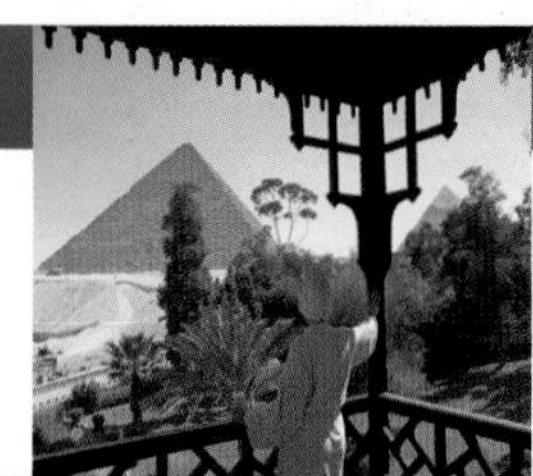

Mena House Oberoi Hotel, Giza, Egypt

This hotel is where Egyptian kings stayed! It is a luxury hotel with the best view of the pyramids, and is the only hotel in Egypt with a golf course. Double rooms from €249.

www.oberoihotels.com

Hotel Danieli, Venice, Italy

This hotel has 91 beautiful rooms. The best rooms are in the old part (ask for Dandolo's palace) and there's a wonderful roof terrace with views over the lagoon. Double rooms from €349.

danieli.hotelinvenice.com

THE RESIDENCE, TUNIS, TUNISIA

This amazing hotel has a sea water spa and beautiful gardens. Famous guests include Sting and Catherine Deneuve. Double rooms from €211.

www.theresidence-tunis.com

b Read Sylvie's e-mail. Which hotel is she writing to?

From Sylvie Vartan sylvievartan@hotmail.com
To ____________
Subject Reservation for November

Dear Sir / [1] *Madam*

I would like to make a [2]______ for a single [3]______ for three [4]______, 24, 25, and 26 November.

I would like a room with a [5]______ of the gardens, if possible. Could you send me some [6]______ about the spa treatments?

[7]______ confirm the reservation.

[8]______

Sylvie Vartan

c Complete the e-mail with these words.

~~Madam~~ information Please nights reservation room Yours view

d Complete the chart.

	Informal e-mails (to a friend)	Formal e-mails (to a hotel)
Beginning	Hi / Hello / Dear (*Antonio*)	______ (*Sir / Madam / Mr. Smith*)
End	Hope to hear from you soon.	Please ______ (*the reservation*).
	All the best / Love	______
Name	First name only	First name and ______

WRITE an e-mail to one of the hotels to make a reservation for you and your partner, family, etc.

Say…
- what room(s) you would like (single, double, how many).
- when you want to go (number of nights and dates).

Ask…
- for a room with a view and information about something.
- the hotel to confirm the reservation.

Check your e-mail for mistakes.

8 What do you remember?

GRAMMAR

Circle the correct sentence, a or b.

(a) Hi. I'm Susanna.
b Hi. I Susanna.

1 a The Earth is hoter than Mars.
b The Earth is hotter that Mars.

2 a Tea is cheaper than coffee.
b Tea is more cheap than coffee.

3 a Driving is dangerouser than flying.
b Driving is more dangerous than flying.

4 a Your English is worse than mine.
b Your English is more bad than mine.

5 a It's the cheapest restaurant in the city.
b It's the cheaper restaurant in the city.

6 a What's the better time to visit?
b What's the best time to visit?

7 a Would you like to do a parachute jump?
b Do you like to do a parachute jump?

8 a I'd like to drive a Ferrari.
b I'd like drive a Ferrari.

9 a You speak very slow.
b You speak very slowly.

10 a She plays tennis very good.
b She plays tennis very well.

☐ 10

VOCABULARY

a adjectives and adverbs

Write the opposite adjective or adverb.

good *bad*
1 quickly ______
2 safe ______
3 well ______
4 noisy ______
5 the best ______

b word groups

Circle the word that is different.

Ireland	(Chinese)	Thailand	Spain
1 careful	tall	serious	generous
2 cold	hot	dry	dangerous
3 bigger	hotter	leader	older
4 friendly	quietly	dangerously	carefully
5 noisy	crowded	expensive	safe

c prepositions

Complete the sentences with *for*, *in*, *than*, *of*, or *up*.

Look *at* the board.
1 It's the hottest country ______ the world.
2 The best time ______ year to visit is the spring.
3 I bought a present ______ my sister.
4 Would you like to go ______ in a balloon?
5 My brother is taller ______ me.

☐ 15

PRONUNCIATION

a Underline the word with a different sound.

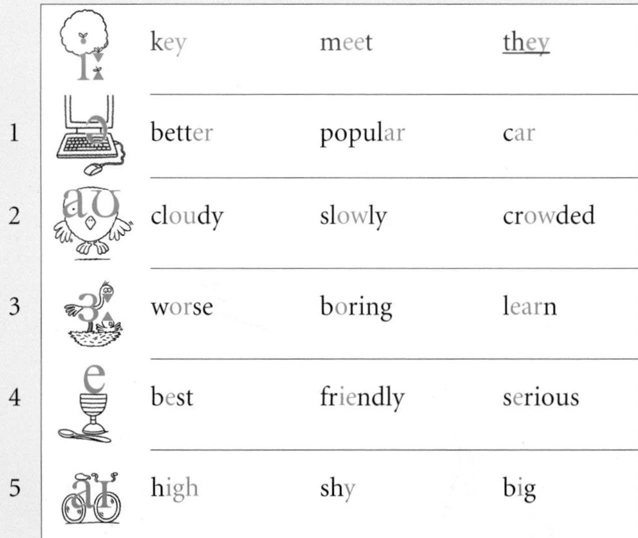

	key	meet	<u>they</u>
1	better	popular	car
2	cloudy	slowly	crowded
3	worse	boring	learn
4	best	friendly	serious
5	high	shy	big

b Underline the stressed syllable.

infor<u>ma</u>tion

aggressive ambitious adventure politely dangerously

☐ 10

CAN YOU UNDERSTAND THIS TEXT?

a Look at the photo and read the article quickly. Would you like to go there?

b Read the article again. Circle a, b, or c.

1 In the Atacama desert...
  a it hardly ever rains.
  b it never rains.
  c it sometimes rains.
2 The only people who live there are...
  a NASA scientists.
  b villagers.
  c builders.
3 The people in Chungungo...
  a have more water than before.
  b have a lot of water.
  c can't water their plants.
4 The Atacama is a very good place to go if you want to...
  a see clouds.
  b see mountains.
  c see stars.

The Atacama desert...

...the perfect place for people who are looking for adventure

The Atacama desert in Chile is a spectacular place. There is very little vegetation, and it looks like the moon – in fact NASA tested their lunar vehicles here. There are some very big volcanoes. Almost nobody lives there, but there are some small villages on the edge of the desert. Life is hard and everything needs to be imported – food, building materials, and of course water.

In 1971 it rained in the Atacama. People were amazed because the last time it rained there was 400 years earlier, in 1570! It is the driest place in the world. But in the village of Chungungo they are now getting water from the fog clouds which come in from the sea. Daisy Sasmaya, a villager, says, 'We are very happy because now we can have a shower every day, and we can water our plants every week.'

The sky over the Atacama desert is hardly ever cloudy, so it is one of the best places in the world to see the stars. The biggest observatory in the world is being built on top of a mountain. 'It's the purest air in the world,' says journalist Hugh O'Shaughnessy. 'At night the sky is incredibly clear – you feel that there is nothing between you and Mars.'

Adapted from a British magazine

CAN YOU HEAR THE DIFFERENCE?

8.18 Nicolas, a French student at university in Edinburgh, talks about his first impressions. Listen. Circle a or b.

1 In Scotland people speak...
  a with a different accent and some different words.
  b with a different accent only.
2 In Edinburgh...
  a it's very windy but it doesn't rain much.
  b it rains more than in Paris.
3 Nicolas's Scottish friends...
  a eat a lot of fruit and vegetables.
  b eat a lot of sweet things.
4 Nicolas...
  a never drinks whisky.
  b drinks whisky when he goes to the pub.
5 When he finishes university he...
  a is going to go home.
  b doesn't know what he is going to do.

CAN YOU SAY THIS IN ENGLISH?

a Can you...? Yes (✓)

- ☐ say what the weather is like today (three sentences)
- ☐ compare your town / city with another (three sentences)
- ☐ say three superlative sentences about cities in your country (e.g. *The biggest city is...*)
- ☐ say three things you would like to do (e.g. *go up in a balloon*)
- ☐ say three different ways that people can drive (e.g. *slowly*)

b Complete the questions.

are do does did would is were do

1 What ______ you do last weekend?
2 How often ______ you do sport or exercise?
3 Where ______ you like to go next summer?
4 ______ your town have many tourist sights?
5 ______ you like cooking?
6 ______ you going to go out tonight?
7 What ______ the teacher wearing today?
8 Where ______ you at ten o'clock last night?

c Interview your partner. When he / she answers, try to ask another question.

9 A Before we met

G present perfect
V *been to*
P sentence stress

Have you been to Madrid?
No, I haven't. But I've been to Barcelona.

1 SPEAKING & READING

a In pairs, answer the questions.

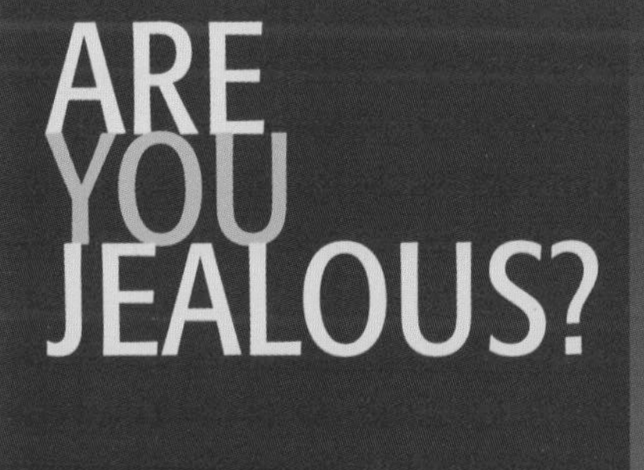

1 Are you jealous?
- often
- sometimes
- hardly ever / never

2 Can you remember a time when you were jealous of…?
a a brother or sister
b a friend
c another person

3 Do you know a very jealous person? Who?

4 Who do you think are more jealous, men or women?

b 9.1 Read and listen to the beginning of a story and answer questions 1–3.

1 Which cities has Rob visited? Tick (✓) the boxes.

Barcelona ☐
Lisbon ☐
Madrid ☐
Rome ☐
Venice ☐
Florence ☐

2 Who is Jessica? Where is she now?

3 Why doesn't Charlotte want to go to these three places?

c In pairs, guess the meaning of the highlighted words. Check with your teacher or a dictionary.

Rob is going out with Charlotte, a woman who works in the same company as him. They want to go away somewhere for the weekend.

It was a Thursday evening in June when we sat down in Charlotte's living room with the holiday brochures. 'I got these from the travel agent's today,' said Charlotte. 'This is going to be fun! Have you been to Italy?'

'Yes, I have,' I replied. 'I've been to Rome and Florence.'

'On holiday?'

'Yes… with Jessica.'

'Oh.' There was a long silence.

'But I haven't been to Venice. What about Venice?'

'No. Forget Italy. Have you been to Spain?'

'Yes. I've been to Barcelona.'

'With Jessica?'

'Yes, but…'

She picked up a brochure for Lisbon. 'Don't tell me. You've been there too. With Jessica.'

'No. I've never been to Portugal. Look, what's the problem? Jessica's not my girlfriend now. She's thousands of miles away. She lives in Canada. Why are you so jealous of her?'

'Me? Jealous? I'm not jealous.'

There was another long silence.

2 GRAMMAR present perfect

a Look at this sentence from the story in 1 and answer questions 1–4.

I've been to Rome and Florence.

1 Does Rob know Rome and Florence? **yes / no**
2 Do we know exactly *when* Rob went to Rome and Florence? **yes / no**
3 What verb is *'ve*?
4 What verb is *been*?

b Look at the story in 1 again. Underline [+], [−], and [?] examples of *have been (to)*.

c Complete the chart with *have, has, haven't*, or *hasn't*.

	[+]	[−]	[?]
I, you, we, they	I ______ been to Rome.	I ______ been to Venice.	______ you been to Lisbon?
he, she, it	She ______ been to Rome.	She ______ been to Venice.	______ he been to Lisbon?

d ➲ **p.138 Grammar Bank 9A.** Read the rules and do the exercises.

3 PRONUNCIATION sentence stress

a 9.2 Listen and repeat this dialogue. Copy the rhythm.

A Have you been to Italy?
B Yes, I have. I've been to Venice.
A Have you been to New York?
B No, I haven't. I haven't been to the USA.

b Play *Have you been to…?*

4 LISTENING

a 9.3 Listen to the rest of the conversation between Rob and Charlotte. Who phones?

b Listen again. Complete the sentences with *Charlotte, Rob*, or *Jessica*.

1 ______ hasn't been to Paris.
2 ______ likes the hotel.
3 ______'s mobile rings.
4 It is ______.
5 ______ doesn't want to talk on the phone to ______.
6 ______ is angry with ______ and leaves the house.

5 SPEAKING

Stand up and move around the class. Ask *Have you been to…?* questions until somebody answers 'yes'. Write their name in the questionnaire.

Find a person who…

has been to a very hot country ______
has been to a karaoke bar ______
has been to a big sports event ______
has been to an opera ______
has been to a spa ______
has been to a fortune teller ______
has been to another continent ______
has been to a big pop concert ______

G present perfect or past simple?
V past participles
P irregular past participles

9B I've read the book, I've seen the film

Have you seen the film? Did you like it?

1 SPEAKING

CINEMA EXPERIENCES

Have you ever…?		Yes	No	
1	*spoken* to a film actor or actress			Who was it? What did you say?
2	_____ a film more than three times			What film? When was the last time you saw it?
3	_____ in a film			What film was it? Why did you cry?
4	_____ a 'soundtrack' from a film			What film was it? Did you like the film?
5	_____ the cinema in the middle of a film			What film was it? Why did you leave?
6	_____ in the cinema			What film was it? Why did you sleep?
7	_____ somebody in the back row			Who was it? Did you see the film?

a Complete the questionnaire above with these past participles.

slept bought cried kissed left ~~spoken~~ seen

b Interview a partner with the questionnaire. If he / she says *'Yes, I have'*, ask the other two questions.

2 VOCABULARY past participles

a Look at the past participles in exercise **a**. Which ones…?

1 are regular _____ _____
2 are irregular (and the same as the past simple)
_____ _____ _____
3 are irregular (and different from the past simple)
_____ _____

b **p.154 Irregular verbs.** Highlight the past participles that are different from the past simple.

3 PRONUNCIATION irregular participles

a Put three irregular past participles in each column.

begun bought broken caught done
driven drunk given known made
paid spoken taken worn written

b 9.4 Listen and check. Practise saying them.

4 GRAMMAR present perfect or past simple?

a Look at the dialogue. In pairs, answer the questions.

1 What tense is question **A**?
2 What tense are questions **B** and **C**?
3 Which question is general?
4 Which questions are specific?

A Have you ever spoken to an actor or actress?
Yes, (I have).
B Who was it?
Jude Law.
C What did you say to him?
I asked him for his autograph.

b **p.138 Grammar Bank 9B.** Read the rules and do the exercises.

5 LISTENING & SPEAKING

a Look at the four books and answer the questions.

- Have you read the book?
- Have you seen the film(s)?

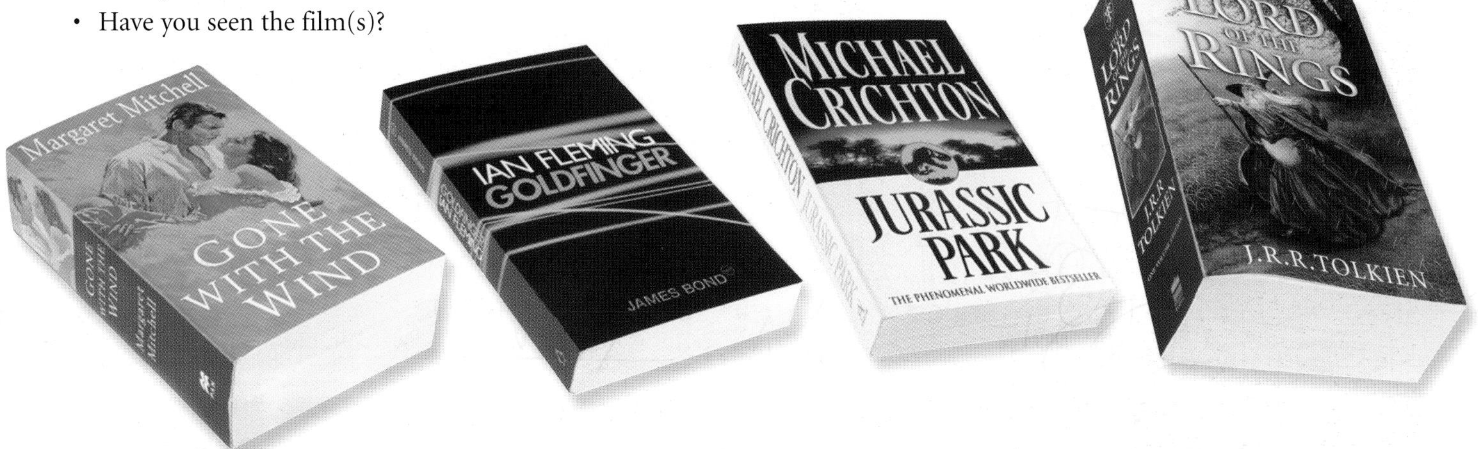

b Read the website information about *The Book Programme* on Radio South. What is tonight's programme about? What are listeners going to do?

The Book Programme – listeners' phone-in.

Our question tonight: Do good books make good films?
When a book becomes a bestseller, we know that a film version is soon going to appear. But which is usually better, the book or the film?
Phone 0845 8769922 and tell us what you think.

c 9.5 Listen to Carl, Linda, and Sam phoning the programme. Which person is *most* positive about films made from books?

d Listen again. Mark the sentences T (true) or F (false).

1 Carl thinks books are usually better than films.
2 He loved the *Lord of the Rings* films.
3 Linda says people read a lot.
4 She thinks people buy books after they see a film.
5 Sam thinks good books make bad films.
6 He preferred the James Bond books.

e In pairs, think of a film based on a book and make a class list on the board.

f Look at the chart. What are the questions?

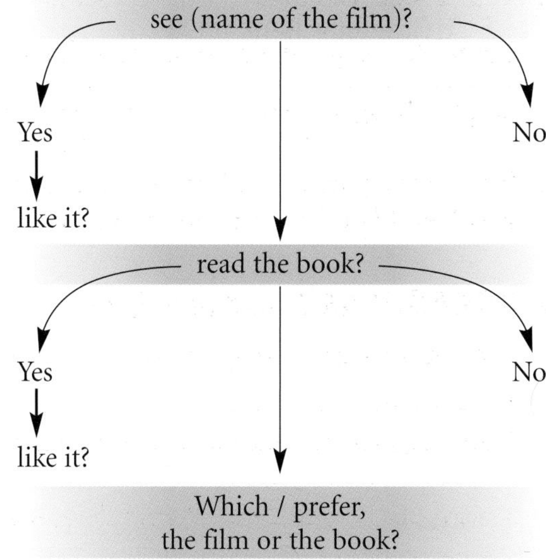

g In pairs, ask and answer about the films in **e**.

FILE 1 Grammar Bank p.122

In pairs or small groups, circle a, b, or c.

1 **A** Where ______ from?
B Italy.
a you are b are you c is you

2 **A** What's ______ name?
B Michael. He's Irish, I think.
a her b your c his

3 **A** What's this?
B It's ______.
a a identity card b an identity card
c identity card

4

a Don't open b Not open c You don't

5 **A** How old are you?
B I ______.
a have twenty years b am twenty years
c am twenty

FILE 2 Grammar Bank p.124

In pairs or small groups, circle a, b, or c.

1 My father ______.
a doesn't cooks b don't cook
c doesn't cook

2 ______ you live with your mother?
a Are b Do c Does

3 **A** What ______?
B I'm unemployed.
a do you do b do you work c do you

4 My father's ______.
a engineer b a engineer c an engineer

5 David is ______.
a my boyfriend's sister b my sister's boyfriend
c boyfriend my sister

FILE 3 Grammar Bank p.126

In pairs or small groups, circle a, b, or c.

1 I love ______!
a cars fast b fast cars c fasts cars

2 What time ______?
a you get up b do you get up c do get up you

3 ______ fruit for breakfast.
a I always have b I have always c Always I have

4 She goes to English classes ______.
a one time a week b one a week c once a week

5 Our local festival is ______ Friday.
a on b at c in

FILE 4 Grammar Bank p.128

In pairs or small groups, circle a, b, or c.

1 **A** ______ read maps?
B Not very well.
a Can you b Do you can c Can

2 My wife hates ______.
a watch football b watching football
c to watching football

3 She says she doesn't love ______.
a him b he c his

4 **A** What do you think of this music?
B ______
a I love. b I love him. c I love it.

5 **A** Is this your bag?
B ______
a Yes, it's my. b Yes, it's mine. c Yes, it's the mine.

FILE 5 Grammar Bank p.130

In pairs or small groups, circle a, b, or c.

1 ______ the first American president?
a Were he b Did he be c Was he

2 They ______ the tickets at a travel agent's.
a didn't book b didn't booked c don't booked

3 I ______ a lot last night.
a studyed b studied c studed

4 **A** What ______ last night?
B I went out.
a you did b did you c did you do

5 What time ______ to bed?
a did you went b did you go c went you

FILE 6 Grammar Bank p.132

In pairs or small groups, circle a, b, or c.

1 How many bathrooms ______ in the house?
a is there b are there c there are

2 ______ a good film on TV last night.
a There is b There was c There were

3 Listen! The neighbours ______ again!
a argue b arguing c are arguing

4 **A** What ______?
B They're doctors.
a are they doing b do they do c they do

5 The museum ______ at 9 o'clock.
a opens b is opening c open

FILE 7 Grammar Bank p.134

In pairs or small groups, circle a, b, or c.

1 There isn't ______ milk.
a some b an c any

2 I ______ water.
a don't drink many b don't drink much
c drink quite

3

______ coffee do you drink?

a How much b How many c How

4 Where ______ to go next summer?
a do you go b you going c are you going

5 I'm sure you ______ very happy.
a are going to be b go to be c are going be

FILE 8 Grammar Bank p.136

In pairs or small groups, circle a, b, or c.

1 Are cars ______ in Britain than in the USA?
a expensiver b most expensive
c more expensive

2 Butter is ______ for you than olive oil.
a badder b worse c worst

3

This is ______ building in the city.

a the old b the most old c the oldest

4 ______ fly a plane?
a Do you like b Would you like to
c You would like

5 Americans drive ______.
a carefully b careful c carefuly

FILE 9 Grammar Bank p.138

In pairs or small groups, circle a, b, or c.

1 ______ Paris or Rome?
a Have you been b Have you been to
c Have you be to

2 I've read the book but I haven't ______ the film.
a see b saw c seen

3 **A** Have you ever met anyone famous?
B Yes, I ______.
a have b do c did

4 ______ she driven a Ferrari before?
a Did b Has c Do

5 We ______ to Italy last year.
a go b have been c went

9 Vocabulary

Do the exercises in pairs or small groups.

a Circle the word that is different.

	Ireland	(Chinese)	Thailand	Spain
1	France	Brazil	Polish	Spain
2	lawyer	footballer	cooker	teacher
3	grandmother	son	uncle	brother
4	angry	fast	tired	hot
5	usually	often	sometimes	yesterday
6	saw	buy	got	heard
7	sofa	armchair	living room	mirror
8	chemist's	art gallery	supermarket	square
9	carrots	beans	strawberries	potatoes
10	carefully	good	fast	aggressively

b Write the next word.

one, two, *three*

1 thirty, forty, ______
2 Sunday, Monday, ______
3 first, second, ______
4 tenth, twentieth, ______
5 morning, afternoon, ______
6 once, twice, ______
7 second, minute, ______
8 summer, autumn, ______
9 February, March, ______
10 last week, this week, ______

c Answer the questions.

What's the opposite of *big*? *small*

1 What's the sixth month of the year?
2 Who is your mother's sister?
3 In which room do you have a shower?
4 What's the opposite of *clean*?
5 What's the past tense of *think*?
6 Where can you buy stamps and send a letter?
7 What language do they speak in Argentina?
8 Who is the person who serves you in a restaurant?
9 What's the opposite of *love*?
10 What do you call a person who likes giving presents?

d Complete the verbs.

play football

1 g______ married
2 h______ breakfast
3 g______ shopping
4 d______ housework
5 m______ a noise
6 t______ photos
7 t______ off your mobile phone!
8 g______ someone a present
9 p______ the piano
10 w______ for the bus

e What can you see? Label the pictures.

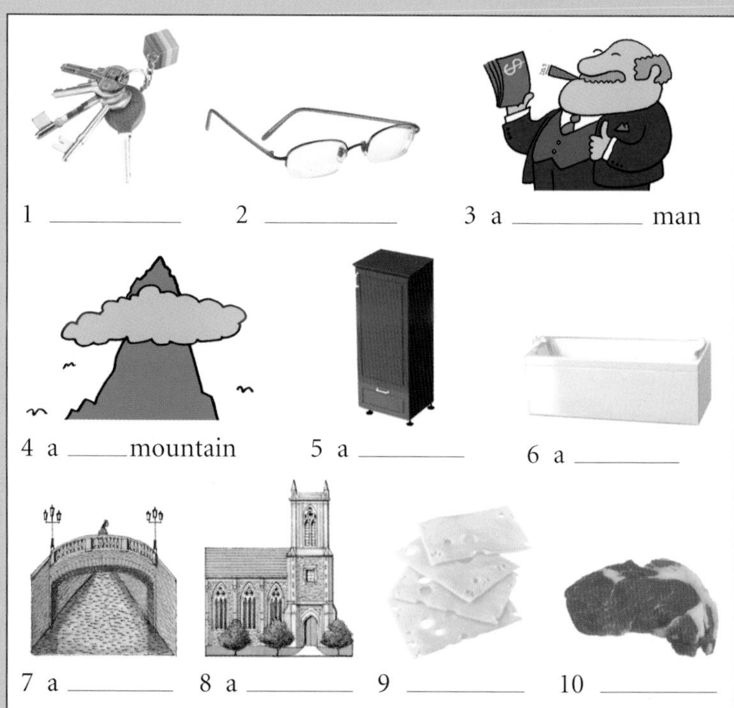

f Complete the sentences with a preposition.

1 Marco's Italian. He's ______ Venice.
2 The British often talk ______ the weather.
3 My brother's ______ university. He's studying French.
4 How often do you listen ______ music?
5 What time did you get ______ this morning?
6 There's a TV ______ the bedroom.
7 I drink a lot ______ water.
8 What did you have ______ breakfast?
9 His flat is next ______ mine.
10 Have you ever been ______ Morocco?

Pronunciation

Do the exercises in pairs or small groups.

a Underline the word with a different sound.

	iː	key	meet	they
1	iː	meat	speak	bread
2	ɑː	garden	glasses	famous
3	ɔː	work	bought	saw
4	ɜː	word	first	four
5	ð	three	this	there
6	dʒ	German	job	get
7	əʊ	home	love	know
8	h	how	hour	hairdresser
9	ʃ	see	sugar	she
10	aɪ	five	give	mine
11	eɪ	play	have	make
12	aʊ	house	daughter	shower
13	ɒ	what	not	don't
14	k	cinema	cards	music
15	ʊ	cooker	footballer	food

b Underline the stressed syllable.

information

1 American
2 afternoon
3 thirteen
4 breakfast
5 July
6 musician
7 between
8 bathroom
9 tomorrow
10 pronunciation
11 sunglasses
12 magazine
13 chocolate
14 umbrella
15 receptionist
16 grandmother
17 dangerous
18 museum
19 supermarket
20 newspaper

Communication

3B What's the time? **Student A**

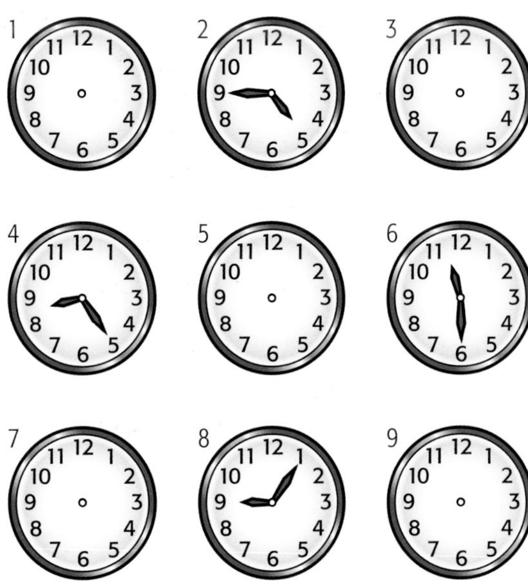

Ask and answer questions with **B** to complete the times on the clocks.

Clock 1: What's the time? / What time is it?

3B Louisa's day **Student A**

Ask **B** these questions.

1 What time does Louisa get up? (6.30.)
2 How does she get to work? (She cycles.)
3 What does she have for breakfast? (A sandwich.)
4 Does she go out in the evening? Why (not)? (No – a babysitter is very expensive.)
5 What time does she cook dinner? (6.30.)

3C The Okinawa way

1	a 2	b 1	c 0
2	a 2	b 1	c 0
3	a 2	b 1	c 0
4	a 0	b 2	c 1
5	a 2	b 1	c 0
6	a 0	b 2	c 1
7	a 0	b 1	c 2
8	a 2	b 1	c 0
9	a 2	b 1	c 0
10	a 0	b 1	c 2

What your score means:

0–7 Your philosophy is 'a short life and a happy one'. Have a good time!

8–14 Your lifestyle is OK but you don't live the Okinawa way. You need to change some things if you want to have a very long life.

15–20 Congratulations! You live the Okinawa way. You have a very good chance of living until you are 100 years old (or more!).

3D When…? **Student A**

a Ask **B** these questions.

When do you usually…?	What time do you normally…?
study	get up
have a shower or bath	go to work / school
drink champagne	start work / school
see all your family	have dinner
listen to the radio	
do housework	
go to the beach	

b Answer **B**'s questions with a preposition + a time word. Ask *What about you?*

When do you usually study?
In the evening. What about you?
It depends…

5A Three Presidents **Student A**

Ask and answer questions with **B** to complete the information about Presidents Washington, Lincoln, and Roosevelt. You start.

What was Washington's first name?

President	Washington	Lincoln	Roosevelt
First name?	________	Abraham	________
Which president?	First	________	26th
born (year)?	________	1809	________
born (place)?	Westmoreland, Virginia	________ ________	New York City, New York
parents from?	Virginia	Virginia	________

5D Police interview **Student A**

Work in pairs with another **A**. You are police officers. There was a robbery last night. **B** and **B** are two friends. You think they were responsible. They say that they went out for dinner and went to the cinema last night. You want to know if this is true.

a Look at the Police interview form and prepare to ask the **Bs** the questions. Think of more questions to get more details about the evening, e.g. *What did you wear? What did you eat and drink? What film was it?*

b Interview *one* of the **Bs**. Write down his / her answers in the form. (Your partner interviews the other **B**.)

Police interview form

Name: **Date:**

	What time?	Where?	More details
/ meet?			
/ have dinner?			
/ go to the cinema?			

What / do after the cinema?	
What time / get home?	

c Compare with your partner. Did the two **Bs** tell exactly the same story? If not, arrest them!

6B Memory test **Student A**

a Write questions from the prompts.

1 / a cupboard in the room?
Was there a cupboard in the room?
2 How many tables / ?
3 / a lamp on the table?
4 Where / the TV?
5 What colour / the walls?
6 / any pictures? How many?

b Ask **B** your questions.

c Answer **B**'s questions. Who has the best memory?

6C They're having a party! **Student A**

You and **B** have the same picture but with eight differences.

a Tell **B** what is happening in the **left** side of your picture. **B** will tell you what is different in his / her picture. Circle the differences.

b Listen to **B** telling you what is happening in the **right** side of his / her picture. Look at your picture. Tell **B** the differences. Circle them on your picture.

c When you've finished, compare the two pictures.

8A The True False Show **Student A**

€10,000 €20,000 €30,000 €40,000 €50,000 €60,000 €70,000 €80,000

a Complete the sentences with the comparative of the **bold** adjective.

1 **fast** A horse is ______________________ than a tiger. (**False**)
2 **expensive** Tokyo is ______________________ than New York. (**True**)
3 **near** The Earth is ______________________ the Sun than Mars is. (**True**)
4 **big** Africa is ______________________ than Asia. (**False**)
5 **common** The letter *i* is ______________________ than *e* in English. (**False**)
6 **bad** Black coffee is ______________________ for you than white coffee. (**False**)
7 **dangerous** Rugby is ______________________ than skiing. (**True**)
8 **rich** Switzerland is ______________________ than Saudi Arabia. (**True**)

b Roleplay *The True False Show*. You are the quiz presenter, **B** is the contestant.

- Read sentence 1 to **B**. **B** says if it's true or false.
- If **B** is right, he / she gets €10,000. Continue with sentence 2, etc.
- If **B** gets the answer wrong, he / she loses everything and starts from the beginning again.

c Change roles. Now **B** is the presenter.

d Who won more money, you or **B**?

1C Interview **Students A+B**

A is the receptionist. Ask **B** questions and complete the form.

What's your first name?

First name	______________
Surname	______________
Country / City	________ / ________
Student	Yes ☐ No ☐
Age	________
Address	______________
Postcode	______________
E-mail address	______________
Phone number	______________
Mobile phone	______________

Change roles. Now **B** is the receptionist. Ask **A** questions and complete the form.

3B What's the time? **Student B**

Ask and answer questions with **A** to complete the times on the clocks.

Clock 2: What's the time? / What time is it?

3B Louisa's day **Student B**

Ask **A** these questions.

1 Does Louisa have breakfast at home? Why (not)? (No – she doesn't have time.)
2 Why does she cycle to work? (Because the bus is expensive.)
3 What time does she finish work? (5.00.)
4 What does she do after dinner? (She does housework or answers e-mails.)
5 What time does George go to bed? (9.00.)

3D When...? **Student B**

a Answer **A**'s questions with a preposition + a time word. Ask *What about you?*

b Ask **B** these questions.

When do you usually...?	What time do you normally...?
have coffee	go to bed
come to your English class	have lunch
go shopping	finish work / school
have a holiday	have dinner
watch TV	
do homework	
relax	

When do you usually have coffee?

In the morning. What about you?

I don't drink coffee.

6B Room 11 **Students A+B**

Memory test **A** p.109 **B** p.112

Communication

5A Three Presidents **Student B**

Ask and answer questions with **A** to complete the information about Presidents Washington, Lincoln, and Roosevelt. **A** starts.

President	**Washington**	**Lincoln**	**Roosevelt**
First name?	George	________	Theodore
Which president?	________	16th	________
born (year)?	1732	________	1858
born (place)?	________ ________	Hodgenville, Kentucky	________ ________
parents from?	________	Virginia	New York

5B Sydney

Sydney, Nova Scotia, population 26,000

Raoul and Emma were in Sydney, but not Sydney, Australia. They were in Sydney, Nova Scotia, in north-east Canada!

The story of Emma and Raoul was on television and in newspapers around the world. They stayed in Sydney, Nova Scotia, for four days and then travelled home on Air Canada to London, England (not London, Canada).

5D Police interview **Student B**

Work in pairs with another **B**. You are friends. Last night you met, had dinner, and went to the cinema. There was a robbery last night. **A** and **A** are police officers. They think you were responsible, and they want to interview you separately. If you both tell the same story, you are innocent.

a Prepare your story. Use these questions. Think of extra details, e.g. *What did you wear? What did you eat and drink? What film was it?*

- What time / where did you meet?
- What time / where did you have dinner?
- What time / where did you go to the cinema?
- What did you do after the cinema?
- What time did you get home?

b Answer **A**'s questions.

c Did you and your friend tell the same story?

6B Memory test **Student B**

a Write questions from the prompts.

1 / a carpet in the room?
Was there a carpet in the room?
2 How many beds / ?
3 / the door open or closed?
4 What / on the bed?
5 What colour / the curtains?
6 / any books in the room?

b Answer **A**'s questions.

c Ask **A** your questions. Who has the best memory?

6C They're having a party! **Student B**

You and A have the same picture but with eight differences.

a Listen to **A** telling you what is happening in the **left** side of his / her picture. Look at your picture. Tell **A** the differences. Circle them on your picture.

b Tell **A** what is happening in the **right** side of your picture. **A** will tell you what is different in his / her picture. Circle the differences.

c When you've finished, compare the two pictures.

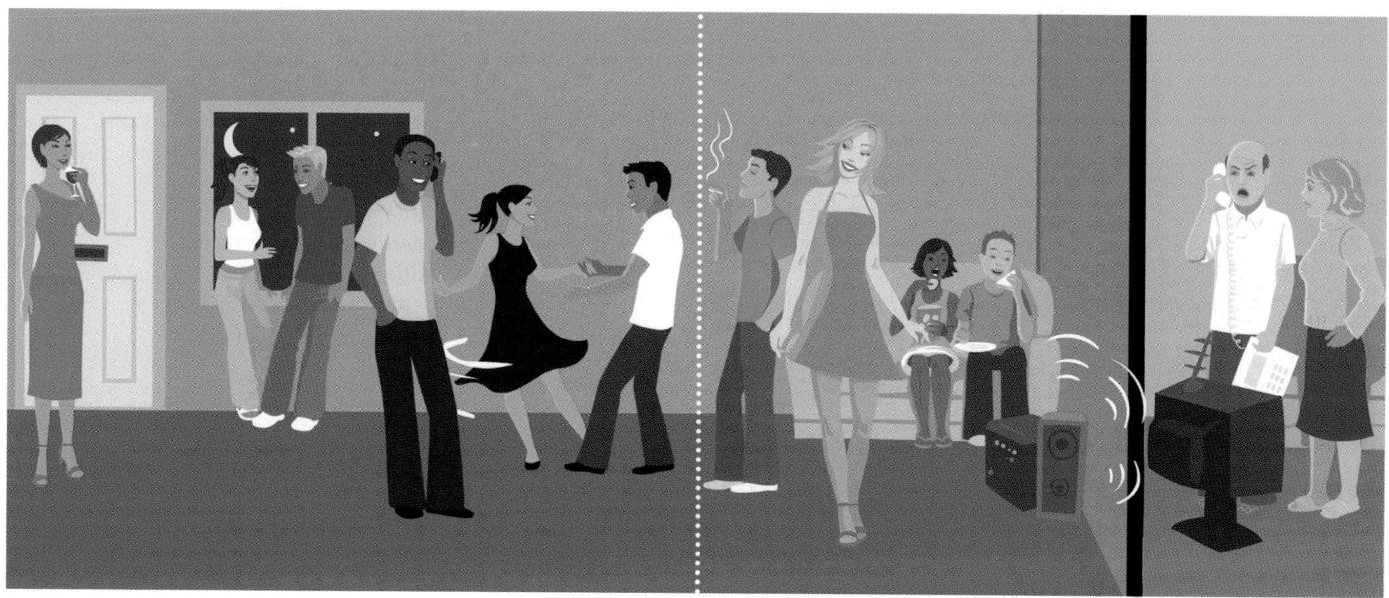

8A The True False Show **Student B**

€10,000 €20,000 €30,000 €40,000 €50,000 €60,000 €70,000 €80,000

a Complete the sentences with the comparative of the **bold** adjective.

1 **good** Red wine is ______________ for you than white wine. **(True)**
2 **safe** Driving is ______________ than flying. **(False)**
3 **old** The Parthenon is ______________ than the Pyramids. **(False)**
4 **intelligent** Dolphins are ______________ than chimpanzees. **(True)**
5 **small** Spain is ______________ than Germany. **(False)**
6 **short** The Second World War was ______________ than the First World War. **(False)**
7 **popular** Basketball is ______________ than football. **(True)**
8 **long** A kilometre is ______________ than a mile. **(False)**

b Roleplay *The True False Show*. **A** is the quiz presenter, you are the contestant. Say if **A**'s sentences are true or false.

c Change roles. Now you are the presenter.

- Read sentence 1 to **A**. **A** says if it's true or false.
- If **A** is right, he / she gets €10,000. Continue with sentence 2, etc.
- If **A** gets the answer wrong, he / she loses everything and starts from the beginning again.

d Who won more money, you or **A**?

Listening

1.7

1 **A** A cheese and tomato sandwich, please.
B That's 3 euros and 20 cents.
2 British Airways flight to Madrid is now boarding at gate number 9.
3 **A** Where to, love?
B Manchester Road, please. Number 16.
4 **A** Here's your key, sir. Room 12.
B Thank you.

1.8

Tom OK, bye.
Anna Yes, goodbye.
Tom See you tomorrow.
Anna Not tomorrow, Saturday.
Tom Oh yeah. See you on Saturday.
Anna See you.
Tom Goodnight.

1.18

1 The train waiting at platform 13 is the Eurostar to Paris.
2 **A** Excuse me! How far is it to San José?
B It's about 40 kilometres.
A Thanks a lot.
3 15 love.
4 **A** How much is that?
B A pizza and a Coke. That's 17 euros.
5 **A** What's your address?
B It's 80 Park Road.
A Sorry? What number?
B 80, 8 oh.
6 **Teacher** OK. Can you be quiet, please? Open your books on page 90.
Student 1 What page?
Student 2 Page 90.

1.19

Receptionist Hello. Are you a new student?
Mario Yes, I am.
Receptionist Sit down, then. I'm just going to ask you a few questions.
Mario OK.
Receptionist Right. What's your first name?
Mario Mario.
Receptionist What's your surname?
Mario Benedetti.
Receptionist Benedetti. How do you spell it?
Mario B-E-N-E-D-E-double T-I.
Receptionist B-E-N-E-D-E-double T-I. OK. Where are you from?
Mario I'm from Italy. From Rome.
Receptionist Are you a student?
Mario Yes, I am.
Receptionist And how old are you?
Mario I'm 20.
Receptionist What's your address?
Mario In Rome?
Receptionist Yes.
Mario It's Via Foro 25.
Receptionist What's your postcode?
Mario Sorry?
Receptionist Is there a postcode? You know, a number?
Mario Ah yes. It's Rome 00132.
Receptionist 00132. Great. What's your e-mail address?
Mario It's mario.benedetti@hotmail.com.
Receptionist And what's your phone number?
Mario My mobile number or my home number in Rome?
Receptionist Both – home and mobile.
Mario My phone number in Rome is 06 840 5517.
Receptionist 06 840 5517.
Mario Yes. And my mobile number is 348 226 7341.
Receptionist 348 226 7341. That's great, Mario. Thank you. Now come and meet the Director of Studies, we need to give you a test…

1.32

1 **Teacher** Hello. Hello. Can you close the door please, Susanna?
Student Sorry?
Teacher Close the door, please.
2 **Teacher** Can you sit down, please? Can you sit down? SIT DOWN!
3 **Teacher** OK, open your books. It's lesson 1C. Lesson 1C.
4 **Teacher** OK, now read the text. You can use your dictionary for any new words.
5 **Teacher** Miguel and Maria, don't speak Spanish, this is an English class! Please speak in English.
6 **Teacher** All right now, stand up. STAND UP. OK, now ask What's your name? to five other students.
7 **Teacher** OK, now go to page 84.
Students What page?
Teacher 84, page 84.
8 **Teacher** OK, can you look at the board, please? Look at the board.
9 **Teacher** All right, now listen and repeat the letters. A (A), B (B) C…
10 **Teacher** Maria, please turn off your mobile phone! TURN OFF YOUR MOBILE, MARIA!

1.37

Allie Hello. Are you Mark Ryder?
Mark Yes. Are you Allie?
Allie Yes, I am.
Mark Nice to meet you.
Allie And you. Welcome to the UK. Your hotel's in the city centre.
Mark How far is it?
Allie It's about 30 minutes if the traffic's OK.
Mark Great!
Allie Would you like a coffee first?
Mark No, I'm fine, thanks.
Allie All right. Let's go. My car's in the car park. Can I help you with your bags?
Mark No, it's OK, thanks.

2.5

Natasha You work with computers Darren, is that right?
Darren Yes, that's right.
Natasha Do you like your job?
Darren Yes, I do. I love it. Computers are very interesting, don't you think?
Natasha Um, not really. I don't like computers. Er, what do you do in the evenings?
Darren I play computer games, or I watch television.
Natasha What do you do at the weekend?
Darren I… play computer games and watch television.
Natasha Do you go to the cinema?
Darren No, I don't. I watch films on television or DVD. Do you watch TV?
Natasha No, I don't have a television.
Darren What do you do at the weekend?
Natasha I go to the cinema.
Darren Oh.

Natasha Ah, coffee, great. Cigarette, Darren?
Darren No, thanks. I don't smoke. Er, Natasha, can I ask you a question?
Natasha Yes, OK.
Darren How old are you? 28?
Natasha Yes, that's right.
Darren And, er, how old are you in the photo – the photo on the Internet? 19? 20?
Natasha Look, Darren, it's two o'clock – time to go back to work. Bye.
Darren Natasha, wait, wait… Natasha!

2.11

And now on Radio 4, *Guess my job.*

Compère Good evening and welcome again to the jobs quiz, *Guess my job.* And our team tonight are Brian, a teacher (Hello), Liz, who's unemployed (Hi), and Marylin, who's a writer (Good evening). And our first guest tonight is…

Phil Phil.

Compère OK, team, you have *two* minutes and *ten* questions to guess Phil's job, starting now. Let's have your first question.

Brian Hi, Phil. Do you work in an office?

Phil No, I don't.

Liz Do you work in the evening?

Phil It depends. Yes, sometimes.

Marylin Do you work with your hands?

Phil No, I don't. Not with my hands.

Liz Do you wear a uniform?

Phil Er yes – well, a kind of uniform.

Marylin Do you drive?

Phil No, I don't. Not in my job.

Brian Do you write letters or e-mails?

Phil No, I don't.

Liz Do you work with other people?

Phil Yes, I do.

Brian Do you speak any languages?

Phil No, only English.

Marylin Do you have special qualifications?

Phil No, I don't.

Compère You have *one more question.*

Brian Er, do you earn a lot of money?

Phil Yes, I do.

2.12

Compère That's ten questions! So, Brian, Liz, and Marylin – *what's his job?*

Marylin OK Phil. We think you're … an actor.

Compère Are you an actor, Phil?

Phil No, I'm not. I'm a professional footballer.

2.13

1 He's Hugh Grant's brother.
2 She's Naomi Campbell's mother.
3 He's J.K. Rowling's husband.
4 She's Antonio Banderas's ex-wife.
5 He's Will Smith's father.
6 She's Kate Winslet's sister.

2.15

Sarah This is my mother, in our garden at home.

Guy Let's see. Is that your father?

Sarah No, it's Martin, her partner. My Mum's divorced.

Guy Does your mother work?

Sarah Yes, she's a nurse. And Martin's a doctor at the same hospital. I don't like him very much. This is my sister Lisa and her husband Philip. And their daughter, Sophie.

Guy Ah – she's really sweet. How old is she?

Sarah She's three.

Guy Do you have any more nieces or nephews?

Sarah No, just Sophie for the moment.

Guy Is that you?

Sarah Don't laugh! Yes, that's from last Christmas, at my grandparents' house.

Guy Who's that?

Sarah That's my cousin Adam. Adam and I are really good friends. He's a singer in a band. They play in local pubs and clubs…

2.18

Allie Where are you from in the United States, Mark?

Mark The West Coast. San Francisco.

Allie Is it nice?

Mark Oh yeah. It's a great city. Are you from London?

Allie No, I'm from Cambridge. My family live there but I live here in London.

Mark Sorry. Hello darling, how are you? ……… I'm fine, yeah. ……… Don't worry. ……… Fine, fine. ………. That's great. ………. Bye, darling. I love you. ………. Sorry.

Allie That's OK. Your wife?

Mark No, no, my daughter. She always phones me when I'm travelling.

Allie How old is she?

Mark She's nine. She lives with her mother in Los Angeles. We're divorced. Are you married?

Allie No, I'm not.

Mark How old are you?

Allie That's very personal! What do you think?

Mark 25? 26?

Allie Thanks, I'm 27. How old are you?

Mark I'm 34. Would you like another drink?

Allie No, thanks. I have to go now, Mark. Our first meeting's at 10.00. See you tomorrow.

Mark See you tomorrow, Allie. Goodnight.

Allie Goodnight.

3.2

1 It's an easy exercise.
2 I live in an old house.
3 She's an American actress.
4 She has an expensive flat.
5 It's a nice evening.
6 I have a black and white cat.

3.5

1 **Husband** Vicky, it's seven o'clock. Wake up.

2 **Husband** Vicky, wake up!
Vicky Oh no! It's quarter past seven! I'm late again.

3 **DJ** This is Dave Martin on Breakfast Special and the time now on Radio 1 is twenty-five past seven.
Vicky Oh where's my bag?

4 **Vicky** Taxi! Do you have the right time?
Taxi Driver Yes, love. It's half past seven.
Vicky Half past seven! Oh no, I'm late. Please hurry!

5 **Vicky** A white coffee, please.
Assistant Here you are. That's 1.80.
Vicky Oh no, is that clock right?
Assistant Yes, it's quarter to eight.
Vicky Help!
Assistant Careful with your coffee.

6 **Man** Hurry up Vicky, you're late. It's five to eight.

7 **Vicky** Good morning. It's eight o'clock and this is Vicky McGuire with the news on CTV.

3.6

1 I travel 55 miles to work!
2 I don't see my daughters – they're in bed.
3 I walk from the station to work.
4 I'm very worried about my contract.
5 I usually go to sleep in front of the TV.

3.7

Professor Where do you do work, Simon?
Simon I work for a computer company in London – but I live in Brighton.
Professor Are you married?
Simon Yes, I have three daughters.
Professor So you travel from Brighton to London every day?
Simon Yes. I travel 55 miles to work!
Professor Tell me about a typical day.
Simon Well, I get up at six o'clock and I have a shower and get dressed. I don't see my daughters – they're in bed.
Professor Do you have breakfast?
Simon No, I don't have time. I have to get the train to London at half past seven.
Professor What time do you get to London?
Simon The train usually arrives at half past eight. Then I walk from the station to work. That's about half an hour.
Professor What time do you start work?
Simon At 9.00. I start work and I have a coffee. I drink about six cups of coffee a day.
Professor Do you go out for lunch?
Simon No, I'm very busy. I have a sandwich in the office.
Professor Do you like your job?
Simon It's OK, but I'm very worried about my contract. It finishes in six months.
Professor What time do you finish work?
Simon I finish work at half past five. Then I walk to the station again to get the train.
Professor Do you have dinner with your family?
Simon No, I don't. My family have dinner at six – but I'm on the train then. I don't get home until quarter to eight.
Professor What do you do after dinner?
Simon After dinner I sit and watch TV. I'm very tired. I usually go to sleep in front of the TV.
Professor What time do you go to bed?
Simon About 11.00.

3.8

Professor Have breakfast in the morning, Simon, it's very important. But don't drink six cups of coffee – that's too much. Don't have lunch in the office, go out to a sandwich bar or restaurant. And finally, if possible find a new job in Brighton, not in London.

3.16

Cristina
My favourite time of day is 10 o'clock at night, because it's when I finish training and I can start to relax and enjoy the evening. My favourite day of the week is Thursday, because I don't work on Friday, so for me the weekend begins on Thursday night. My favourite month is July, because it's the month when I have my holiday. My favourite season is the spring. One of my hobbies is gardening and my garden is really beautiful in the spring. My favourite public holiday is Christmas. My family live very far away, and it's the only time when I can see them.

Udom
My favourite time of the day is the morning, because I get up early and feel full of energy. My favourite day of the week is Friday because it's the end of the week and I can go home for the weekend. My favourite month is December, because here in Thailand it's when you can see a lot of flowers. My favourite season is winter because in winter it's a nice temperature and it's when I feel comfortable. The summer here is very hot. My favourite public holiday is the Thai New Year in April. It's a water festival, and people throw water at each other and everyone is very happy.

3.19

Allie Thanks, Mark.
Mark You're welcome. Look, there's a free table over there. Here you are. Oh, I'm really sorry!
Allie Don't worry. It's always the same. When I wear white something like this always happens.
Mark Look, first I'll get you another coffee, then we can go shopping.
Allie Shopping?
Mark Yeah. I want to buy you a new shirt. You can't go to a meeting like that.
Allie But we don't have time – the next meeting's at 12.30.
Mark We have time. It's only 11.00.
Allie Are you sure?
Mark Yes. Sit down and relax. Let's have coffee and then go.
Allie Well, OK.

4.4

1 I can't sing.
2 She can dance very well.
3 He can't cook.
4 My boyfriend can't speak English.
5 Her brother can play the piano.
6 I can't drive.

4.5

1 **A** Mandy, where's the sugar?
B In the cupboard, on the right.
A I can't see it. It isn't there.
B Yes, it is. Look for it.
A I can't find it. It's definitely not there.
B I *know* it's there. It's on the second shelf.
A I can't hear you.
B Turn the radio off then. It's on the second shelf.
A Well, I'm sorry, but it isn't there.
B The sugar!
A Oh.

2 **A** Tony. Can you come here a minute? Tony!
B What?
A Can you help me?
B What is it?
A It's the computer. The printer doesn't work.
B Can you wait a minute?
A TONY!
B Coming. What's the problem?
A It's the printer – it doesn't work.
B It helps if you turn it on!

4.6

1 **A** Do you like shopping?
B No, I don't. I hate it. It's boring. I hate going to clothes shops with my girlfriend. We always argue.

2 **A** Do you like shopping?
B It's OK. I like buying food, and things for the house. I don't like shopping for clothes. I can never find things I like, and clothes are very expensive.

3 **A** Do you like shopping?
B Yeah! I go shopping every Saturday. I love buying clothes, music, books, food – everything. Shopping's fun. I love it.

4 **A** Do you like shopping?
B It depends. I like trying on clothes with my friends. That's fun but I don't like going shopping with my mother, and I hate going to the supermarket.

4.8

1 I *love* talking on the phone.
2 I like playing computer games.
3 I don't like doing housework.
4 I *hate* watching football.

4.16

Allie Thank you very much, Mark.
Mark You're welcome. I'm really sorry about the coffee.
Allie That's OK. It's late. Our meeting's at 12.30.
Mark We can take a taxi.
Allie OK. Do you like the shirt?
Mark Well, yeah, it's exactly the same as the other one.
Allie The same? It's completely different!
Mark Sorry!
Allie Typical man!
Mark Allie, can I ask you something?
Allie Yes. What?
Mark Would you like to have dinner with me tonight?
Allie Tonight?
Mark Yeah. You see, it's my birthday.
Allie Oh! Happy birthday! I'm sorry, but I can't have dinner tonight. I'm busy.
Mark Oh. How about Friday night?
Allie Friday? Well ... OK.
Mark Do you know a good restaurant?
Allie Let me think. Do you like Italian food?
Mark I love it.
Allie Well, there's a new Italian restaurant. We can go there.
Mark Good idea. Taxi!

5.1

We are now at Mount Rushmore, in South Dakota, and you can see in front of you, from left to right, the heads of George Washington, Thomas Jefferson, Theodore Roosevelt, and Abraham Lincoln. As you know, all four men were Presidents of the United States of America. George Washington was the first president…

5.6

They walked to the information desk and they showed their tickets to the woman.
Raoul When is our next flight?
Woman The next flight? This is the end of your journey. Where did you want to go?
Raoul Where are we?
Woman You're in Sydney.
Raoul We're in Australia?
Woman Australia? No, you're in Canada!
Raoul Canada!

5.11

Interviewer Sílvia, from Rio de Janeiro, went out with four friends, Karina, Mônica, Ana, and Thelma. Sílvia, can you tell us about your girls' night out?
Sílvia Sure.
Interviewer What did you wear?
Sílvia I wore jeans and a jacket – and two friends wore the same!
Interviewer And what did you do?
Sílvia Well, first we went to a restaurant in Ipanema. It's a place where a lot of famous people go and we saw an actor there, called Fernando Pinto. Karina really likes him – in fact she's crazy about him! Then we went to a beach bar and we had some drinks. And then later we went to a party.
Interviewer What did you have to eat and drink?
Sílvia At the restaurant we had beer and we had some French fries. And at the beach bar we had beer and coconut water.
Interviewer What did you talk about?
Sílvia About men, of course! What else?
Interviewer How did you go home?
Sílvia By taxi. I have a car, but I don't like driving at night.
Interviewer What time did you get home?
Sílvia Very, very late – I don't remember exactly what time.
Interviewer So, did you have a good time?
Sílvia Yes, it was good. Not fantastic, but good – seven out of ten!

5.17

Then the inspector questioned Barbara Travers.
Inspector What did you do after dinner yesterday evening?
Barbara After dinner? I played cards with Gordon, and then I went to bed.
Inspector What time was that?
Barbara It was about half past eleven. I remember I looked at my watch.
Inspector Did you hear anything in your father's room?
Barbara No. I didn't hear anything.
Inspector Did you have any problems with your father?
Barbara No, no problems at all. My father was a wonderful man and a perfect father.
Inspector Thank you, Miss Travers.

5.18

Next the inspector questioned Gordon Smith.
Inspector What did you do after dinner, Gordon?
Gordon I played cards with Barbara. Then she went to bed.
Inspector Did you go to bed then?
Gordon No. I stayed in the sitting room and I had a glass of whisky. Then I went to bed.
Inspector What time was that?
Gordon I don't remember exactly. I didn't look at the time.
Inspector Did you hear anything during the night?
Gordon No, I didn't. I was very tired. I slept very well.
Inspector You and Mr Travers were business partners, weren't you?
Gordon Yes, that's right.
Inspector And it's a very good business I understand.
Gordon Yes, inspector, it is.
Inspector And now it is *your* business.
Gordon Listen, inspector, I did not kill Jeremy. He was my partner and he was my friend.

5.19

Finally the inspector questioned Claudia Simeone.
Inspector What did you do yesterday evening, after dinner?
Claudia I went to my room and I had a bath and I went to bed.
Inspector What time was that?
Claudia About 11.00.
Inspector Did you hear anything?
Claudia Yes. I heard somebody go into Jeremy's room. It was about 12.00.
Inspector Who was it?
Claudia It was Amanda, his wife.
Inspector Are you sure? Did you see her?
Claudia Well no, I didn't see her. But I'm sure it was Amanda.
Inspector You were Mr Travers' secretary, Claudia.
Claudia Yes, I was.
Inspector Were you *just* his secretary?
Claudia What do you mean?

Inspector Were you in love with Mr Travers?
Claudia No, I wasn't.
Inspector The truth please, Claudia.
Claudia Very well, inspector. Yes, I was in love with him and he said he was in love with me. He said he wanted to leave his wife – Amanda – and marry me. I was stupid. I believed him. He used me, inspector! I was very angry with him.
Inspector Did you kill him?
Claudia No, inspector, I loved Jeremy.

5.20

Before dinner, Gordon had a drink with Jeremy in the library.
Gordon Cheers, Jeremy. Happy birthday.
Jeremy Ah, thanks, Gordon.
Gordon Listen, Jeremy, I want to talk to you about Barbara.
Jeremy Barbara? What's the problem?
Gordon It's not exactly a problem. I am in love with her, and I want to marry her.
Jeremy Marry Barbara? Marry my daughter! Are you crazy? Never. You don't love Barbara. You only want her money!
Gordon That's not true, Jeremy. I love her.
Jeremy Listen to me. If you marry Barbara, when I die all my money goes to Claudia.
Gordon To Claudia? To your secretary?
Jeremy Yes.
Gordon Is that your last word, Jeremy?
Jeremy Yes, it is.
Amanda Dinner everybody!

At midnight Gordon finished his whisky and went upstairs.
Jeremy Who is it? Gordon?

5.23

Mark Hi, Allie. Wow! You look great. Nice dress!
Allie Oh, thank you. Er, this is for you – for your birthday. I bought you a little present. Oh! Oh no. I hope it's not broken.
Mark It's a mug! It *was* a mug. Thanks, Allie!
Allie I don't believe it! I'm sorry, Mark.
Mark No problem. It was really nice of you.
Allie I'll get you another one tomorrow.
Mark Don't worry. Listen, did you call a taxi to go to the restaurant?
Allie No, I have my car outside. Come on, it's time to go. I booked the table for 8.00 and I'm not sure exactly where the restaurant is.
Mark Hey, Allie, relax. This isn't work. This is a night out.
Allie Sorry. I'm a bit stressed today. OK. Let's go.

6.2

Estate agent OK. Let's have a look upstairs now. Follow me.
Louise It's very old.
Estate agent Yes, madam, the house is a hundred years old. The Travers family lived here for nearly eighty years. There are five bedrooms. This was Mr Travers' bedroom.
Larry It's cold in here.
Louise Yes, very cold.
Estate agent Don't worry, madam. There is central heating in the house. And this room here is the second bedroom.
Larry OK, well what do you think, Louise?
Louise I like it.
Larry Me too. Yup. We want it.
Estate agent Excellent! Let's go back to my office and we can sign the contract.

6.4

Larry Good evening.
Barman Good evening, sir, madam. What would you like to drink?
Larry Do you have champagne?
Barman Yes, sir.
Larry A bottle of champagne, please.
Barman Here you are!
Louise Cheers, Larry.
Larry Cheers. To our new house.
Barman You're Americans, aren't you?
Louise Yes, that's right. We're from Washington.
Larry My wife and I just rented the big house in the village. Tonight is our first night there.
Barman The Travers family's old house?
Larry Yes.
Barman Oh.
Louise Is there a problem?
Barman Didn't they tell you?
Larry Tell us what?
Barman About the murder.
Louise Murder??
Barman Yes, Mr Travers was murdered in that house in 1938… in his bed.
Louise Oh, how horrible!
Barman That's why they always rent that house.
Larry Why?
Barman Because nobody wants to buy it.
Louise Come on, Larry. Let's go and find a hotel.
Larry A hotel?
Louise Yes – I don't want to sleep in a house where somebody was murdered. Come on.
Larry Louise… your champagne… Louise…

6.6

Stephen In the middle of the night I suddenly woke up! It was 2.00. The television was off! But how? There was no remote control, and I certainly didn't get up and turn it off. The light was still on, but suddenly the light went off too. Now I was really frightened! I couldn't see anything strange, but I could feel that there was somebody or something in the room. I got out of bed and turned on the TV again. Little by little I started to relax, and I went to sleep again. When I woke up it was morning. I had breakfast and I left the hotel about 10.00.
Interviewer So the question is, did you see the ghost?
Stephen No, I didn't see the ghost, but I definitely felt something or somebody in the room when I woke up in the night.
Interviewer Were you frightened?
Stephen Yes, I was! Very frightened!
Interviewer Would you like to spend another night in the hotel?
Stephen Definitely, yes.
Interviewer Why?
Stephen Well, I'm sure there was something strange in that room. I can't explain the television and the light. I want to go back because I want to see the ghost.

6.12

Hi Bill, it's Rob. What are you doing?… I'm going to London… Who are you talking to?… I'm having a coffee… Is the baby crying?… My train's arriving. Bye!

6.14

1 I'm from Edinburgh.
2 He's from London.
3 They live in Brighton.
4 We went to Oxford for the weekend.
5 She was born in Dublin.
6 We're studying in Cambridge.
7 I want to go to Manchester.
8 Do you like Birmingham?

6.18

Allie OK. It's this street. No, it isn't. I'm sure she said the first on the right.
Mark No, she said the *second* on the right. Relax, Allie.
Allie Look, let's ask that man there.
Mark I don't think he knows. He's a tourist.
Allie Just ask him, please.
Mark OK, OK. Excuse me! We're lost. Do you know where King Street is?
Man Sorry, I don't live here – I'm a tourist.
Mark You see. I was right.
Allie OK, let's try the second on the right.
Mark Here it is. King Street. I *knew* she said the second on the right.
Allie There's the restaurant, Donatella's. Can you see anywhere to park?
Mark That white car's going over there! Do you think you can park in that space?
Allie Are you saying I can't park?
Mark Allie, I'm only joking.
Allie OK, OK, I'm sorry.

7.2

Bob Good evening. My name's Bob, and welcome to another edition of … *Can men cook?*
Audience Yes, they can!
Bob Well, Belinda, who's our first guest tonight?
Belinda This is Colin Davidson and he's from Bristol!
Bob Hello, Colin! What can you cook?
Colin Hello, Bob. My speciality is spaghetti bolognese.
Bob And what do you need to make it, Colin?
Colin Well, for four people you need some spaghetti. About half a kilo, Bob. And then for the bolognese sauce you need an onion, some butter, a carrot, some mushrooms, some tomato ketchup…
Bob Tomato *ketchup*, Colin?
Colin Yes, that's right, and you also need some red wine.
Bob Do you need any meat, Colin?
Colin Yes, Bob. You need some meat – about 300 grams. And some cheese.
Bob What kind of cheese?
Colin Any kind. It doesn't matter.
Bob OK. So those are all the ingredients. The question now is – *Can men cook?*
Audience Yes, they can!
Bob Colin, you have exactly 30 minutes to make us… spaghetti bolognese!
Colin Well, Bob, first you cut up the onion and you fry it. Then you take the…
Bob OK, Colin. That's your thirty minutes. And now it's time to taste the spaghetti bolognese. And it looks… mm, delicious. Belinda, can you try it for us? Well, Belinda, what do you think of it? Can men cook?
Belinda Mmm. Yes, Colin, it's er very interesting. I'm sure your wife loves your cooking.
Colin I'm not married, Belinda. Would you like to have dinner with me?
Bob Well, that's all we have time for. Until *next* week. It's goodbye from me Bob Keen, Belinda Leyton, and Colin Davidson from Bristol.

7.6

Jerry Hello?
Peter Hello! Is that Jerry Harte?
Jerry Speaking.
Peter This is Peter Douglas from the programme *Changing Holidays*.
Jerry Oh, hello!
Peter Is your holiday planned for next week, Jerry?
Jerry Yes, it is.
Peter Where are you going to go?
Jerry We're going to go to Norway.
Peter Who are you going to go with?
Jerry With Sue, my girlfriend.
Peter How are you going to get there?
Jerry By train.
Peter What are you going to do there?
Jerry We're going to clean a river and plant some trees. It's a working holiday!
Peter Oh, very interesting. Where are you going to stay?
Jerry We're going to stay at a campsite.
Peter Well, Jerry, you're not going to go camping, because you're not going to go to Norway. We're going to *change your holiday*!
Jerry Oh, so where are we going to go?

7.8

Peter Well, here we are at the airport with Lisa and Jon and Jerry and Sue. And this is the moment of truth. I've got two envelopes here, and now I'm going to give the two couples their *new* holiday plans! Are you ready to play 'Changing Holidays'?
All Yes.
Peter OK, so now you can open the envelopes. Jon and Lisa first.
Jon A working holiday in Norway.
Lisa Oh no!
Peter Oh yes! You're going to help clean a river and plant some trees.
Jon Oh great. Working all day!
Lisa Where are we going to stay?
Peter You're going to stay at a campsite!
Lisa A campsite? Oh no, I hate camping!
Peter And now Sue and Jerry.
Sue Oh! A week in New York.
Jerry New York?
Peter That's right. You're going to spend a week in the Big Apple, shopping, going out, and seeing the sights! Do you like shopping, Jerry?
Jerry Not much.
Sue What are we going to wear? We don't have the right clothes for New York.

7.9

Peter OK, so it's hello again to our two couples from last week, Lisa and Jon, and Sue and Jerry. Welcome back. So what we all want to know is, did you have a good time? Jon and Lisa, what about you?
Jon No, we didn't have a good time. It wasn't a holiday. I mean, we worked every day.
Lisa And it was hard work. That's not my idea of a holiday.
Jon And we hated camping!
Lisa The people were very nice but…
Jon It rained every day. We went to bed at 10.00 every night – not exactly exciting!
Lisa The thing is, what we really like is shopping, nightlife, big cities – and if that's what you want, Norway's not the place to go.
Peter OK, OK. What about Sue and Jerry. Did *you* have a good time?
Sue Well, we don't usually like big cities. But New York is special!
Jerry Yeah. The hotel wasn't very good – it was very big and impersonal. But we liked all the tourist sights – the Guggenheim was fantastic.

Sue And the people were great, and we loved the food.

Jerry Yeah, we even liked the nightclub! We usually go to bed early, we're not really 'night' people, but the New York nightlife is great.

Peter So where are you going to go next summer? Lisa and Jon?

Lisa Next summer we're really going to go to New York!

Peter And Jerry and Sue?

Sue We really liked New York. Next year we're going to go to another city, maybe Amsterdam or Barcelona!

7.19

Mark How was the pasta?

Allie It was delicious.

Mark Listen, Allie. There's something I want to ask you.

Allie Yes? What?

Waiter Would you like a dessert?

Allie Yes, please. What is there?

Waiter Tiramisu, ice cream, or fruit salad.

Allie Fruit salad, please.

Waiter And you, sir?

Mark Nothing for me, thanks. Allie?

AllieYes. Go on, Mark.

Mark Well, tomorrow's my last day. And I think we… I mean, I really liked meeting you and…

Waiter Here you are. Fruit salad. Would you like any coffee?

Allie Yes, an espresso, please.

Mark The same for me, please.

Allie Sorry, Mark.

Mark Do you want to come to California next month? There's a big conference. I'm going to be there. Why don't you come? What do you think?

Waiter Two espressos. Anything else? A little brandy? A grappa?

Mark No, thank you. What do you say, Allie?

Allie I'm not sure, Mark. I need some time to think about it, OK?

Mark All right. But please tell me before I go.

Allie OK.

Mark Could we have the check, please?

Waiter Sorry? The check?

Allie The bill, Mark. We're in Britain, remember?

Mark Sorry. Could we have the bill, please?

Waiter Yes, sir.

8.1

Presenter Good evening. Welcome to *The True False Show*. Tonight's show comes from Dublin. My name's Annie O'Brian and I ask the questions. Remember, after each question you have ten seconds to say 'true' or 'false'. If you get the first answer right, you win 10,000 euros. If you get the second answer right, you win 20,000 euros, and you win 30,000 euros for the third correct answer. For eight correct answers you win 80,000 euros. But if you get an answer wrong, you go home with ... nothing. Our first contestant is Darren from London. Right, Darren, for 10,000 euros. Mosquitoes are more dangerous than sharks. True or false?

Darren Er, true.

Presenter Correct. Mosquitoes are more dangerous than sharks. More people die every year from mosquito bites than from shark attacks. Now, for 20,000 euros, brown eggs are healthier than white eggs. True or false?

Darren Er… false.

Presenter Correct. It's false. Brown eggs *look* nicer than white ones, but they are exactly the same. For 30,000 euros, the Earth is hotter than Mars.

Darren I think it's true, Annie.

Presenter Correct. The Earth is much hotter than Mars. Next, for 40,000 euros, coffee is more popular than tea in the UK. True or false?

Darren Er, false.

Presenter Correct. British people drink 185 million cups of tea every day. Next, for 50,000 euros, tigers are better swimmers than cats. True or false?

Darren Er… false. No – true.

Presenter Is that your answer?

Darren Yes, true.

Presenter Correct. Tigers are very good swimmers. For 60,000 euros, an adult is shorter in the morning than in the evening.

Darren Er… false.

Presenter Correct. Adults are one centimetre *taller* in the morning than in the evening. OK Darren, for 70,000 euros. White cars are safer than yellow cars. True or false?

Darren Er, I'm sure that's false, Annie.

Presenter Correct. Yellow cars are safer – they are easier to see during the day, so they don't have as many accidents. And finally, the last question. Be very careful, Darren. If you get it right, you win 80,000 euros, but if you get it wrong, you lose everything. Are you ready?

Darren Yes, ready.

Presenter OK, so for 80,000 euros. The word 'yes' is more common than the word 'no'. True or false?

Darren Er… er…

Presenter Quickly Darren, time's running out.

Darren True.

Presenter No, Darren. It's false. 'No' is more common than 'yes'. You *had* 70,000 euros, but now you go home with *nothing*.

8.4

Presenter Hello again. Today we talk to Dr Alan Baker, a psychologist, about car colour and personality. Good evening, Dr Baker.

Dr Baker Good evening!

Presenter So, what does the colour of our cars say about our personality?

Dr Baker Well, let's start with yellow. People who drive yellow cars are usually very friendly. This colour is more popular with women than with men.

Presenter And white?

Dr Baker A white car shows that you are careful. It's the favourite colour car for doctors – they buy more white cars than any other colour.

Presenter What about other colours?

Dr Baker Well, let's take red. People who choose red cars are usually more aggressive drivers than normal. With blue cars, it's the opposite. If you have a blue car it means you are probably quiet.

Presenter What about green?

Dr Baker People with green cars are usually generous.

Presenter And what about black?

Dr Baker Well, people who like black cars are usually serious people. Business people often choose black cars.

Presenter We've got time for one more colour. What about silver?

Dr Baker Yes, well if you have a silver car it means you are stylish.

Presenter Er, what colour is your car, Dr Baker? White?

Dr Baker No, it's red, actually.

Presenter Thank you very much, Dr Baker. And now we turn our attention…

8.11

Interviewer Russell, can you describe your day?
Russell Well, first we had some classes and we learned how to land.
Interviewer What happened then?
Russell Well, when we finished the classes we went up in the plane.
Interviewer How high did you go up?
Russell About 800 metres.
Interviewer Then what happened?
Russell Well, I sat on the floor and waited.
Interviewer How did you feel?
Russell Very frightened! That was the worst part, waiting to jump.
Interviewer And then?
Russell Then the instructor said 'Jump!' and I jumped.
Interviewer How was it?
Russell It was incredible. First I fell very fast. I couldn't think. I forgot all the instructions. Suddenly the parachute opened, and I floated down.
Interviewer Did you land OK?
Russell Yes, I did – perfectly.
Interviewer How did you feel afterwards?
Russell Great – I felt fantastic. I was really happy. I thought 'I did it!'
Interviewer Would you like to do it again?
Russell Well no, I wouldn't.
Interviewer Why not?
Russell Because it can be dangerous. One of the people in my group broke his leg. And two months after that I heard that someone died.
Interviewer How?
Russell His parachute didn't open and he fell…

8.17

Mark Hello?
Allie Hi, Mark, it's Allie. I'm really sorry but the traffic this morning is terrible. I'm going to be very late.
Mark OK.
Allie I think the best thing is for you to take a taxi to the station and then get the train to the airport.
Mark No problem, I'll call a taxi. Well, thanks for everything…
Allie No listen, I'll meet you at the airport – we can say goodbye there.
Mark All right. Where can we meet?
Allie At the information desk.
Mark OK, see you there.
Allie Bye.
Mark Excuse me, change of plan. Could you call me a taxi, please? To the station.

Hello. Sorry I can't take your call. Please leave a message after the tone.
Mark Hi, Allie, this is Mark. Where are you? I'm at the information desk. My flight leaves in forty minutes.
Allie Mark! Mark! Sorry I'm late!
Mark Don't worry – I'm just happy you got here.
Allie Come on. You're going to miss your flight.
Mark Wait a minute. Are you going to come to the conference in California? Am I going to see you again?
Allie The plane's going to leave without you.
Mark Allie?
Allie I asked my boss this morning, and he said yes. I can go!
Mark Great! Oh, I don't have your home phone number.
Allie Don't worry. I'll e-mail it to you tomorrow.
This is the final call for all passengers on flight BA287 to San Francisco. Please proceed immediately to Gate 12.
Mark Goodbye, Allie. And thanks for everything.
Allie Goodbye, Mark. Have a safe trip!
Mark See you in California. Bye.

9.3

Rob Why don't we go to Paris? I haven't been there.
Charlotte Are you sure?
Rob Look, I promise. I've never been to Paris.
Charlotte OK. Let's look at the brochure. I love Paris. It's one of my favourite cities.
Rob You choose a hotel then.
Charlotte What about this one? It's very near the Eiffel Tower. It looks nice. Very romantic. Let's go there.
Rob Is that your phone?
Charlotte No, it's yours.
Rob Oh yeah. You're right. Hello?… Who?… Oh hi. What a surprise… Fine, fine. How are you?… Sorry?… It's seven o'clock here. In the evening. What time is it in Canada?… Sorry?… No, I'm not. I'm with… I'm with a friend… Can I call you back later?… I said, can I call you back later this evening?… Sorry? I can't hear you… OK I'll call you back later… Yes, OK. Bye… Sorry, Charlotte, what did you say about the hotel?
Charlotte Forget it, Rob. I don't want to go away with you this weekend. In fact I don't want to do anything with you. See you sometime.
Rob Charlotte, don't go. Listen, I can explain. It isn't what you think…

9.5

Presenter Our next caller is Carl from Essex. Hello, Carl.
Carl Hi.
Presenter What do you think, Carl? Do good books make good films?
Carl Well, I've read a lot of books and then seen the films, and I usually think that the books are better. For example, I loved the *Lord of the Rings* books but I didn't like the films very much.
Presenter Thank you, Carl. Our next caller is Linda from Manchester. Hello, Linda.
Linda Hi. Well, what I think is that today people don't read very much. But they do go to the cinema. And sometimes *after* they've seen a film of a book then they go and buy the book, so that's a good thing because they read more.
Presenter But do you think good books make good films?
Linda Yes. I've read a lot of good books and then I've seen the films and I've loved them all, *The Exorcist*, *Harry Potter*, *Gone with the Wind*. They're all great books and great films.
Presenter Thank you, Linda. And our last caller is Sam from Cardiff. Hello, Sam. What do you think about our question today?
Sam I think it depends. I think good books *don't* usually make good films. But I've seen some films which I think are *better* than the books. That's usually because the book *wasn't* very good.
Presenter So bad books can make good films?
Sam That's right.
Presenter Give me an example.
Sam Well, the James Bond films. The books aren't very good but some of the films are great, like *Goldfinger*, or *From Russia with Love*.
Presenter Thank you, Sam. Bye.

1A present tense verb *be* [+]

Full form	Contraction
I **am** your teacher.	I'**m** your teacher.
You **are** in room 13.	You'**re** in room 13.
He **is** James.	He'**s** James.
She **is** Marta.	She'**s** Marta.
It **is** a school.	It'**s** a school.
We **are** students.	We'**re** students.
You **are** in Class 2.	You'**re** in Class 2.
They **are** teachers.	They'**re** teachers.

- Use capital *I*. *I'm your teacher.* NOT ~~i'm~~.
- *you* = singular and plural.
- Use *he* for a man, *she* for a woman, and *it* for a thing.
- Use *they* for people and things.
- In contractions ' = a missing letter, e.g. *'m* = *am*.
- Use contractions in conversation.

1B present tense verb *be* [−] and [?]

Full form	Contraction	
I **am not**	I'**m not**	
You **are not**	You **aren't**	Italian.
He / She / It **is not**	He / She / It **isn't**	Spanish.
We **are not**	We **aren't**	British.
You **are not**	You **aren't**	
They **are not**	They **aren't**	

- Put *not* after the verb to make negatives [−].
- You can also contract *are not* and *is not* like this:
  *You are not Italian. – You'**re not** Italian.*
  *She is not Polish. – She'**s not** Polish.*

[?] [✔] [✘]

?		✔		✘	
Am I			I **am**.		I'**m not**.
Are you	German?		you **are**.		you **aren't**.
Is he / she / it	Russian?	Yes,	he / she /it **is**.	No,	he / she / it **isn't**.
Are we	Polish?		we **are**.		we **aren't**.
Are you			you **are**.		you **aren't**.
Are they			they **are**.		they **aren't**.

- In questions, put *be* before *you*, *he*, etc.
  ***Are you** Spanish?* NOT ~~You are Spanish?~~
  *Where **are you** from?* NOT ~~Where you are from?~~
  Don't use contractions in [✔] short answers.
  *Are you Scottish? Yes, **I am**.* NOT ~~Yes, I'm.~~

1C possessive adjectives: *my*, *your*, etc.

I'm Italian.	**My** family are from Rome.
You're in level 1.	This is **your** classroom.
He's the director.	**His** name is Michael.
She's your teacher.	**Her** name is Tina.
It's a school.	**Its** name is Queen's School.
We're an international school.	**Our** students are from many different countries.
They're new students.	**Their** names are David and Emma.

- *his* = of a man, *her* = of a woman, *its* = of a thing.
- *their* = of men, women, or things.
- Possessive adjectives don't change with plural nouns.
  ***our** students* NOT ~~ours students~~

⚠ Be careful with *it's* and *its*.
it's = it is — **It's** a school.
its = possessive — **Its** name is…

1D articles: *a* / *an*, *the*, plurals, *this* / *that* / *these* / *those*

a / *an* (indefinite article)

It's	**a**	bag.
		pen.
	an	**i**dentity card.
		umbrella.

- Use *a* / *an* with a singular noun.
- Use *an* with a noun beginning with a vowel (*a*, *e*, *i*, *o*, *u*).

the (definite article)

Open	**the**	door.
Close		windows.

- Use *the* when we know which (door, windows).
  *Open **the** door.*
  NOT ~~Open a door.~~
- Use *the* with singular and plural nouns.

plurals

Singular	Plural	Spelling
a book a key	books keys	add *-s*
a wat**ch** a bo**x**	watch**es** box**es**	add *-es* after *ch*, *sh*, *s*, *x*
a countr**y** a dictionar**y**	countr**ies** dictionar**ies**	consonant + *y* > *ies*

- Add *-s* to make plural nouns.
  It's a pen.
  They're pens.
- Don't use *a* / *an* with plural nouns.
  They're keys.
  NOT ~~They're a keys.~~

this / *that* / *these* / *those*

What's **this**? It's a lighter.
That car is Italian.
These watches are Japanese.
What are **those**? They're tables.

- Use *this* / *these* for things near you.
- Use *that* / *those* for things far away.
- *this* / *that* = singular, *these* / *those* = plural.

1A

a Complete with *am*, *is*, or *are*.

I *am* French.
1 My surname ______ López.
2 We ______ from Madrid.
3 I ______ Anna.
4 Antonio and Juan ______ in room 7.
5 The teacher ______ English.
6 You ______ in Class 3.
7 She ______ a student.

b Write the sentences with contractions.

I am from Italy. *I'm from Italy.*
1 It is a nice school. ______
2 We are in Class 2. ______
3 You are in room 6. ______
4 He is Paulo. ______
5 They are students. ______
6 She is the teacher. ______
7 I am fine. ______

1B

a Write the sentences in the negative.

She's American. *She isn't American.*
1 I'm British.
2 They're Brazilian.
3 It's Mexican food.
4 She's Italian.
5 We're from England.
6 You're Japanese.
7 He's from the USA.

b Make questions and short answers.

/ you Spanish? *Are you Spanish?* ✔ *Yes, I am.*
1 / I in room 13? ______? ✔ ______
2 / it German? ______? ✘ ______
3 / they from Italy? ______? ✘ ______
4 / we in Class 2? ______? ✔ ______
5 / she Chinese? ______? ✔ ______
6 / you Irish? ______? ✘ ______
7 / he from Scotland? ______? ✘ ______

1C

a Complete the sentences with a possessive adjective.

My name's Stephen.
1 Angela, please turn off ______ mobile phone.
2 The students are from Italy. ______ names are Susanna and Tito.
3 London is famous for ______ red buses.
4 She's French, but ______ mother is English.
5 We're in Class 3. ______ teacher is Bob.
6 ______ name is Ian. He's from Scotland.
7 I'm Mike. ______ family are from Dublin.

b Write the questions.

you how are ? *How are you?*
1 his what's name ?
2 German mother is her ?
3 from your are where parents ?
4 surname Zablowski is your ?
5 spell do how your name you ?

1D

a Complete with *a* or *an*. Write the plural.

	singular	plural
	a file	*files*
1	___ bag	
2	___ country	
3	___ identity card	
4	___ watch	
5	___ e-mail	
6	___ sandwich	
7	___ key	
8	___ umbrella	

b Complete the dialogues with *this*, *these*, *that*, or *those*.

Teacher What's ______, Tim?
Tim It's a lighter.
Teacher And what are ______, Tim?
Tim They're cigarettes.
Teacher Give them to me. ______ is a no-smoking school.

Man What's ______?
Woman It's a cat.
Man Who are ______ boys?
Woman They're your students. Put your glasses on!

2

2A present simple all verbs + and −

+	−
I **work**. You **work**. He / She / It **works**. We **work**. You **work**. They **work**.	I **don't work**. You **don't work**. He / She / It **doesn't work**. We **don't work**. You **don't work**. They **don't work**.

- **Contractions:** *don't = do not, doesn't = does not.*
- Use the present simple for things that are generally true or habitually happen.
  *British people **like** animals. He **works** from 9.00–5.00.*
- To make negatives use *don't / doesn't* + the infinitive.
  *He doesn't **work**.* NOT ~~He doesn't works~~.

spelling rules for *he / she / it*

I work / play / live. I watch / finish / go / do. I study.	He **works** / **plays** / **lives**. She **watches** / **finishes** / **goes** / **does**. She **studies**.

⚠	
I have	He has NOT ~~He haves~~
I go	He goes /gəʊz/
I do	He does /dʌz/

- The spelling rules for the *he / she / it* forms are the same as for plurals (Grammar Bank 1D).

2B present simple all verbs ?

?		✔		✘
Do I work? **Do** you work? **Does** he / she / it work? **Do** we work? **Do** you work? **Do** they work?	Yes,	I **do**. you **do**. he / she / it **does**. we **do**. you **do**. they **do**.	No,	I **don't**. you **don't**. he / she / it **doesn't**. we **don't**. you **don't**. they **don't**.

- Remember word order = **ASI** (auxiliary, subject, infinitive) or **QUASI** (question word, auxiliary, subject, infinitive).

Question word	Auxiliary	Subject	Infinitive (= verb)
	Do	you	live with your parents?
	Does	Jenny	like Chinese food?
Where	do	you	live?
What food	does	Jenny	like?

2D possessive *s*

She is Naomi Campbell**'s** mother. It's James**'s** house. They are my parent**s'** friends.

- Use *'s* with a person to talk about relatives and possessions.
  *Naomi Campbell**'s** mother* NOT ~~the mother of Naomi Campbell~~
- Use *'s* with irregular plural people, *men, women, children, people.*
  *That's my children**'s** school.* NOT ~~That's my childrens' school~~.
- Use *s'* with regular plural people.
  *They're my parent**s'** friends.* NOT ~~They're my parent's friends.~~
- Don't use *'s* with things.
  the end of the film NOT ~~the film's end~~

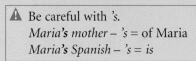

⚠ Be careful with *'s*. *Maria's mother* – *'s* = of Maria *Maria's Spanish* – *'s* = is

2A

a Change the sentences.

We like animals. — He *likes animals.*
1 I listen to the radio. — She ______.
2 He lives in a flat. — We ______.
3 They have two children. — He ______.
4 She doesn't drink coffee. — They ______.
5 I don't smoke. — My father ______.
6 The shop closes at 5.00. — The shops ______.
7 I go to the pub. — He ______.
8 I do housework. — She ______.

b Complete the sentences with a [+] or [–] verb.

study have ~~like~~ drive speak play do eat read

[+] He *likes* animals.
1 [+] My father ______ *The Times.*
2 [–] Her house is big, but it ______ a garden.
3 [+] We ______ French very well.
4 [–] I ______ fast food.
5 [+] She ______ a BMW.
6 [–] I ______ computer games.
7 [–] My father ______ housework.
8 [+] He ______ economics at university.

2B

a Complete the questions with *do* or *does.*

Do you have a car?
1 ______ you like Chinese food?
2 ______ your father cook?
3 ______ your mother work?
4 ______ you speak French?
5 ______ you play the piano?
6 ______ people in your country like animals?
7 ______ your teacher smoke?
8 ______ you study another language?

b Order the words to make questions.

a you car have do ? *Do you have a car?*
1 drink you coffee do ?
2 your does brother work ?
3 work you where do ?
4 music she like what does ?
5 newspaper you what read do ?
6 the go you cinema do to ?
7 does father watch your on TV sport ?
8 mother glasses wear your does ?

2D

a ~~Cross out~~ the wrong form.

It's **Kate's bag** / ~~**bag's Kate**~~.
1 Do you like **Jane's cats** / **cat's Jane**?
2 I drive **my mother's car** / **my car's mother**.
3 Amelia is **my wife's sister** / **my sister's wife**.
4 This is **my flat's friend** / **my friend's flat**.
5 **A** Who are you?
B I'm **Daniel's brother** / **brother's Daniel**.
6 He works for **his father's company** / **his company's father**.
7 She's **the wife's policeman** / **the policeman's wife**.
8 Don't do **your sister's homework** / **your homework's sister**!

b Complete with *'s* (possessive), *'s* (*is*), *s* (plural / third person *s*), or –.

My friend*'s* father work*s* in Germany.
1 My brother__ a lawyer. He__ 24. He work__ for BP.
2 He live__ in Paris with his three children__. He has two boy__ and a girl.
3 My brother__ wife__ name is Pauline. She__ a teacher.
4 Pauline__ parent__ live__ in Paris too. My brother like__ Pauline__ mother but not her father.

3

3A adjectives

It's a **big** house.
They're **pretty** flowers.

- Adjectives go before a noun. NOT It's ~~a house big~~.
- Adjectives don't change before a plural noun. NOT They're ~~prettys flowers~~.

3B telling the time

What's the time?

 It's seven o'clock.

 It's half past nine.

 It's quarter to two.

 It's twenty-five past one.

 It's twenty to four.

- Use *It's* + time to say what time it is.
- You can ask *What's the time?* or *What time is it?*
- Use *at* + time to say when you do something.
  A *What time do you get up?*
  B *I get up* ***at*** *half past seven.*

⚠ You can also say the time like this.
1.25 = *It's one twenty-five.*

3C adverbs of frequency

I **always** have toast for breakfast.
Do you **usually** go to work by bus?
She doesn't **often** go to bed late.
They're **sometimes** late.
She **hardly ever** watches TV.
He is **never** stressed.

- Use adverbs of frequency to answer the question *How often…?*
- Adverbs of frequency go before all verbs (except *be*). after *be.*

⚠ Use a [+] verb with *never* and *hardly ever.*
He ***never*** *smokes.* NOT ~~He doesn't never smoke~~.

3D prepositions of time

in
the morning
the afternoon
the evening
December
the summer
1998

on
Monday (morning)
the 12th of July
my birthday

at
three o'clock
midday / midnight
lunchtime
night
the weekend
Christmas / Easter / New Year

- Use *in* for parts of the day, months, seasons, and years.
- Use *on* for days and dates.
- Use *at* for times of the day, *night*, *the weekend*, and festivals.

3A

a Underline the adjectives in these sentences.

She's a beautiful actress.
1 Hi. I'm Carla. Nice to meet you.
2 Do you like Japanese food?
3 It's an international school.
4 They're a typical British family.
5 My father makes fantastic pasta.
6 Do you work with other people?
7 I'm a professional footballer.
8 We're good friends.

b Are the highlighted phrases right (✔) or wrong (✘)? Correct the wrong phrases.

She has hair red. ☒ *She has red hair.*
1 Do you like fast cars? ☐ ______
2 They're French girls. ☐ ______
3 I have a family big. ☐ ______
4 He's an English actor. ☐ ______
5 They're news boots. ☐ ______
6 It's a flat expensive. ☐ ______

3B

What's the time? Match the times with the clocks.

It's quarter to six. *g*
1 It's five past two. ___
2 It's quarter past four. ___
3 It's ten to three. ___
4 It's twenty-five to five. ___
5 It's seven o'clock. ___
6 It's twenty past one. ___
7 It's half past eight. ___

a b c d e f g h

3C

a Complete the sentences with an adverb of frequency.

never always hardly ever sometimes usually

They *never* drive – they don't have a car.
1 I ______ drink champagne – only at Christmas.
2 She ______ eats meat. She's a vegetarian.
3 He doesn't have a watch so he's ______ late.
4 We ______ get up at 7.30, except at weekends.
5 I don't do a lot of exercise but I ______ go swimming.

b Order the words to make sentences.

always she at six up gets *She always gets up at six.*
1 for late always I am class
2 meet ever hardly we
3 what work you usually time do finish ?
4 morning in the hungry I am never
5 often I read don't the newspaper
6 restaurants sometimes expensive to go we
7 wine good usually very is this

3D

a Complete with *in*, *on*, or *at*.

on July 9th
1 ______ 6.30
2 ______ the evening
3 ______ the weekend
4 ______ the 1st of January
5 ______ the winter
6 ______ 2005
7 ______ lunchtime
8 ______ September
9 ______ night
10 ______ Thursday morning
11 ______ Easter
12 ______ Saturday

b Complete with *in*, *on*, or *at* and a time expression.

five o'clock July 4th Christmas Sundays
the summer midnight the afternoon ~~nine o'clock~~

In the UK people usually start work *at nine o'clock*.
1 On December 31st many people drink champagne ______.
2 In the USA they celebrate Independence Day ______.
3 Many people all over the world give presents ______.
4 In Italy it's usually very hot ______.
5 In many countries shops are closed ______.
6 In Spain many people have a siesta ______.
7 Traditionally, British people have a cup of tea ______.

4

4A *can / can't*

+		−	
I You He / She / It We You They	**can** swim. **can** come. **can** help.	I You He / She / It We You They	**can't** swim. **can't** come. **can't** help.

?			✔			✘		
Can	I you he / she / it we you they	swim? come? help?	Yes,	I you he / she / it we you they	**can.**	No,	I you he / she / it we you they	**can't.**

- **Contraction:** *can't* = *cannot.*
- *can* has different meanings:
  I can swim. = I know how to.
  I can come. = It's possible for me (I'm not busy).
  Can you help me? = Please help me.

⚠ Don't use *to* after *can.*
*I **can swim**.* NOT ~~I can to swim~~.

4B *like* (+ verb + *-ing*)

☺☺	I **love**	**shopping**.
☺	I **like**	**going** to the cinema.
☹	I **don't like**	**doing** housework.
☹☹	I **hate**	**driving** at night.

- Use verb + *-ing* after *like, love,* and *hate.*

spelling rules for the *-ing* form

Infinitive	Verb + *-ing*	Spelling
cook study	I like cook**ing**. She hates study**ing**.	add *-ing*
dance	I love danc**ing**.	~~e~~ + *-ing*
shop	I don't like shop**ping**.	one vowel + one consonant = double consonant + *-ing*

4C object pronouns: *me, you, him,* etc.

I	me	Wait for **me**.
you	you	I love **you**.
he	him	She isn't in love with **him**.
she	her	He kisses **her**.
it	it	I don't like **it**.
we	us	Can you help **us**?
you	you	See **you** tomorrow.
they	them	Phone **them** this evening.

- Object pronouns take the place of nouns.
  She meets John. She invites him to her house.
- Object pronouns go after the verb.
  *I **love you**.* NOT ~~I you love~~.
- You also use object pronouns after prepositions (*with, to, from,* etc.).
  *Listen to **me**! I'm in love with **her**.* NOT ~~I'm in love with she~~.

4D possessive pronouns: *mine, yours,* etc.

Subject pronouns	Possessive adjectives	Possessive pronouns
I	It's **my** car.	It's **mine**.
you	It's **your** car.	It's **yours**.
he	It's **his** car.	It's **his**.
she	It's **her** car.	It's **hers**.
we	It's **our** car.	It's **ours**.
they	It's **their** car.	It's **theirs**.

- Use possessive pronouns to talk about possession.
  A *Whose book is it? Is it **yours**?*
  B *Yes, it's **mine**.*
- Use possessive pronouns in place of a possessive adjective + noun.
  *It's **my car**.* OR *It's **mine**.*

⚠ Don't use *the* with possessive pronouns.
This is yours. NOT ~~This is the yours.~~

4A

a Complete the sentences with *can* or *can't*.

I can sing but I *can't* dance.

1 We ______ play tennis on Saturday. I'm free.
2 **A** ______ I smoke here?
B No, it's a no-smoking restaurant.
3 I'm sorry. I ______ remember your name.
4 I ______ speak French but not German.
5 ______ you help me? This case is very heavy.
6 I ______ see you tonight. I'm very busy.
7 Sorry? I ______ hear you.
8 Look! We ______ buy some milk in that shop.

b Write a [+] or [–] sentence for each picture.

camp drive have pay smoke ~~park~~ take use

You can't park here.
1 ______ a coffee here.
2 ______ here.
3 ______ photographs.
4 ______ here.
5 ______ in this street.
6 ______ with a credit card.
7 ______ mobiles here.

4B

a Write the *-ing* form of the verbs in the chart.

~~write~~ run talk play have sit get cook make swim study phone

work work**ing**	live liv**ing**	shop shop**ping**
	writing	

b Write sentences about Matt with *love*, *not like*, *like*, or *hate* and a verb.

He loves playing chess.
1 ______
2 ______
3 ______
4 ______
5 ______
6 ______
7 ______

Matt's likes and dislikes
☺☺ ~~chess~~, TV
☺ photos, the cinema
☹ exercise, the radio
☹☹ housework, fast food

4C

a Complete the sentences with an object pronoun (*me*, *you*, etc.)

I love *you*.

1 He's in love with ______ but she doesn't love ______.
2 It's a good film. Do you want to see ______?
3 You speak very quickly. I can't understand ______.
4 We have a problem. Can you help ______?
5 I try to talk to ______ but she doesn't listen to ______.
6 They're nice people. Do you know ______?

b Change the highlighted words to pronouns.

I see John every day. *I see him every day.*

1 I know Linda.
2 She lives with her father.
3 I usually see my parents on Sunday.
4 I can't remember your e-mail address.
5 I don't like this actress.
6 Can you book a table for my friend and me?

4D

a Look at the pictures. Complete the sentences with *mine*, *yours*, etc.

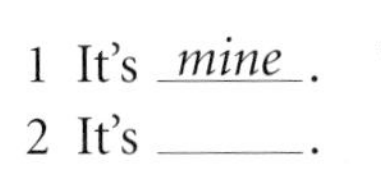

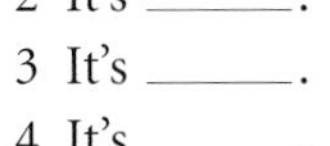

1 It's *mine*.
2 It's ______.
3 It's ______.
4 It's ______.
5 It's ______.
6 Is it ______?

b ~~Cross out~~ the wrong word.

This is **my** / ~~**mine**~~ son, David.

1 **A** Are these **your** / **yours** keys?
B No, these are **my** / **mine**.
2 She's French and **her** / **hers** husband is British. **Their** / **Theirs** children speak French and English.
3 **A** I can't find **my** / **mine** mobile.
B Is this **your** / **yours**?
4 **A** Whose car is that?
B It's not **our** / **ours**. **Our** / **Ours** car is in the garage.

5A past simple of *be*: *was / were*

+

I You He / She / It We You They	**was** **were** **was** **were** **were** **were**	famous.	I You He / She / It We You They	**wasn't** **weren't** **wasn't** **weren't** **weren't** **weren't**	famous.

(− columns: right half)

- **Contractions**: *wasn't = was not, weren't = were not.*
- Use *was / were* to talk about the past.
  *My grandfather **was** born in London.*

? ✔ ✘

Was **Were** **Was** **Were** **Were** **Were**	I you he / she / it we you they	famous?	Yes,	I **was**. you **were**. he / she / it **was**. we **were**. you **were**. they **were**.	No,	I **wasn't**. you **weren't**. he / she / it **wasn't**. we **weren't**. you **weren't**. they **weren't**.

5B past simple regular verbs

+ −

I You He / She / It We You They	**worked** yesterday.	I You He / She / It We You They	**didn't work** yesterday.

spelling rules for regular verbs

Infinitive	Past	Spelling
watch play	watch**ed** play**ed**	add *-ed*
live smoke	live**d** smoke**d**	add *-d*
stop	stop**ped**	one vowel + one consonant = double consonant
study	stud**ied**	consonant + *y* > *ied*

? ✔ ✘

Did	I you he / she / it we you they	**work** yesterday?	Yes,	I you he / she / it we you they	**did**.	No,	I you he / she / it we you they	**didn't**.

- **Contraction**: *didn't = did not.*
- Use the past simple for finished actions.
- Regular verbs in the past + end in *-ed*, e.g. *worked, lived, played.*
- The past is the same for all persons.
- Use *did / didn't* + infinitive for past ? and −.

5C past simple irregular verbs

Infinitive	Past +	Past −
go	**went**	**didn't go**
have	**had**	**didn't have**
get	**got**	**didn't get**
buy	**bought**	**didn't buy**
leave	**left**	**didn't leave**
drive	**drove**	**didn't drive**
meet	**met**	**didn't meet**
see	**saw**	**didn't see**
wear	**wore**	**didn't wear**
do	**did**	**didn't do**

- Use the irregular past form only in + sentences.
  *I **saw** a film last night.*
- Use the infinitive after *did / didn't.*
  ***Did** you **see** a film last night?* NOT ~~*Did you saw…?*~~
- Remember word order = **ASI** (auxiliary, subject, infinitive) or **QUASI** (question word, auxiliary, subject, infinitive).
  Did you go out last night?
  Where did you go?

⚠ Past of *can = could.*
− = *couldn't* NOT ~~*didn't can*~~
? = *Could you…?* NOT ~~*Did you can…?*~~

5A

a Change the sentences from present to past.

Present simple	Past simple
I'm tired.	I *was* tired last week.
1 Today is Sunday.	Yesterday ______ Saturday.
2 Where are you now?	Where ______ you yesterday?
3 We are in Munich today.	We ______ in Berlin yesterday.
4 I'm in Italy this month.	I ______ in France last month.
5 My father's a pilot.	My grandfather ______ a pilot too.
6 It isn't open now.	It ______ open this morning.
7 Why aren't you at work today?	Why ______ you at work yesterday?

b Complete the dialogues with *was, wasn't, were,* or *weren't.*

A *Were* you and Susan at the party last night?
B Yes, we [1] ______.
A [2] ______ it good?
B No, it [3] ______. The music [4] ______ awful. Where [5] ______ you?
A I [6] ______ ill.

A Where [7] ______ you born?
B I [8] ______ born in Australia in 1919.
A [9] ______ your parents Australian?
B No, they [10] ______. My mother [11] ______ Italian and my father [12] ______ Greek.

5B

a Rewrite the sentences in the past simple with *yesterday.*

Present	Past
I use the Internet.	*I used the Internet yesterday.*
1 I watch TV.	______
2 Do you listen to the radio?	______
3 We study English.	______
4 He doesn't work.	______
5 The film finishes at 7.00.	______
6 I don't like the film.	______
7 Does she smoke?	______
8 They play tennis.	______

b Complete the sentences with a verb in the past simple.

arrive not book land live stay
not remember turn on want watch

I *turned on* the TV.
1 We ______ in a three-star hotel last year.
2 They ______ a table and the restaurant was full.
3 ______ you ______ the football on TV last night?
4 Sorry. I ______ it was your birthday yesterday.
5 I ______ with my parents when I was a student.
6 Why ______ you ______ to be a doctor?
7 He ______ late for work and the boss was angry.
8 When the plane ______ she ______ her mobile phone.

5C

a Complete the text with the verbs in brackets in the past simple.

Yesterday *was* my birthday. (be)
My boyfriend [1] ______ me a beautiful jacket. (buy)
In the evening we [2] ______ out. (go)
I [3] ______ my new jacket. (wear)
We [4] ______ for a Chinese restaurant (look)
but we [5] ______ find one, (not can)
so we [6] ______ dinner in our favourite Italian restaurant. (have)
After that we [7] ______ a film. (see)
Then we [8] ______ two friends at a nightclub. (meet)
We [9] ______ for two hours. (dance)
We [10] ______ home until 3.00. (not get)
I [11] ______ very tired, (be)
and I [12] ______ straight to bed. (go)

b Complete the questions in the past simple.

Did you go out last night? (you / go out)
1 What ______? (you / wear)
2 Where ______? (you / go)
3 What ______? (you / do)
4 ______ with you? (your sister / go)
5 What ______ to eat? (you / have)
6 What time ______? (the party / finish)
7 What time ______? (you / get home)
8 ______ a good time? (you / have)

6

6A *there is / there are*

	Singular	Plural
+	**There's** a piano.	**There are** some glasses in the cupboard.
−	**There isn't** a fridge.	**There aren't** any pictures.
?	**Is there** a TV?	**Are there** any glasses?
✔ ✘	Yes, **there is**. No, **there isn't**.	Yes, **there are**. No, **there aren't**.

- We often use *there is / are* with *a / an, some,* and *any*.
- Use *some* and *any* with plural nouns. *Some* = not an exact number.
- Use *some* in + sentences and *any* in − and ?.

⚠ Be careful. *There is* and *It is* are different.
***There's** a key on the table. **It's** the key to the kitchen.*

6B *there was / there were*

	Singular	Plural
+	**There was** an old TV.	**There were** only three guests.
−	**There wasn't** a remote control.	**There weren't** any more people.
?	**Was there** a ghost?	**Were there** any lights?
✔ ✘	Yes, **there was**. No, **there wasn't**.	Yes, **there were**. No, **there weren't**.

- *there was / were* is the past of *there is / are*.

6C present continuous: *be* + verb + *-ing*

+

Full form	Contraction	
I **am**	I'**m**	
You **are**	You'**re**	**crying**.
He / She / It **is**	He / She / It'**s**	**having** a party.
We **are**	We'**re**	**arguing**.
You **are**	You'**re**	
They **are**	They'**re**	

−

Full form	Contraction	
I **am not**	I'**m not**	
You **are not**	You **aren't**	**crying**.
He / She / It **is not**	He / She / It **isn't**	**having** a party.
We **are not**	We **aren't**	**arguing**.
You **are not**	You **aren't**	
They **are not**	They **aren't**	

?		✔		✘	
Am I			I **am**.		I'**m not**.
Are you	**crying**?		you **are**.		you **aren't**.
Is he / she / it	**having** a party?	Yes,	he / she /it **is**.	No,	he / she / it **isn't**.
Are we	**arguing**?		we **are**.		we **aren't**.
Are you			you **are**.		you **aren't**.
Are they			they **are**.		they **aren't**.

- Use the present continuous for things that are happening now. *It's **raining**. The baby's **crying**.*
- For the spelling of the *-ing* form see Grammar Bank 4B.

6D present simple or present continuous?

Present simple	Present continuous
My sister **works** in a bank.	Today she'**s working** at home.
What **do you** usually **wear** to work?	What **are you wearing** now?

- Use the present simple to say what you usually do.
- Use the present continuous to say what you are doing now.

⚠ Be careful with *do*.
A *What **do you do**? (= What's your job?)*
B *I'm a teacher.*
A *What **are you doing**?* (= now, at the moment)
B *I'm waiting for a friend.*

6A

a Complete the sentences with *There's* or *There are.*

There's ________ a sofa in the living room.
1 ________ four cups in the cupboard.
2 ________ a clock in the kitchen.
3 ________ lots of chairs.
4 ________ a garage.
5 ________ some pictures on the wall.
6 ________ a desk in the study.

b Write [+], [−], or [?] sentences with *there is / are.*

[+] chairs / the garden *There are some chairs in the garden.*
1 [+] table / the kitchen
2 [?] fireplace / the living room
3 [−] plants / the living room
4 [?] cupboards / the kitchen
5 [−] shower / bathroom
6 [+] shelves / study

6B

a Look at the hotel information. Write a [+] or [−] sentence with *There was / were.*

There weren't any single rooms.
1 ________
2 ________
3 ________
4 ________
5 ________

Hotel Astoria	
single rooms	✗
double rooms	✓
swimming pool	✓
restaurant	✓
car park	✗
shops	✗

b Complete with the correct form of *there was* or *there were.*

A How many guests *were there* in the hotel?
B [1] ______ ______ four including me. [2] ______ ______ a French tourist and [3] ______ ______ two businessmen.
A [4] ______ ______ a restaurant?
B No, [5] ______ ______, but [6] ______ ______ a bar.
A What [7] ______ ______ in your room?
B [8] ______ ______ a minibar and a TV.
A [9] ______ ______ two beds?
B No, [10] ______ ______. [11] ______ ______ a double bed.

6C

a Write a question and answer for each picture.

1 *What's he doing?* He ________.
2 ________? ________.
3 ________? ________.

b Put the verbs in brackets in the present continuous.

A Hello.
B Oh, hi Dad. Where are you?
A I'm in my hotel. *I'm having* a drink in the bar. (have)
It [1] ________ a lot here. Is Mum there? (rain)
B Yes, but she [2] ________ to somebody on the mobile just now. (talk)
A Oh. What [3] ______ you ______? (do)
B My friend Matt is here.
A Matt? Why [4] ______ you ______ your homework? (not do)
B Don't worry. We [5] ________ together. (study)
A Where's Jenny?
B She [6] ________ for Kevin to come. (wait)
They [7] ________ a party tonight. (have)
A Oh. What [8] ______ she ______? (wear)
B Nothing special. OK Dad, here's Mum. Bye.

6D

a Right or wrong? Tick (✓) or cross (✗) the sentences.

It rains at the moment. ✗
1 Listen! The baby's crying. ☐
2 My neighbours often argue. ☐
3 John's on holiday. He has a great time. ☐
4 My brother's staying with us at the moment. ☐
5 I'm normally going to the gym after work. ☐
6 **A** Where are you going? **B** To the shops. ☐
7 **A** What are you doing? **B** I'm a teacher. ☐

b Put the verbs in brackets in the present simple or continuous.

Where *are* you *going*? (go) To play football – see you later!
1 **A** Hi, Sarah! What ________ you ________ here? (do)
B I ________ for my boyfriend. (wait)
2 **A** What ______ your mother ______? (do)
B She's a nurse. She ________ at the local hospital. (work)
3 Listen! They ________ a party upstairs again. (have)
They ________ a party at least once a month! (have)
4 I ________ to the supermarket. (go)
________ you ________ anything? (want)

7

7A countable / uncountable nouns

- There are two kinds of noun in English, countable (C) and uncountable (U).
  C = things you can count. C nouns can be singular or plural.
  ***one apple**, **two** apples, **three** apples.*
  U = things you can't count. U nouns can't be plural.
  butter, meat NOT ~~two butters, three meats~~
- Some nouns can be C or U but the meaning is different.

a / an, some / any

		Countable	Uncountable
+	We need	**an** apple. **some** apples.	**some** butter. **some** milk.
−	We don't need	**a** tomato. **any** tomato**es**.	**any** rice. **any** sugar.
?	Do we need	**a** tomato? **any** tomato**es**?	**any** rice? **any** sugar?

- Use *a / an* with singular C nouns.
- Use *some* with plural C nouns and U nouns in +.
- Use *any* with plural C nouns and U nouns in − and ?.

⚠ We can also use *some* in ? to ask for and offer things.
*Can I have **some** coffee?*
*Would you like **some** biscuits?*

7B *how much / how many?*

Uncountable (singular)	Full answers	Short answers
How much water do you drink?	I drink **a lot of** water. I drink **quite a lot of** water. I don't drink **much** water. I don't drink **any** water.	**A lot.** **Quite a lot.** **Not much.** **None.**
Countable (plural)		
How many sweets did you eat?	I ate **a lot of** sweets. I ate **quite a lot of** sweets. I didn't eat **many** sweets. I didn't eat **any** sweets.	**A lot.** **Quite a lot.** **Not many.** **None.**

- Use *How much...?* with uncountable (U) nouns and *How many...?* with plural countable (C) nouns.
- Use: *a lot (of)* with C and U nouns for **a big quantity**.
  quite a lot (of) for **quite a big quantity**.
  not...much with U nouns for **a small quantity**.
  not...many with C plural nouns for **a small quantity**.
  not...any (*none* in short answers) for **zero quantity**.

7C *be going to* (plans)

Full form	Contraction	
I **am** You **are** He / She / It **is** We **are** You **are** They **are**	I**'m** You**'re** He / She / It**'s** We**'re** You**'re** They**'re**	**going to have** a holiday next month.

−

Full form	Contraction	
I **am not** You **are not** He / She / It **is not** We **are not** You **are not** They **are not**	I**'m not** You **aren't** He / She / It **isn't** We **aren't** You **aren't** They **aren't**	**going to have** a holiday next month.

?		✔		✘	
Am I **Are** you **Is** he / she / it **Are** we **Are** you **Are** they	**going to have** a holiday next month?	Yes,	I **am**. you **are**. he / she /it **is**. we **are**. you **are**. they **are**.	No,	I**'m not**. you **aren't**. he / she / it **isn't**. we **aren't**. you **aren't**. they **aren't**.

- Use *be going to* + verb (infinitive) to talk about future plans.
- With the verb *go* you can say *I'm going to go* OR *I'm going ~~to go~~.*
- We often use future time expressions with *going to*.
  tomorrow, next week, next year, etc.

⚠ next year NOT ~~the next year~~

7D *be going to* (predictions)

You can also use *be going to* + verb (infinitive) for predictions.

*(I think) They**'re going to be** very happy.*

*(I think) It**'s going to rain.***

7A

a Write *a*, *an*, or *some* + a food / drink word.

1 *some cereal* 6 ______
2 ______ 7 ______
3 ______ 8 ______
4 ______ 9 ______
5 ______ 10 ______

b Complete the dialogue with *a*, *an*, *some*, or *any*.

A I invited my sister for dinner. Is that OK?
B No, it isn't. We don't have *any* food!
A There are [1] ______ eggs and [2] ______ cheese. I can make [3] ______ omelette.
B There aren't [4] ______ eggs. I had the last two.
A We can make [5] ______ pasta. Are there [6] ______ tomatoes?
B Yes. And there's [7] ______ onion. What about drink? Is there [8] ______ wine?
A Yes, there's [9] ______ bottle of red wine. And there's [10] ______ Coke too.

7B

a Complete with *How much* / *How many*.

How much fruit do you eat?

1 ______ people were there at the party?
2 ______ milk does she drink?
3 ______ coffee did you drink yesterday?
4 ______ eggs are there in the fridge?
5 ______ cents are there in a euro?
6 ______ money do you have with you?
7 ______ hours does your baby usually sleep?
8 ______ free time do you have during the week?

b ~~Cross out~~ the wrong words.

I don't eat ~~**much**~~ / **many** apples.

1 I eat **a lot of** / **much** fruit.
2 Do you drink **much** / **many** water?
3 We don't buy **much** / **many** vegetables.
4 **A** How much meat do you eat?
B **None** / **Any**. I'm a vegetarian.
5 I eat **quite a lot of** / **quite** fish.
6 **A** How much exercise do you do?
B **No much** / **Not much**.

7C

a Write sentences about Susan's holiday plans.

She's going to go to Rome. (go)

1 ______ Italian. (speak)
2 ______ a hotel. (stay in)
3 ______ photos. (take)
4 ______ spaghetti. (eat)
5 ______ Colosseum. (see)

b Complete the sentences with (*be*) *going to* + a verb.

buy cook do not have study not fly

Our car is ten years old. We *'re going to buy* a new one.

1 My mother's at work so my father ______ the lunch.
2 I ______ tonight. I have an exam tomorrow.
3 ______ you ______ a present for Bill?
4 We ______ to Edinburgh. It's too expensive.
5 What ______ your brother ______ after school?
6 It's her birthday next week, but she ______ a party.

7D

a Write predictions for the pictures.

1 *It's going to* ______
2 ______
3 ______
4 ______

b Complete the predictions with (*be*) *going to* and a verb.

be break have not pass wake up win

It's my dream holiday! I know I*'m going to have* a good time.

1 They're playing very well. I think they ______ the match.
2 She's a very bad student. She ______ the exam.
3 Look at the blue sky. It ______ a beautiful day.
4 You're driving very fast! We ______ an accident!
5 Be careful with that glass! You ______ it!
6 The baby's very tired. I don't think she ______ tonight.

8

8A comparative adjectives

White cars are **safer than** yellow cars.
Mosquitoes are **more dangerous than** sharks.
Tigers are **better** swimmers **than** cats.

- Use comparative adjectives + *than* to compare two people / things.

Adjective	Comparative	
old cheap	old**er** cheap**er**	one-syllable adjectives: add *-er*
big hot	big**ger** hot**ter**	adjectives ending one vowel + one consonant: double consonant, add *-er*
healthy happy	health**ier** happ**ier**	one- or two-syllable adjectives ending consonant + *y* > *-ier*
famous expensive	**more** famous **more** expensive	two- or more syllable adjectives: *more* + adjective
good bad far	**better** **worse** **further**	irregular

8B superlative adjectives

It's **the hottest** country in the world.
The most dangerous time is the spring.

- Use *the* + superlative adjective to say which is the (*biggest*, etc.) in a group.

Adjective	Comparative	Superlative	
cold high	colder higher	**the** cold**est** **the** high**est**	add *-est*
hot big	hotter bigger	**the** hott**est** **the** bigg**est**	double consonant, add *-est*
pretty sunny	prettier sunnier	**the** pretti**est** **the** sunni**est**	> *-iest*
dangerous	**more** dangerous	**the most** dangerous	*the most* + adjective
good bad far	**better** **worse** **further**	**the best** **the worst** **the furthest**	irregular

8C *would like to*

[+]

I You He She We They	**'d like to** fly a plane.

[−]

I You He She We They	**wouldn't like to** fly a plane.

[?] [✔] [✘]

Would	I you he she we they	**like to** fly a plane?	Yes,	I you he she we they	**would**.	No,	I you he she we they	**wouldn't**.

- **Contractions**: *'d = would, wouldn't = would not.*
- *I would like to = I want to* (now or in the future).
- Use the infinitive with *to* after *would like.*
  *I **would like to learn**.* NOT ~~I would like learn.~~
- You can also use *Would you like to…?* for invitations.
  ***Would you like to** have dinner with me tonight?*

⚠ *Would like* and *like* are different.
***I'd like** to dance.* (= I want to dance now or in the future)
***I like** dancing.* (= I enjoy it, I like it in general)

8D adverbs

I drive **slowly**.
They speak very **quietly**.
People dress very **well**.

- Use adverbs to say *how* people do things.
- Adverbs usually go after the verb.
  I speak English very well.
  NOT ~~I speak very well English.~~
- Look at the chart for how to make adverbs.

Adjective	Adverb	
slow quick bad careful	slow**ly** quick**ly** bad**ly** careful**ly**	+ *-ly*
healthy easy	health**ily** eas**ily**	consonant + *y* > *-ily*
good fast hard	**well** **fast** **hard**	irregular

- Remember the difference between adjectives and adverbs.
  *I'm a **careful** driver.* (adjective)
  *I drive **carefully**.* (adverb)

⚠ Not all words that end in *-ly* are adverbs, e.g. *friendly* = adjective.
*He's a **friendly** person.*

8A

a Write the comparative form of these adjectives.

hot *hotter*

1 short ______
2 difficult ______
3 beautiful ______
4 noisy ______
5 thin ______
6 near ______
7 easy ______
8 rich ______

b Write comparative sentences.

The Nile / the Amazon (long)
The Nile is longer than the Amazon.

1 Canada / Brazil (big)
2 Tessa / Deborah (pretty)
3 Driving / flying (dangerous)
4 My English / your English (bad)
5 This chair / that chair (comfortable)
6 Her husband / her (young)
7 Buses / trains (cheap)
8 French wine / English wine (good)

8B

a Write the opposite superlative adjectives.

the hottest *the coldest*

1 the biggest ______
2 the lowest ______
3 the cheapest ______
4 the youngest ______
5 the easiest ______
6 the wettest ______
7 the ugliest ______
8 the richest ______

b Complete the sentences with a superlative. Use the adjectives in brackets.

It's *the most dangerous* country in the world. (dangerous)

1 I am ______ in my family. (tall)
2 That house is ______ in the street. (old)
3 The Scots make ______ whisky in the world. (good)
4 This is ______ part of the country. (hot)
5 This is ______ building in the city. (famous)
6 He's ______ student in the class. (bad)
7 Chinese is one of ______ languages to learn. (difficult)
8 It's ______ dress in the shop. (pretty)

8C

a Write sentences and questions with *would like.*

I / go to New York
I'd like to go to New York.

1 I / be a millionaire.
2 you / be famous?
3 I / not / go up in a balloon
4 he / learn to cook
5 she / not / be on TV
6 they / have children?
7 I / not / live in a foreign country
8 We / like / buy a bigger flat

b Complete these sentences with a verb in the correct form (infinitive or *-ing*).

be get open cook go (x 2) see live have fly learn

I'd like *to learn* to fly a plane.

1 Would you like ______ dinner with me tonight?
2 I'd like ______ to Australia but I don't like ______.
3 She wouldn't like ______ a teacher. She hates children.
4 Do you like ______ wild animals? Would you like ______ on a safari?
5 We'd like ______ married in June.
6 I would like ______ a restaurant because I like ______.
7 Does your sister like ______ in Paris?
8 Would you like ______ another language?

8D

a Adjective or adverb? ~~Cross out~~ the wrong word.

He's very **polite** / ~~**politely**~~.

1 Our teacher speaks very **slow** / **slowly**.
2 Her German is **perfect** / **perfectly**.
3 Everything happened very **quick** / **quickly**.
4 The food was very **good** / **well**.
5 Please drive **careful** / **carefully**.
6 You can walk **safe** / **safely** at night in this city.
7 My sister dresses very **good** / **well**.
8 The weather is **terrible** / **terribly** tonight.

b Complete the sentences with adverbs from these adjectives.

bad ~~good~~ careful hard easy healthy slow quiet beautiful

I don't speak French very *well*.

1 We played ______ in the semi-final and we lost 5–1.
2 Hurry up! You're walking very ______.
3 Can you talk ______, please? Your father is asleep.
4 We had a good map and we found their house ______.
5 The boss likes him because he works ______.
6 Open the bag ______. There are eggs inside.
7 He eats very ______ – lots of fruit and vegetables.
8 She sings ______. I'm sure she's going to be famous.

9

9A present perfect: verb *be*

+

Full form	Contraction	
I **have** You **have** He / She / It **has** We **have** You **have** They **have**	I**'ve** You**'ve** He / She / It**'s** We**'ve** You**'ve** They**'ve**	**been** to Rome.

−

Full form	Contraction	
I **have not** You **have not** He / She / It **has not** We **have not** You **have not** They **have not**	I **haven't** You **haven't** He / She / It **hasn't** We **haven't** You **haven't** They **haven't**	**been** to Venice.

? ✔ ✘

Have I **Have** you **Has** he / she / it **Have** we **Have** you **Have** they	**been** to Paris?	Yes,	I **have**. you **have**. he / she / it **has**. we **have**. you **have**. they **have**.	No,	I **haven't**. you **haven't**. he / she / it **hasn't**. we **haven't**. you **haven't**. they **haven't**.

- Use the present perfect for general past experiences.
- To make the present perfect use *have* / *has* + past participle.
- *'s* = *has* in present perfect (but can also be *is* or possessive *'s*).

⚠ Compare the present perfect of *be* and the present perfect of *go*.
*He's **been** to Italy.* = He visited Italy and came back.
*He's **gone** to Italy.* = He's in Italy now.

9B present perfect: regular and irregular verbs

	Infinitive	Present perfect
Regular verbs	cry kiss queue	**have cried** **have kissed** **have queued**
Irregular verbs	buy leave see speak	**have bought** **have left** **have seen** **have spoken**

- For regular verbs the past participle is the same as the past simple (+ *-ed*).
- For irregular verbs the past participle is sometimes the same as the past simple, e.g. *buy, bought, bought,* and sometimes different, e.g. *see, saw, seen.*

present perfect or past simple?

Have you seen the film? When **did you see** it?	Yes, **I have**. I **saw** it last week.

- Use the present perfect to talk / ask about a general experience in the past.
- Use the past simple to talk / ask about a specific moment in the past.
*I **saw** the film **last week**.*
- Don't use the present perfect with *when* and past time expressions, e.g. *yesterday, last week.*
***When did** you see it?* NOT ~~When have you seen it?~~
*I **saw** it **last week**.* NOT ~~I've seen it last week.~~

APPENDIX

1 *have got*

+

Full form	Contraction	
I **have got** You **have got** He / She / It **has got** We **have got** You **have got** They **have got**	I**'ve got** You**'ve got** He's / She's / It**'s got** We**'ve got** You**'ve got** They**'ve got**	a car.

−

Full form	Contraction	
I **have not got** You **have not got** He / She / It **has not got** We **have not got** You **have not got** They **have not got**	I **haven't got** You **haven't got** He / She / It **hasn't got** We **haven't got** You **haven't got** They **haven't got**	a car.

? ✔ ✘

Have I **got** **Have** you **got** **Has** he / she / it **got** **Have** we **got** **Have** you **got** **Have** they **got**	a car?	Yes,	I **have**. you **have**. he / she /it **has**. we **have**. you **have**. they **have**.	No,	I **haven't**. you **haven't**. he / she / it **hasn't**. we **haven't**. you **haven't**. they **haven't**.

- You can use *have got* instead of *have* for possession.
I've got a bike. = I **have** a bike.
***Have you got** a car?* = **Do you have** a car?
- *have got* is more common in the UK, *have* is more common in the USA and in international English.

9A

a Write the sentences with contractions.

I have been to Brazil. *I've been to Brazil.*

1 She has not been to the USA.
2 They have not been to China.
3 He has been to an opera.
4 You have not been to my house.
5 I have not been there.
6 We have been to Madrid.

b Write [+], [−], and [?] sentences with *been*.

[+] She / Italy *She's been to Italy.*

1 [−] I / Rome
2 [?] you / Barcelona
3 [−] Mark / South America
4 [+] My parents / Africa
5 [?] Ann / Argentina
6 [−] We / Budapest

9B

a Complete the sentences with the past participles of the verbs in brackets.

Have you *seen* my car keys? (see)

1 Have you ______ his new girlfriend? I don't like her. (meet)
2 I've ______ *War and Peace* three times. (read)
3 Have you ever ______ in love? (fall)
4 I've never ______ in the cinema. (cry)
5 My wife has ______ all over the world. (travel)
6 He's ______ a lot of famous people in his work. (meet)
7 She's ______ George Clooney's new film four times. (see)
8 I've ______ a lot of poems but I never show them to anybody. (write)

b Put the verbs in brackets in the present perfect or past simple.

A *Have you ever been* to the opera? (be)
B Yes, I *went* last year. (go)
A 1______ you ever ______ to a famous actor or actress? (speak)
B Yes, I 2______.
A Who 3______ it? (be)
B Jeremy Irons.
A Where 4______ you ______ him? (see)
B I 5______ him at an airport. (see)
A What 6______ you ______ to him? (say)
B I 7______ him for his autograph. (ask)

A 8______ your brother______ to South Korea? (be)
B Yes, he 9______. He 10______ to Seoul. (be)
A When 11______ he ______ there? (go)
B He 12______ there in 2002, to see the World Cup. (go)
A 13______ he ______ it? (like)
B Yes, he 14______ it. (love)

Study Link **MultiROM** www.oup.com/elt/englishfile/elementary

2 *will* (future)

[+]		[−]	
I You He She It We They	**'ll write.**	I You He She It We They	**won't write.**

[?]			[✔]			[✘]		
Will	I you he she it we they	**write?**	Yes,	I you he she it we they	**will.**	No,	I you he she it we they	**won't.**

- **Contractions:** *'ll = will, won't = will not.*
- Use *will* + infinitive for:

instant decisions **I'll call** a taxi.
offers **I'll help** you.
promises **I'll e-mail** you tomorrow.

Numbers

1 Numbers 1–20

Match the words with the numbers.

twelve	twenty	eleven	~~three~~
eighteen	five	fifteen	seven

1 one
2 two
3 *three*
4 four
5 ______
6 six
7 ______
8 eight /eɪt/
9 nine
10 ten
11 ______ /ɪ'levn/
12 ______
13 thirteen /θɜː'tiːn/
14 fourteen
15 ______
16 sixteen
17 seventeen
18 ______
19 nineteen
20 ______

p.5

2 Numbers 20–1,000

Write the numbers.

30 thirty /'θɜːti/
______ thirty-one
______ forty
______ forty-seven
______ fifty
______ fifty-nine
______ sixty
______ sixty-three
______ seventy
______ seventy-two
______ eighty
______ eighty-six
______ ninety
______ ninety-four
______ a / one hundred /ə 'hʌndrəd/
______ two hundred and fifty
______ a / one thousand /ə 'θaʊzənd/

p.7

40 28 783 120 81 499 376 68 55 34 42 977

Countries and nationalities

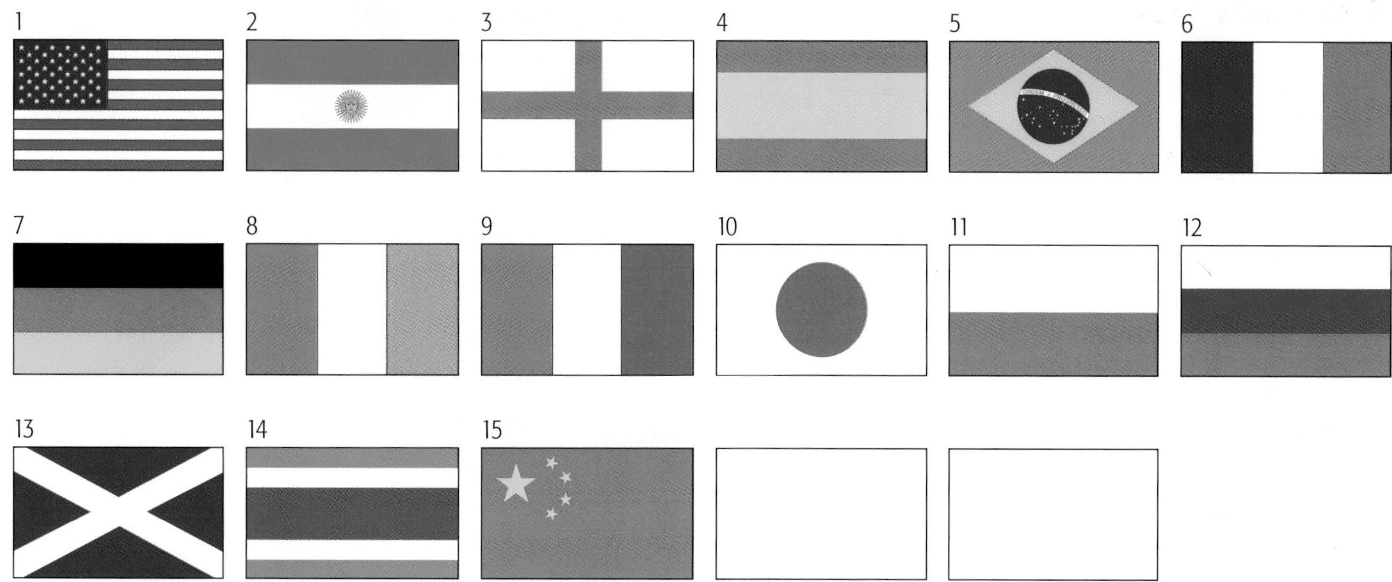

a Match the flags with the countries. Write the number in the box.

	Country	Nationality	Language
		-ish	
	England	English	English
	Ireland /ˈaɪələnd/	Irish	English / Irish Gaelic
	Poland	Polish	Polish
	Scotland	Scottish	English
	Spain	Spanish	Spanish
		-an	
	Germany /ˈdʒɜːməni/	German	German
1	the United States (the USA)	American	English
		-ian	
	Argentina	Argentinian	Spanish
	Brazil	Brazilian	Portuguese
	Italy	Italian	Italian
	Russia /ˈrʌʃə/	Russian	Russian
		-ese	
	China	Chinese	Chinese
	Japan /dʒəˈpæn/	Japanese	Japanese
	France /frɑːns/	French	French
	Thailand /ˈtaɪlænd/	Thai	Thai
	______	______	______
	______	______	______

b Add two more countries. Draw the flags.

c Cover the words and look at the flags. Can you remember the countries, nationalities, and languages?

- Use CAPITAL letters for countries, nationalities, and languages.
- (Great) Britain = England, Scotland, and Wales
- the United Kingdom (the UK) = England, Scotland, Wales, and Northern Ireland

p.6

Common objects

a Match the words and pictures.

- 12 an address book
- a book
- 3 cigarettes
- 5 coins
- a comb /kəʊm/
- a credit card
- a diary /ˈdaɪəri/
- a dictionary
- a file
- glasses /ˈglɑːsɪz/
- an identity card
- 25 keys /kiːz/
- 27 a lighter
- 23 a lipstick
- a magazine /mægəˈziːn/
- matches
- 4 a mobile (phone)
- a newspaper
- a pen
- a pencil
- a photo
- 7 a purse /pɜːs/
- stamps
- sunglasses
- tissues /ˈtɪʃuːz/
- an umbrella
- a wallet /ˈwɒlɪt/
- a watch

b Cover the words and look at the pictures. In pairs, ask and answer.

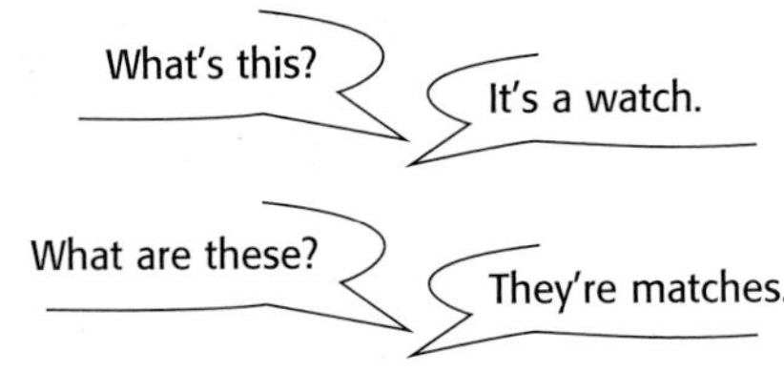

p.10

1

2

3
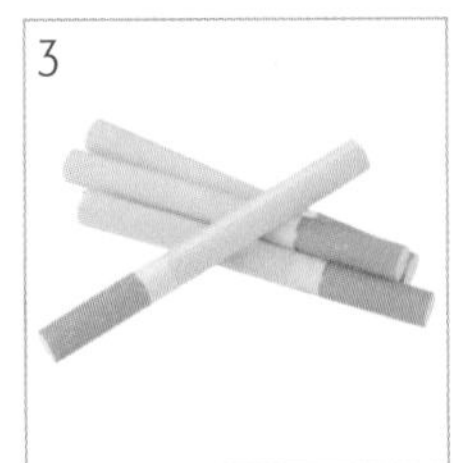

4

5

6

7

8
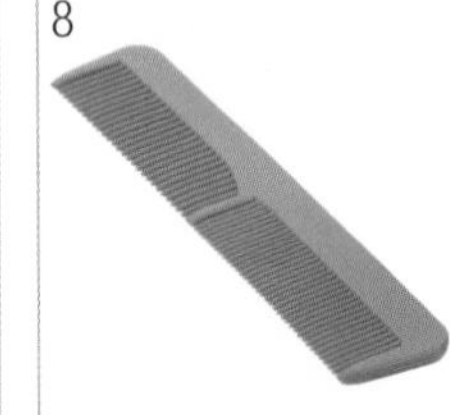

9

10

11
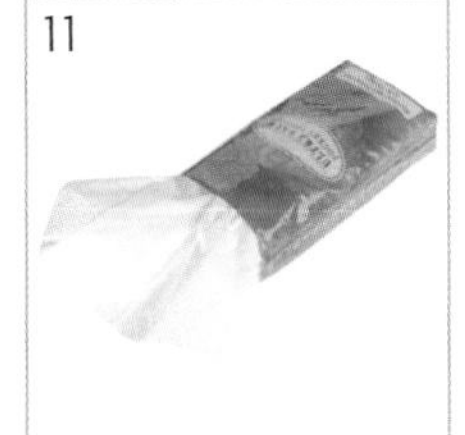

12

13

14
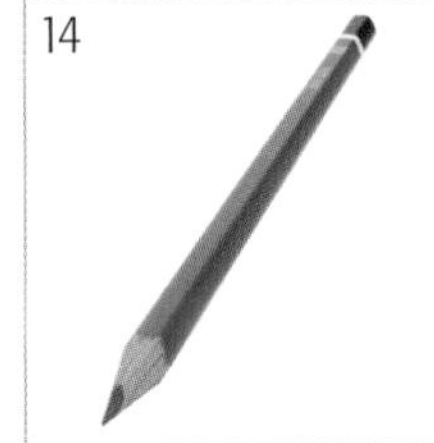

15

16

17

18
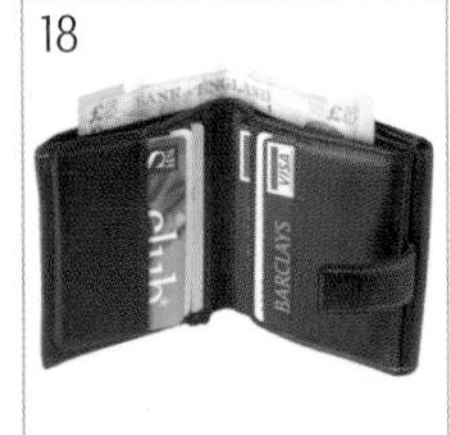

19

20
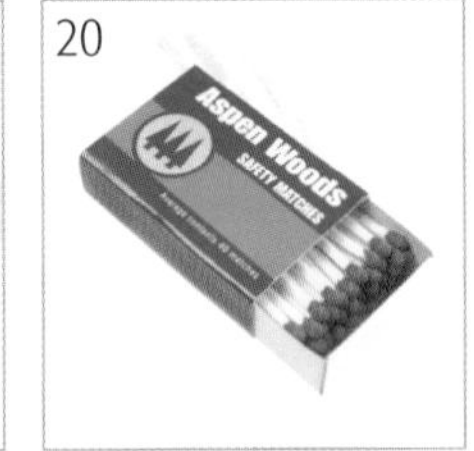

21

22
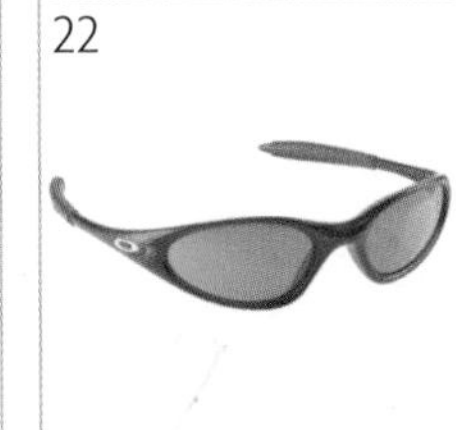

23

24

25

26

27
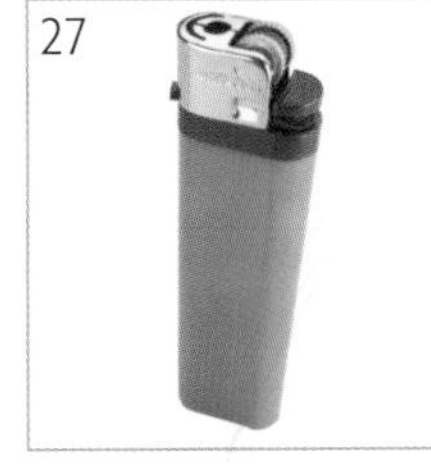

28

Verb phrases

a Match the verbs and pictures.

		cook
		do
		drink
		drive
		eat
	9	go
		have
	8	like
		listen /'lɪsən/
	1	live /lɪv/
		play
	7	read
	13	smoke
		speak
		study
	10	watch
		wear /weə/
		work

b Cover the verbs. Test yourself or a partner.

p.16

1 
in a flat

2 
in an office

3 
children

4 

economics

5 

German

6 
a VW

7 

a newspaper

8 
animals

9 

to the cinema

10 

television

11 
to the radio

12 
the guitar

13 
a cigarette

14 
exercise

15 
tennis

16 
a sandwich for lunch

17 
coffee

18 
fast food

19 
dinner

20 
housework / homework

21 
glasses

Jobs

a Match the words and pictures.

- [ ] an actor[1]
- [ ] a builder /ˈbɪldə/
- [7] a doctor
- [ ] an engineer
- [5] a footballer
- [3] a hairdresser /ˈheədresə/
- [ ] a housewife
- [ ] a journalist /ˈdʒɜːnəlɪst/
- [ ] a lawyer /ˈlɔɪə/
- [ ] a (bank) manager
- [13] a musician /mjuˈzɪʃn/
- [ ] a nurse /nɜːs/
- [11] a pilot /ˈpaɪlət/
- [15] a police officer[2]
- [ ] a politician /pɒlɪˈtɪʃn/
- [ ] a receptionist
- [ ] a secretary /ˈsekrətri/
- [ ] a shop assistant
- [ ] a student /ˈstjuːdnt/
- [ ] a waiter[3]

> 1 for women you can use actor or actress
> 2 people often say policeman / policewoman
> 3 for women you can use waiter or waitress

b Which words don't have the stress on the first syllable? Practise saying them.

c Cover the jobs. In pairs, ask and answer with the pictures.

What does he do?

He's an actor.

p.20

The family

a Look at the two family trees. Number the people in relation to Robert.

1 aunt /ɑːnt/
2 brother /ˈbrʌðə/
3 cousin /ˈkʌzn/
4 father /ˈfɑːðə/
5 grandfather
6 grandmother
7 mother /ˈmʌðə/
8 sister
9 uncle /ˈʌŋkl/

10 daughter /ˈdɔːtə/
11 nephew /ˈnefjuː/
12 niece /niːs/
13 son /sʌn/
14 wife

b Cover the words. In pairs, ask and answer.

Who's Martha?

She's Robert's grandmother.

c Complete with *children, grandparents, parents*. How do you pronounce them?

1 my father and my mother → my ______________ /ˈpeərənts/
2 my grandfather and my grandmother → my ______________
3 my son and my daughter → my ______________

My wife's mother = my mother-in-law
My husband's sister = my sister-in-law, etc.

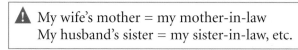

p.23

Common adjectives

1 Colours and common adjectives

a What colour is it? Match the words and colours.

	black		orange /'ɒrɪndʒ/
	blue		pink
	brown /braʊn/	*1*	red
	green		white
	grey /greɪ/		yellow /'jeləʊ/

1 2 3 4 5 6 7 8 9 10

b Match the words and pictures 1–13.

	bad	________
	beautiful /'bjuːtɪfl/	________
1	big	________
	dangerous	________
	dirty /'dɜːti/	________
	easy	________
	empty	________
	expensive	________
	fast /fɑːst/	________
	high	________
	old	________
	rich	________
	wet	________

c Match these adjectives with their opposites in **b**.

cheap clean difficult dry full /fʊl/ good
low /ləʊ/ new poor safe slow small ugly

d Test your partner.

What's the opposite of cheap? Expense. What's the...?

p.28

2 Appearance, *quite / very*

a Match the words and pictures.

	fair	dark
	fat	thin
	long	short (hair)
	old	young /jʌŋ/
	tall	short

b Cover the adjectives and look at the pictures. Test yourself or a partner.

c How tall are they? Complete the sentences.

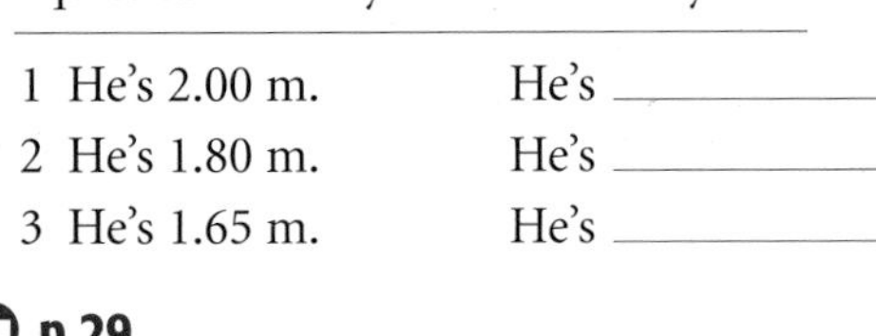

quite tall very tall not very tall

1 He's 2.00 m. He's ________.
2 He's 1.80 m. He's ________.
3 He's 1.65 m. He's ________.

p.29

Daily routine

a Match the verbs and pictures.

	do her Italian homework
	finish work / school
4	get dressed /drest/
	get home
	get to work / school
2	get up
	go home
	go shopping
	go to bed
	go to her Italian class
	go to the gym /dʒɪm/
6	go to work / school
	have a coffee
3	have a shower / a bath
5	have breakfast /ˈbrekfəst/
	have dinner
	have lunch
	make the dinner
	sleep (*for seven hours*)
	start work / school
	take (*the dog for a walk*)
1	wake up (*early / late*)
	watch TV

b Cover the verbs. In pairs, use the pictures to describe Vicky's day.

p.30

1 Time words and expressions

a Complete the expressions.

How often do you see your friends?

MTWThFSS	every *day* /'evri/
week 1, week 2, etc.	every w______
Jan, Feb, March, etc.	every m______
2001, 2002, 2003, etc.	every y______
only on Mondays	once a ______ /wʌns/
on Mondays and Wednesdays	twice a ______
on Mondays and Wednesdays and Fridays	three times a ______
in January, April, July, and October	four times a ______

b Cover the right-hand column. Test yourself.

p.33

2 The date

a Match the words and pictures.

- ☐ spring
- ☐ summer
- ☐ autumn /'ɔːtəm/
- ☐ winter
- ☐ Easter
- ☐ Christmas
- ☐ New Year

b Complete the months. Remember to use CAPITAL letters!

*J*anuary /'dʒænjuəri/	_uly /dʒu'laɪ/
_ebruary /'februəri/	_ugust /'ɔːgəst/
_arch	_eptember /sep'tembə/
_pril /'eɪprɪl/	_ctober /ɒk'teʊbə/
_ay	_ovember /nəʊ'vembə/
_une	_ecember /dɪ'sembə/

c Complete the numbers and words.

1st	first /fɜːst/
2nd	______ /'sekənd/
______	third /θɜːd/
4th	______
______	fifth /fɪfθ/
6th	______
7th	______
______	eighth
______	ninth
10th	______
11th	______
______	twelfth /twelfθ/
13th	______
14th	______
______	twentieth /'twentɪəθ/
21st	______
______	twenty-second
23rd	______
______	twenty-fourth
30th	______ /'θɜːtɪəθ/
______	thirty-first

All other ordinal numbers = number + *th*, e.g. fifteenth, sixteenth.

d Look at the example. What's the date today?

12/3 = ***the*** *twelfth* ***of*** *March* OR *March* ***the*** *twelfth*

p.34

More verb phrases

a Match the verbs and pictures.

	buy (*a newspaper*) /baɪ/
	call / phone (*a taxi*)
	come (*here*)
19	dance (*the tango*)
	draw (*a picture*) /drɔː/
	find (*some money*) /faɪnd/
	give (*someone a present*)
	hear (*a noise*) /hɪə/
	help (*someone*)
	look for (*your keys*)
	meet (*a friend*)
	paint (*a picture*) /peɪnt/
	play (*chess*)
	ride (*a bike*)
1	run (*a race*)
	see (*a film*)
20	sing (*a song*)
	swim (*every day*)
	take (*photos*)
	take (*your umbrella*)
	talk (*to a friend*)
	tell (*someone a secret*)
	travel (*by plane*)
	turn on / off (*the TV*)
	use (*a computer*)
	wait for (*a bus*)
	walk (*home*)

b Cover the verbs and look at the pictures. Test yourself or a partner.

p.41

1

2

3

4

5

6

7

8
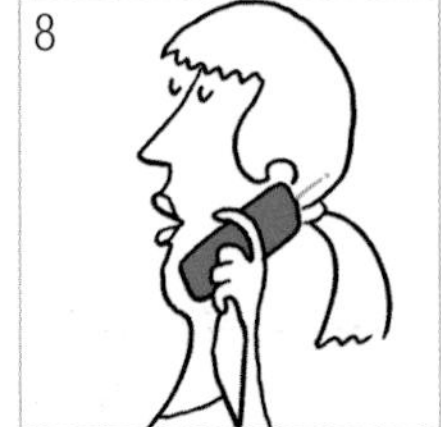
9

10

11

12

13

14

15

16

17

18

19

20

21

22

23

24

25

26

27

Go, have, get

a Match the verbs and pictures.

- away (*for the weekend*)
- by bus
- for a walk
- home (*by bus* / *car*)
- out (*on Friday night*)
- *1* shopping
- to a restaurant /ˈrestrɒnt/
- to bed (*late*)
- to church / to mosque /mɒsk/
- to the beach

- *15* breakfast / lunch / dinner
- a car
- a drink
- a good time
- a sandwich
- a shower

- a newspaper (= buy)
- a taxi / bus / train (= take)
- an e-mail / letter (= receive)
- dressed
- home (= arrive)
- to a restaurant (= arrive)
- *23* up

b What's the difference between *go home* and *get home*?

c Cover the expressions and look at the pictures. Test yourself or a partner.

p.56

Flats and houses

1 Rooms

Match the words and pictures.

3	the bathroom /ˈbɑːθruːm/
1	the bedroom
	the dining room /ˈdaɪnɪŋ/
	the garage /ˈgærɑːʒ/
	the garden
	the hall /hɔːl/
8	the kitchen /ˈkɪtʃɪn/
	the living room
	the study
	the toilet

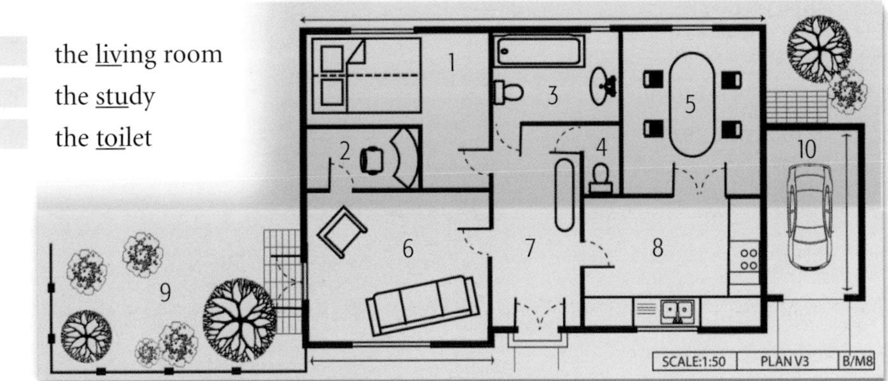

2 Furniture and decoration

a Match the words and pictures.

	an armchair
	a desk
	a fireplace
	a lamp
	a picture /ˈpɪktʃə/
	a plant
	a sofa /ˈsəʊfə/
	a bath /bɑːθ/
	a mirror /ˈmɪrə/
	a shower
	a bed
	a light
1	shelves (a shelf)
	a clock
	a cooker
	a cupboard /ˈkʌbəd/
	a fridge /frɪdʒ/
	carpet
	central heating
	floor
	stairs
	a wall /wɔːl/

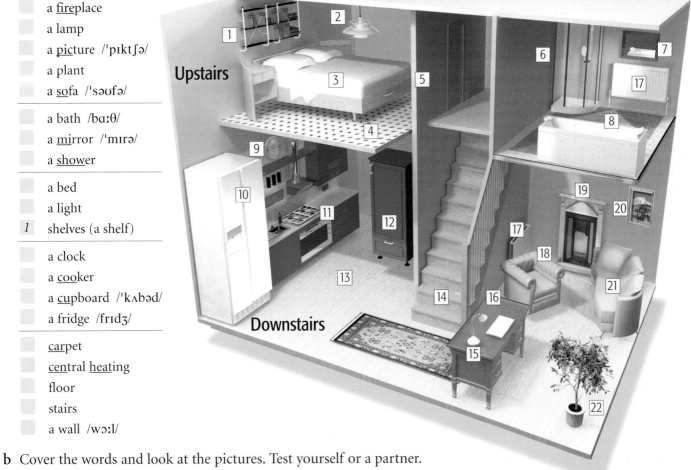

b Cover the words and look at the pictures. Test yourself or a partner.

c What things do you have in your house / flat?

p.64

Town and city

a Match the words and pictures.

- [ ] an art gallery
- [ ] a castle /ˈkɑːsl/
- [ ] a cinema /ˈsɪnəmə/
- [ ] a museum /mjuˌziəm/
- [ ] a theatre /ˈθɪətə/

- [ ] a bank
- [ ] a chemist's / pharmacy /ˈkemɪsts/
- [ ] a department store
- [ ] a market
- [ ] a shopping centre /ˈsentə/
- [ ] a supermarket

- [ ] a bridge /brɪdʒ/
- [ ] a park
- [ ] a river /ˈrɪvə/
- [ ] a road
- [ ] a square /skweə/
- [ ] a street

- [ ] a bus station
- [ ] a railway station
- [ ] a travel agent's

- [ ] a church
- [ ] a mosque

- [ ] a hospital
- *1* a police station
- [ ] a post office
- [ ] a school
- [ ] a sports centre
- [ ] a town hall

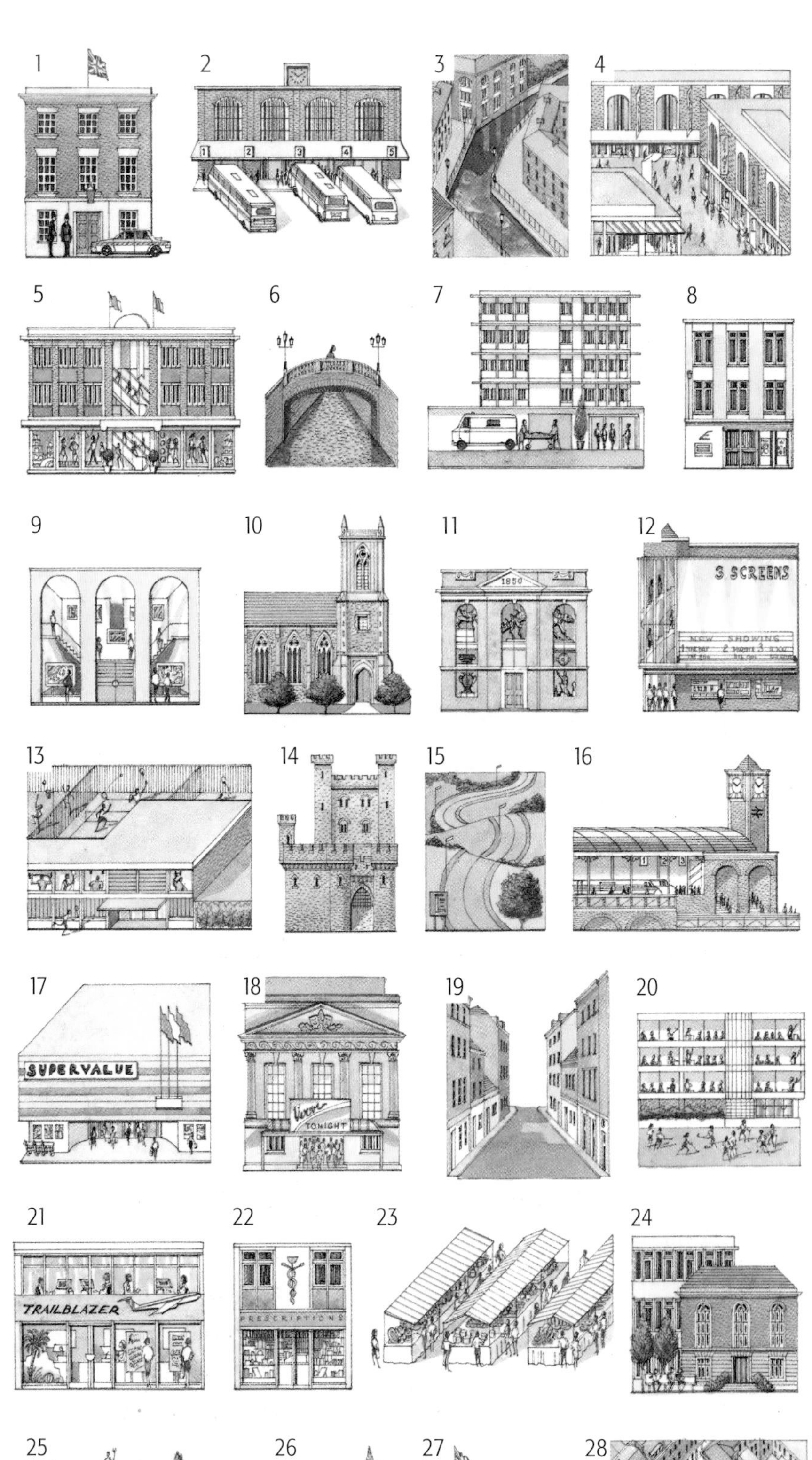

b Cover the words and look at the pictures. Test yourself or a partner.

p.71

a Match the words and pictures.

Breakfast

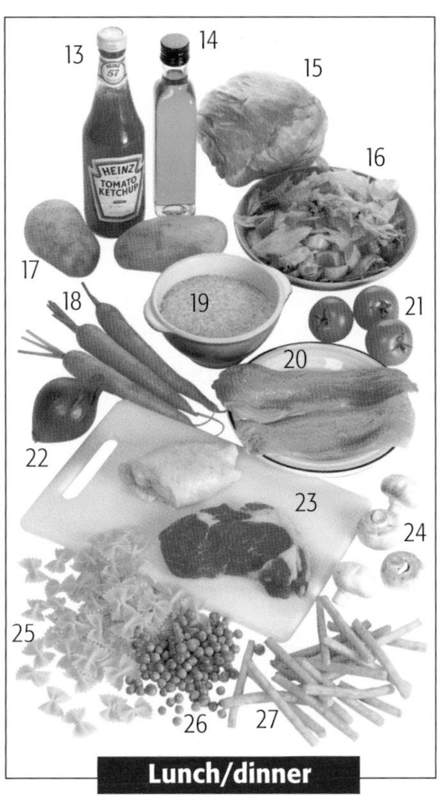
Lunch/dinner

Desserts/snacks

Breakfast

- bread /bred/
- 8 butter
- cereal /ˈsɪəriəl/
- cheese
- 2 coffee
- 12 eggs
- jam /dʒæm/
- (*orange*) juice /dʒuːs/
- milk
- 6 sugar /ˈʃʊɡə/
- tea
- toast

Lunch / dinner

- fish
- ketchup
- 23 meat (steak and chicken)
- (*olive*) oil
- pasta
- 19 rice
- a salad /ˈsæləd/

Vegetables /ˈvedʒtəblz/

- carrots /ˈkærəts/
- chips (French fries)
- a lettuce /ˈletɪs/
- mushrooms
- an onion /ˈʌnjən/
- peas /piːz/
- potatoes /pəˈteɪtəʊz/
- 21 tomatoes /təˈmɑːtəʊz/

Desserts / snacks /dɪˈzɜːts/

- 37 biscuits /ˈbɪskɪts/
- cake
- chocolate /ˈtʃɒklət/
- crisps
- fruit salad
- ice cream
- sandwiches
- sweets

Fruit /fruːt/

- 29 apples
- 28 bananas
- grapes
- oranges
- a pineapple

b Cover the words and look at the pictures. Test yourself or a partner.

p.76

Irregular verbs

PRESENT	PAST SIMPLE	PAST PARTICIPLE
He **is** in Rome. (**be**)	was	been
They **are** in Rome. (**be**)	were	been
The film **begins** at 7.00.	began	begun
She **breaks** his heart.	broke	broken
They **bring** the papers.	brought /brɔːt/	brought
We **build** roads.	built /bɪlt/	built
I **buy** the bread.	bought /bɔːt/	bought
I **can** swim.	could /kʊd/	—
They **catch** the bus.	caught /kɔːt/	caught
She **comes** with her sister.	came	come
It **costs** a lot.	cost	cost
I **do** the housework.	did	done /dʌn/
They **drink** a lot of beer.	drank	drunk
He **drives** a Rolls.	drove	driven
I **eat** a lot.	ate	eaten
She **falls** in love.	fell	fallen
I **feel** angry.	felt	felt
He **finds** a job.	found	found
I **forget** things.	forgot	forgotten
We **fly** with British Airways.	flew /fluː/	flown /fləʊn/
I **get** e-mails.	got	got
He **gives** her presents.	gave	given
They **go** away every weekend.	went	gone /gɒn/
I **have** a car.	had	had
He **hears** a noise.	heard /hɜːd/	heard
I **know** him well.	knew /njuː/	known /nəʊn/

PRESENT	PAST SIMPLE	PAST PARTICIPLE
The train **leaves** at 9.00.	**left**	**left**
I **lose** my keys.	**lost**	**lost**
We **make** mistakes.	**made**	**made**
They **meet** famous people.	**met**	**met**
I **pay** the phone bill.	**paid**	**paid**
I **put** my car in the garage.	**put** /pʊt/	**put**
She **reads** *Time* magazine.	**read** /red/	**read** /red/
I **ring** him every day.	**rang**	**rung**
He **runs** marathons.	**ran**	**run**
He **says** hello.	**said** /sed/	**said**
I **see** my friends every day.	**saw** /sɔː/	**seen**
She **sends** a lot of e-mails.	**sent**	**sent**
He **sings** very well.	**sang**	**sung**
They **sit** on the sofa.	**sat**	**sat**
I **sleep** for eight hours.	**slept**	**slept**
We **speak** French.	**spoke**	**spoken**
You **spend** a lot on clothes.	**spent**	**spent**
She **stands** up.	**stood** /stʊd/	**stood**
I **swim** every day.	**swam**	**swum**
I **take** the dog for a walk.	**took** /tʊk/	**taken**
They **tell** lies.	**told**	**told**
She **thinks** of an idea.	**thought** /θɔːt/	**thought**
They **throw** tomatoes.	**threw** /θruː/	**thrown** /θrəʊn/
I **wake up** in the night.	**woke**	**woken**
He **wears** a hat.	**wore**	**worn**
I **win** competitions.	**won** /wʌn/	**won**
She **writes** to him.	**wrote**	**written**

Vowel sounds

short vowels
long vowels
diphthongs

1 fish /fɪʃ/	2 tree /triː/	3 cat /kæt/	4 car /kɑː/
5 clock /klɒk/	6 horse /hɔːs/	7 bull /bʊl/	8 boot /buːt/
9 computer /kəmp'juːtə/	10 bird /bɜːd/	11 egg /eg/	12 up /ʌp/
13 train /treɪn/	14 phone /fəʊn/	15 bike /baɪk/	16 owl /aʊl/
17 boy /bɔɪ/	18 ear /ɪə/	19 chair /tʃeə/	20 tourist /'tʊərɪst/

Sounds and spelling

	usual spelling		but also
fish	i	his this film six big swim	English women busy
tree	ee ea e	meet three speak eat me we	people police key niece
cat	a	thanks flat black Japan have stamp	
car	ar a	garden party start father glasses dance	aunt
clock	o	hot stop coffee long not box	what watch want
horse	or al aw	sport door talk small saw draw	water four bought thought
bull	u oo	full put good book look room	could would woman
boot	oo u* ew	school food June use new flew	do fruit juice shoe
bird	er ir ur	her verb first third nurse turn	learn work world word
computer	Many different spellings. /ə/ is always unstressed. <u>tea</u>cher um<u>brel</u>la A<u>mer</u>ica <u>fa</u>mous <u>se</u>cond a<u>go</u>		

* especially before consonant + **e**

	usual spelling		but also
egg	e	yes help ten pet very red	friend bread breakfast any said
up	u	bus lunch ugly run lucky cut	come brother son does young
train	a* ai ay	name make rain paint play day	break steak great eight they grey
phone	o* oa	home drove old don't road toast	slow low
bike	i* y igh	nine twice my why high night	buy
owl	ou ow	out thousand house count how brown	
boy	oi oy	coin noise toilet toy enjoy	
ear	eer ere ear	beer engineer here we're year hear	really idea
chair	air are	airport stairs fair hair square careful	their there wear
tourist	A very unusual sound. euro Europe poor sure plural		
/i/	A sound between /ɪ/ and /iː/. Consonant + **y** at the end of words is pronounced /i/. happy any thirsty		
/u/	An unusual sound. education usually situation		

Consonant sounds

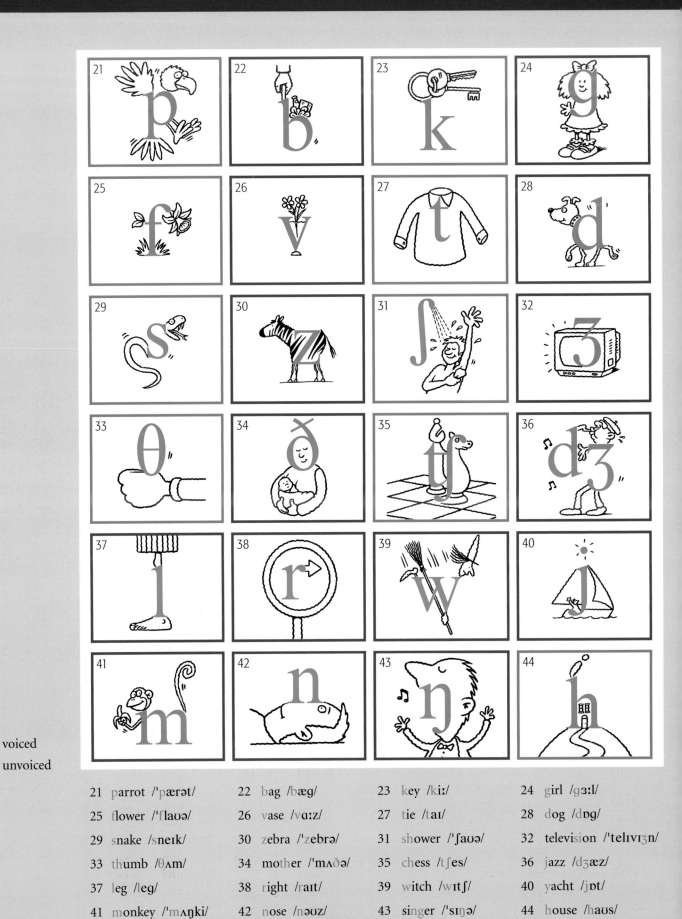

■ voiced
■ unvoiced

21 parrot /ˈpærət/	22 bag /bæg/	23 key /kiː/	24 girl /gɜːl/
25 flower /ˈflaʊə/	26 vase /vɑːz/	27 tie /taɪ/	28 dog /dɒg/
29 snake /sneɪk/	30 zebra /ˈzebrə/	31 shower /ˈʃaʊə/	32 television /ˈtelɪvɪʒn/
33 thumb /θʌm/	34 mother /ˈmʌðə/	35 chess /tʃes/	36 jazz /dʒæz/
37 leg /leg/	38 right /raɪt/	39 witch /wɪtʃ/	40 yacht /jɒt/
41 monkey /ˈmʌŋki/	42 nose /nəʊz/	43 singer /ˈsɪŋə/	44 house /haʊs/

Sounds and spelling

	usual spelling		but also
parrot	p pp	paper pilot Poland sleep apple happy	
bag	b bb	be table job builder number rubber	
key	c k ck	credit card actor kitchen like black pick	Christmas chemist's
girl	g gg	green get angry big eggs bigger	
flower	f ph ff	Friday fifteen wife photo elephant office coffee	
vase	v	very eleven live travel river love	of
tie	t tt	tea take student sit letter bottle	liked dressed
dog	d dd	dance understand bad read address middle	played tired
snake	s ss	sister starts smoke stress actress	nice city cinema police
zebra	z s	zero Brazil music please dogs watches	
shower	sh ti (+ vowel)	shopping shoes Spanish fish station information	sugar sure
television	An unusual sound. revision decision confusion usually garage		

	usual spelling		but also
thumb	th	think thirty throw bathroom fourth tenth	
mother	th	the these then other that with	
chess	ch tch t (+ure)	cheap children church watch match picture adventure	
jazz	j dge	January juice July enjoy bridge fridge	German manager
leg	l ll	like little plane girl small spelling	
right	r rr	red rich problem try sorry terrible	write wrong
witch	w wh	window twenty Wednesday win why when	one once
yacht	y before u	yellow yesterday young yes use university	
monkey	m mm	man Monday money swim summer swimming	
nose	n nn	no never nine ran dinner thinner	know
singer	ng	song England language thing long going	think bank
house	h	happy hungry hotel behind hall head	who whose

OXFORD
UNIVERSITY PRESS

Great Clarendon Street, Oxford OX2 6DP

Oxford University Press is a department of the University of Oxford. It furthers the University's objective of excellence in research, scholarship, and education by publishing worldwide in

Oxford New York

Auckland Bangkok Buenos Aires Cape Town Chennai Dar es Salaam Delhi Hong Kong Istanbul Karachi Kolkata Kuala Lumpur Madrid Melbourne Mexico City Mumbai Nairobi São Paulo Shanghai Taipei Tokyo Toronto

Oxford and Oxford English are registered trade marks of Oxford University Press in the UK and in certain other countries

First published 2004

ISBN 0 19 438425 X

Design and composition by Stephen Strong

Printed in Spain by Gráficas Estella

The Authors would like to thank all the teachers and students around the world whose feedback has helped us to shape New English File. We would also like to thank Carla Guelfenbein, Cristina Mayo, Russell and Anna, Ben Silverstone, and Annabel Wright for agreeing to be interviewed, and Joaquin for the short story *It's written in the cards*. The Authors would also like to thank all those at Oxford University Press (both in Oxford and around the world), and the design team who have contributed their skills and ideas to producing this course.

The Publisher and Authors would like to thank the following for their invaluable feedback on the materials:

Beatriz Martin; Michael O'Brien; Lester Vaughan; Tom Stutter; Wendy Armstrong; Javier Santos Asensi; Tim Banks; Brian Brennan; Xosé Calvo; Javier Gesto; Susanna Di Gravio; Jane Hudson; Carlos Leite; Norma Sheila Botelho; Paulo Pimenta Marques; Katarzyna Pawlowska; Graham Rumbelow; Blanca Sanz; Yolanda Gomez; Ágnes Szigetvári; Judit Gadaneczné Szarka

Finally, very special thanks from Clive to Ma Angeles and from Christina to Cristina for all their help and encouragement. Christina would also like to thank her children Joaquin, Marco, and Krysia for their constant inspiration.

Acknowledgements

The Publisher and Authors are grateful to those who have given permission to reproduce the following extracts and adaptations of copyright material:

p.30 'Hidden toll of the daily grind' by Stephen Palmer, *The Times* 16 January 2001 © NI Syndication London 2001. Reproduced by permission.

p.32 'Secrets of the isles of eternal youth' by Cherry Norton, *The Sunday Times* 10 June 2001 © NI Syndication London 2001. Reproduced by permission.

p.43 'Shopping: it's a guy thing' by Margaret Driscoll and Jane Mulkerrins, *The Sunday Times* 30 December 2001 © NI Syndication London 2001. Reproduced by permission.

p.47 *Unchained Melody* by Zaret/North © Frank Music Corp. Reproduced by permission of MPL Communications Limited.

p.54 'A tale of two Sydneys'. Reproduced by kind permission of Emma Nunn and Raoul Sebastian.

p.56 'tfi friday' by Harvey Marcus, *Marie Claire* October 2002 © Harvey Marcus/Marie Claire/IPC Syndication. Reproduced by permission.

p.67 'Friday Nights: Gosforth, Cumbria' by Stephen Bleach, *The Sunday Times* 28 October 2001 © NI Syndication London 2001. Reproduced by permission.

p.75 'My piece of pop history' by Andrew Holgate, *The Sunday Times* 6 October 2002 © NI Syndication London 2002. Reproduced by permission.

p.90 'Extreme Living' by Lucy Ash, *Eve Magazine* 2002. Reproduced by permission of *Eve Magazine*.

The Publisher would like to thank the following for their kind permission to reproduce photographs and other copyright material:

Alamy pp.7bl (Leslie Garland Picture Library), 16b (David Hobart), 16e (Les Polders), 23l (Jim Pickerell/Stock Connection, Inc.), 28d (Foodfolio), 30 (Jon Mitchell/Lightroom Photos), 49 (Jackson Smith), 52l (Andre Jenny), 61 (Gkphotography), 78r (Charlie Newham), 88d (TH Foto); Ann Scott Associates p.97t; Anthony Blake Photo Library pp.7tl (Robert Lawson), 16d (Anthony Blake); Car Photo Library pp.88h, 88i; Clive Oxenden/ Christina Latham-Koenig pp.22 (bag), 23; Corbis UK Ltd. pp.7bc (Gideon Mendel), 7cl (George D. Lepp), 16a (Randy Faris), 16f (Jon Feingersh), 16h (Robert Holmes), 22a (Ron Gallela/Sygma), 22c (Rune Hellestad/Sygma), 22e (Frank Trapper/Sygma), 22h (Murdo Macleod/Sygma), 22i (Rufus F. Folkks), 22j (Ron Galella/Sygma), 22k, 22l (Mitchell Gerber), 22m (Mitchell Gerber), 28a (Alan Schein Photography), 28e (Hurewitz Creative), 28f (George Hall), 29b (Dusko Despotovic/Sygma), 31 (Bill Miles), 32/33 (Dave Bartruff), 34c (Kevin R. Morris), 37 (Marc Garanger), 40c (LWA-Dann Tardif), 40l (Darama), 40r (Steve Prezant), 46bl (Richard Hamilton Smith), 46br (Rune Hellestad/Sygma), 46tc (Lawrence Manning), 46tl (Chuck Savage), 53a (Paul Almasy), 53b (Nik Wheeler), 53d (Araldo de Luca), 53e (Bettmann), 54t (Ray Juno), 58b (Horace Bristol), 58c (Hulton-Deutsch Collection), 58d (Horace Bristol), 73l (Barry Lewis), 73r (Sergio Pitamitz), 78c (Szenes/Sygma), 78l (Ken Redding), 88b (Aaron Horowitz), 88c (Amos Nachoum), 88g (John Conrad), 90c (Dean Conger), 90l (Wolfgang Kaehler), 90r (Balaguer Alejandro/Sygma), 109l/112 (Bequest of Mrs. Benjamin Ogle Tayloe; Collection of The Corcoran Gallery of Art), 109r/112 (Bettmann), 112b (Robert Holmes), 148bc (Susan Rosenthal), 148bl (Steve Chenn), 148br (Robert Essel NYC); Tom Crossley p.20; Dipag News and Sport p.34r (Felice Calabro); Julio Donoso/Carla Guelfenbein p.35; Empics p.7tr; Getty Images pp.58f (Hulton Archive), 70tl (taxi); Gosforth Hall Hotel pp.66, 66l; Hulton Archive/Getty Images p.58e; imageri.com p.58a; Levi Strauss UK Ltd p.28c; Madame Tussauds p.70tr; Magnum Photos p.32t (Chris Steele-Perkins); Marie Claire/IPC Syndication/Kong Qingyan, Frederico Mendes, Nikolai Ignatiev p.56; Mary Lally Associates p.7br; Henry Meyer p.32c; NASA p.88f (Reto Stockli/Alan Nelson/Fritz Hasler); News International Syndication pp.43 (The Times), 75l (Francesco Guidicini/The Times); Nike UK Ltd p.7cr; Oxford Scientific Films p.88a (David M Dennis); Oxford University Press pp.94l, 94r, 95, 148c, 148tl, 148tr; Photofusion Picture Library p.68 (Nigel Goldsmith); Press Association p.148tc; Residence Tunis p.97br; Retna Pictures p.22f; Rex Features pp.9a (Everett Collection), 9b (Everett Collection), 9c, 9d (Lucasfilm/Everett), 9e, 9f (Universal/Everett), 9g (SNAP), 9h (Everett Collection), 22b (Sipa Press), 22d (Richard Young), 22g (Nils Jorgensen), 28g (Peter Heimsath), 29t (Erik C. Pendzich), 34l (Action Press), 44l, 44r, 45a (C.20thC.Fox/Everett), 45c (Everett Collection), 46tr, 51 (Norm Betts), 52r (Patsy Lynch), 53c (Stephen Meddle), 70b (Nils Jorgensen), 70bc, 71 (James D. Morgan), 75r (Crawford Brown), 89 (Nils Jorgensen), 99 (Rob Crandall), 109c/112; Ronald Grant Archive pp.9i, 28h, 45b, 45d, 45e, 63t; Robert Schirmer p.81b; Science Photo Library p.88e (US Geological Survey); Ben Silverstone p.63b; Starwood Hotels & Resorts Worldwide, Inc. p.97bl; WHSmith p.92; Zooid Pictures pp.16c, 16g, 64, 70tc (Dan Sinclair)

Illustrations by:

Jamel Akib: p.17; Nick Baker: pp.27, 30, 31, 33, 39, 45, 64, 65, 69, 76, 85, 87, 104, 105, 123, 147; Stephen Conlin: pp.106 (bridge/church), 152; Mark Duffin: pp.5, 6, 8, 12, 24, 28 (apple), 36, 48, 60, 72, 91, 106, 111, 129 (symbols), 151; Martha Gavin: pp.18, 19, 42, 69 (flats), 88, 94, 95, 110, 113; Ellis Nadler: pp.54, 93, 150, pronunciation symbols; Nigel Paige: p.15; Robert Shadbolt: pp.11, 41 (questionnaire), 43, 47, 66, 67, 78, 79, 95 (actions), 133, 134; Colin Shelbourn: pp.4, 5 (characters), 6, 7, 8, 9, 21, 23, 29, 41, 77, 102, 106 (man), 129, 134, 135, 143, 144, 145, 146, 149; Annabel Wright: pp.20, 29, 34, 35, 82, 100, 101

Commissioned photography by:

Mark Mason: pp.7 (cheese), 10, 22, 59, 76, 80, 85, 103, 106, 135, 142, 153

Picture research by Zooid Pictures

Illustrations commissioned by Cathy Blackie

Commissioned photography organized by Pippa MacNee